INDUSTRIAL EXPERIMENTATION

by

K. A. BROWNLEE, M. A.

1947

CHEMICAL PUBLISHING CO., INC.
BROOKLYN N. Y.

CHEMICAL PUBLISHING CO., INC.
BROOKLYN N. Y.

FOREWORD

The present Monograph is based on an earlier Memorandum produced by the Directorate of Ordnance Factories (Explosives) for the use, primarily, of those concerned with pilot plant and plant scale experiments on chemical manufacturing processes in the Royal Ordnance Factories (Explosives). Much work of this type was being carried out and it had become evident that it was desirable for the results of such experiments to be subjected to critical tests of significance. A convenient account of the straightforward tests of significance, written from the point of view of the individual who has to apply them in practice without necessarily a full knowledge of their theoretical background, was not readily available, and an attempt was therefore made to prepare one.

It was evident that to apply tests of significance conveniently and economically the experiments had to be planned in appropriate forms. It is considered that the methods outlined should be as much a standard tool of the industrial experimenter as a chemical balance is of the laboratory experimenter. In carrying out an industrial experiment the choice is not between using a statistical design with the application of the appropriate tests of significance or the ordinary methods: the choice is between correct or incorrect methods. Even the simplest experiment requires an estimate of the significance of its results.

The practice sometimes followed of consulting the statistician only after the experiment is completed and asking him "what he can make of the results" cannot be too strongly condemned. It is essential to have the experiment in a form suitable for analysis and in general this can only be attained by designing the experiment in consultation with the statistician, or with due regard to the statistical principles involved.

The present Monograph, therefore, is intended to be a guide to both the planning and the interpretation of experiments on the industrial scale, and it is hoped that the methods described will become part of the everyday technique to those who carry out such experiments.

R. C. BOWDEN,
Director of Ordnance Factories (Explosives)
Ministry of Supply.

CONTENTS

CONTENTS—*continued*

Page

CHAPTER X

MULTIPLE CORRELATION

CHAPTER XI

THE GENERAL ANALYSIS OF VARIANCE

CHAPTER XII

MISCELLANEOUS ASPECTS OF THE ANALYSIS OF VARIANCE

CHAPTER XIII

BALANCED INCOMPLETE BLOCKS

Page

CHAPTER XIV

CONFOUNDING: THE PROBLEM OF RESTRICTED BLOCK SIZE IN FACTORIAL EXPERIMENTS

CHAPTER XV

GENERAL CONCLUSIONS

APPENDIX

FROM THE PREFACE TO THE FIRST EDITION

The present monograph is intended to provide for those who carry out investigational work a guide to modern statistical methods, both the use of tests of significance to attain reliability in deductions from experimental data and the use of statistical design to attain the maximum precision with the minimum expenditure.

The subject is treated entirely from the practical point of view.[1] Theory is at a minimum and the only mathematics involved is simple arithmetic. Each statistical method discussed is illustrated with practical examples worked out in detail to show what exactly is involved in its use. Some of the more advanced techniques may appear rather formidable, but it is strongly recommended that they should be approached through the use of the simpler methods. A little practice in these will lead to a familiarity and confidence with which it will be realized that the advanced techniques are merely comparatively easy extensions of the simpler.

The theoretical background on which the author has drawn is of course that largely developed by Professor R. A. Fisher, expounded in his "Statistical Methods for Research Workers" and "The Design of Experiments."

Indebtedness is expressed to Prof. R. A. Fisher and Dr. Frank A. Yates for permission to reprint Tables III-VI from their book "Statistical Tables for Biological, Agricultural, and Medical Research" (Oliver & Boyd, Edinburgh and London), and to the British Standards Institution for permission to reprint certain factors for Quality Control Charts from B.S. 600R, "Quality Control Charts."

The examples used here are all the results of experimental and investigational work in the Royal Ordnance Factories (Explosives), and the author's thanks are due to Mr. A. C. H. Cairns, Mr. A. H. Woodhead, Mr. D. Newman and others whose collaboration has been invaluable in the development of the ideas and outlook presented here. The author is also indebted to Dr. R. C. Bowden, Director of Ordnance Factories (Explosives), for his active interest and encouragement throughout this work.

K. A. B.

PREFACE TO THE SECOND EDITION

The principal additions to this Edition are a substantial enlargement of Chapter I and two new chapters, Chapter XIII on balanced incomplete blocks amd Chapter XIV on confounding. Further additions are the components of variance for unequal column size in Chapter VII (d), the exact formula for the residual variance about a regression line in Chapter IX (h), the Doolittle method of computation in multiple regression in Chapter X (d), and the partitioning of sums of squares in Chapter XII (c).

Minor additions have also been made at many points.

K. A. B.

[1] The reader will find the mathematical theory of the simple statistical tests well dealt with by A. Linder: "Statistiche Methoden fur Naturwissenschäfter, Mediziner, und Ingenieure" (Verlag Birkhauser, Basel). Full and comprehensive treatments are by M. G. Kendall: "The Advanced Theory of Statistics" (Griffin) and S. S. Wilkes: "Mathematical Statistics" (Princeton).

CHAPTER I

INTRODUCTION

(a) Experimental Error

In all experimental work our observations are always subject to experimental error. No experimenter would seriously dispute this statement. This makes it all the more remarkable that only recently has it begun to be generally admitted that in order to judge the trustworthiness of any experimental result it must be compared with an estimate of its error, an operation known to the statistician as a "test of significance." It can be said at once that the lack of this test of significance is the main origin of the unsatisfactory nature of most industrial experimentation: the errors are large, larger than is realised, and the apparent effects, attributed by the experimenter to such factors as he has varied, are in reality arising solely through the accidental fluctuations due to these errors. If rigorous tests of significance were applied, many of the assertions made would be shown to be based on quite inadequate evidence and many would also be found to be fallacious (the fact that an assertion has been made on inadequate evidence of course does not imply that that assertion is incorrect: it may turn out that the asserter was lucky in his gamble. However, the plant manager in taking the advice of his experimenter does want to know whether he is acting on a scientifically proved fact or on a subjective guess).

(b) Classical and Industrial Experimentation

In this question of the importance of error we have one of the principal differences between laboratory and industrial, or plant scale, experimentation. The laboratory experimenter is generally in the fortunate position of being able to have all his independent variables under complete control: his materials can be of the highest possible purity: his measuring apparatus can all be of the highest accuracy, and usually his errors are small.

In referring above to the laboratory experimenter, we meant particularly those working on physical-chemical systems. Any work involving living matter, bacteria, fungi, etc., is always found to have relatively large variability outside the control of the experimenter, and as far as the magnitude of his experimental error is concerned he is more in the position of the industrial experimenter even if he is working on the laboratory scale.

The industrial experimenter, on the other hand, often cannot obtain complete control of all his variables, for frequently the scale of the experiment is so vast that an army of supervisors would be required to keep them under control. The attainment of good control may also be a difficult technical matter: thus it is generally easy in a well-equipped laboratory to control temperatures within very fine limits with the usual thermostatic equipment. For a plant scale experiment this is generally quite impracticable. Again, it is easy enough to provide excellent lagging for any laboratory apparatus: to lag an absorption column 50 feet high, on the other hand, may be absurdly expensive.

Further, for the industrial experimenter it may be in practice essential to carry out the investigation with only the slightest hindrance to normal production. Thus it might be possible to obtain control of the independent variables, but only through taking such time and care on each batch that the throughput through the plant would be seriously reduced. Or we might wish to vary some of the independent variables over a wide range, in order to get points spaced well apart, so that their effect on the dependent variable would show up clearly: this might lead to the production of a large amount of out-of-specification scrap material. It would thus be necessary to work in a narrow range of the independent variable, which means that the magnitudes of the effects that we have to observe will be much reduced and may well be swamped by errors.

These factors result in industrial experiments generally having a much larger error than laboratory work. Under these conditions it is difficult to decide whether a particular result is genuine or due to the error, and this calls for a statistical test of significance. Further, in order to get a significant result (i.e. a result in which the apparent effect is significantly greater than the error in its determination) we need a larger number of experiments (and this is precisely what is so undesirable in industrial work on account of the expense) unless we use a number of special statistical devices.

Finally, it might not be out of place to remark that it has been the author's experience that even in laboratory work the errors, when calculated objectively with exact statistical technique, are often much larger than the experimenter believes or claims them to be.

It is clear from the above considerations that the industrial experimenter has to face a set of problems additional to those of the laboratory experimenter, and hence requires an additional set of techniques. These have been developed in recent years by research workers in agriculture (notably R. A. Fisher and his colleagues at the Rothamsted Experiment Station) who have to contend with the weather and with variations in the fertility of the soil amongst the variables outside their control.

(c) Replication

If the error of our estimate of an effect is too great, generally there are two alternative methods of reducing it. One is to refine the technique, e.g. by using more precise thermostatic equipment, weighing on better balances, taking more meticulous precaution against evaporation, etc. Alternatively, and often on the industrial scale this is the only alternative, we can replicate (repeat) the experiment a number of times and take the average of the results. Unfortunately this process is not very efficient, for the error of the average is inversely proportional to the square root of the number of observations. Thus averaging four observations brings the error of the average down to one-half that of a single observation : the average of sixteen observations has one-quarter of the error of a single observation.

On the laboratory scale, experiments are relatively cheap, and we can afford to take many more observations than are strictly necessary to establish a given conclusion with a given level of significance. We can easily take so many that the error of the average, if it ever was very high, has become so small that an exact test of significance is obviously unnecessary. On the industrial scale, however, the work is so expensive, involving a large consumption of supervisory man-power, raw materials, power, etc., that to take more observations than would suffice for our purpose, defined above as the establishing of a given conclusion with a given level of significance, would be scandalously extravagant.[1]

(d) Experimental Design : Randomised Blocks

Statistical theory has so far only been mentioned in connection with the theory of errors, to which of course it is fundamental. It has, however, a great deal to say on how experiments should be designed so as to allow the obtaining of an unbiassed estimate of error and to allow the error to be at a minimum.

Let us start with one of the simplest conceptions in experimental design, the so-called "Randomised Block."

[1] This aspect of statistics has been developed considerably recently : c.f. "Sequential Analysis of Statistical Data : Applications" : Statistical Research Group, Columbia University : Columbia University Press, and G. A. Barnard : "Sequential Tests in Industrial Statistics" (Supplement to the Journal of the Royal Statistical Society, Vol. VIII, No. 1, p. 1, 1946).

Suppose we wish to compare four "treatments." We are using "treatment" in a generalised sense: the four treatments may e.g. be literally four fertiliser treatments for wheat, or four diets for rats, or four temperatures for a nitration process, or four concentration of plasticiser in a plastic. Further suppose that the material to which the treatments are applied arrives in batches large enough to allow only four experiments per batch. We will suppose that it is probable that successive batches differ appreciably in their quality. We will call these batches by the general term "blocks." In the wheat example quoted above, four adjacent plots of ground may be considered as the "block": they are more likely to resemble each other in their fertility than other plots belonging to other blocks which will be further away, possibly in a different field. In the case of the rats, it is probable that rats from the same litter resemble each other more than rats from other litters. In the case of the nitration process, a tank full of well-stirred acid and a batch of material to be nitrated mixed thoroughly till it is homogeneous would be the equivalent of the "block." Further suppose that we are going to replicate four times (that is, carry out each observation four times[1]). If the Treatments are A, B, C, and D and the Blocks are 1, 2, 3 and 4 we could execute the experiment as in Table 1.1.

Table 1.1

Block	Treatment			
1	A	A	A	A
2	B	B	B	B
3	C	C	C	C
4	D	D	D	D

A moment's thought will show that a scheme such as that in Table 1.1 is obviously absurd, for whatever differences show up are as likely to be due to differences between blocks as to differences between treatments.

A slightly better procedure would be to distribute the treatments completely at random. We can label 16 cards A, B, C, D each 4 times, place them in a hat, and withdraw them one by one, writing them down in order from left to right in successive blocks. The result of one such operation is in Table 1.2.

Table 1.2

Block	Treatments			
1	D	B	B	D
2	C	D	A	B
3	B	A	C	A
4	C	C	D	A

If we take the averages of the four results for each treatment they will be statistically sound if the randomisation was properly carried out, but the error in each mean (average) will be inflated because it includes in itself the differences between blocks. The experiment will thus not be as accurate as it might be.

It would obviously be better to allocate each treatment once to each block, as in Table 1.3.

[1] It will be convenient if we decide that a "single replication" means an experiment carried out once, "double replication" means an experiment carried out twice, and so on.

Table 1.3

Block	Treatment			
1	A	B	C	D
2	A	B	C	D
3	A	B	C	D
4	A	B	C	D

When we take the average of the four A's, and compare it with the average of, say, the four B's, the difference between the average is completely independent of any block differences.

It might, however, be more satisfactory if the order of carrying out the experiments were randomised (as they stand in Table 1.3 it is systematic, the order being A, B, C, D in each block). If there was any tendency for the first experiment in each case to be high, then this would appear as a high result for A which would be fallacious. Randomisation, such as has been carried out in Table 1.4, would avoid this.

Table 1.4

Block	Treatment			
1	D	B	A	C
2	B	C	A	D
3	C	B	A	D
4	A	C	D	B

We have now arrived at the concept of the "randomised block." All treatments to be compared occur an equal number of times in each block, the block being large enough to take all treatments at least once. The replication is achieved by repeating the experiment on further blocks, the order of experiments always being randomised. Of course, if the size of the block is such that several replications can be placed in a single block, then this can be done and nothing is gained by replicating in different blocks.[3]

The analysis of the results of such an experiment, with the testing of the significance of the results, is discussed in Chapter VII (e).

(e) The Latin Square

The hypothetical experiment discussed in the previous section, though now rigorous in design in that it cannot lead to false conclusions, is in some cases capable of further refinement.

To particularise slightly, suppose that in a multi-stage process batches of a ton are split into four sub-batches which are processed simultaneously (approximately) in four reactors, and we wish to compare the effects of four different treatments at this latter stage. With the four treatments on the four sub-batches in each batch we have the randomised block technique, the allocation of the four treatments to the four reactors being decided by randomisation. It is possible, however, to arrange that with such treatment each of the four reactors occurs once and once only, so that the treatment averages are completely independent of any possible differences between reactors. Such an arrangement is that in Table 1.5, where the letters refer to the treatments.

[3] See, however, the end of Chapter XII (e).

Table 1.5

Batch	Reactor 1	Reactor 2	Reactor 3	Reactor 4
1	A	B	C	D
2	C	D	A	B
3	B	A	D	C
4	D	C	B	A

Examining Table 1.5, it will be seen that the four sub-batches of each batch include all four treatments. At the same time, with each of the four treatments all four reactors occur once and only once and all four batches occur once and only once. Possible errors due to differences between Batches and between Reactors are thus eliminated both from the averages, thus allowing unbiassed estimates to be obtained, and also from the error, thus making the latter a minimum.

The computation of the results of a Latin Square is discussed in Chapter XII (g).

(f) Balanced Incomplete Blocks

In the ordinary Randomised Block the block must be large enough to take one complete set of treatments. It may happen, however, that we wish to compare more treatments than can be got into one block.

Suppose we have raw material in batches that are only large enough to allow 4 experiments to be carried out on one batch, and further suppose that there is an appreciable variance between batches. If we wish to carry out a comparison of 2, 3, or 4 treatments this between batch variance would not worry us, as each set of 2, 3 or 4 treatments could be carried out on the same batch. If, however, we wished to compare 5 or more treatments, then one or more of these would have to be carried out on a different batch from that on which the first 4 treatments were tested, and the comparison would be invalidated by the confusing element of the between batch variance. The standard method of avoiding this difficulty is to select one of the treatments as a "standard," and include it in each batch. All treatments are then compared directly with the standard, and of the other comparison some are direct through the treatments occurring in the same block and others are indirect, from treatment M to the standard in its block to the standard in the other block concerned to the treatment N.

Although this procedure does work it is by no means very satisfactory, as there are three different errors for the three different types of comparison. Further, it is not the most efficient possible.

Consider the alternative design in Table 1.6 where we have the five treatments replicated four times in five batches of four.

Table 1.6

Batch Number				
1	2	3	4	5
A	A	A	A	B
B	B	B	C	C
C	C	D	D	D
D	E	E	E	E

There are a number of points about this design :—

(a) Each treatment occurs once and only once in 4 of the 5 batches.

(b) Any specified pair of treatments, e.g. A and B, or C and E, occur together in 3 of the 5 batches. Thus direct comparisons between B and D are possible in Batches 1, 3 and 5.

(c) Direct comparisons between a specified pair of treatments is not possible in the other 2 batches ; thus there is no D in Batch 2 and no B in batch 4. Nevertheless a very satisfactory comparison can be made, for A, C and E occur in both Batches 2 and 4 and we can in effect use the average of these three as a "standard." It will be noted that to use the average of three as a standard is more satisfactory than using a single individual.

These experimental designs are known as balanced incomplete blocks. They are balanced because each treatment occurs to exactly the same extent : they are incomplete because no block contains the full number of treatments. They suffer from the restriction that balanced arrangements are not possible for all experimental set-ups. Broadly speaking, if we fix the number of treatments that we wish to compare, and if the number of experiments per batch (or "block") is also fixed, then the number of replication of each treatment is thereby determined. This is the principal disadvantage of these designs : the number of replications they require may be greater than we think are necessary to attain sufficient accuracy.

Some of the designs are more satisfactory from this point of view than others. In general, for a given number of treatments, the larger the block we can use the smaller the number of replications that are required to establish balance. Thus if we have 21 treatments to be compared, then working with blocks of 3 we require 10 replications. Working with blocks of 4 we could use the scheme for 25 treatments (duplicating 4 of the most important if we wished to bring the total up to 25) which would require 8 replications. Blocks of 5 are a very satisfactory size as only 5 replications are required. It is a curious property that blocks of 6 and 7 are less desirable, requiring 8 and 10 replications respectively. The exact requirements in any particular instance are a consequence of the combinatorial properties of numbers.

The computation for these designs is discussed in Chapter XIII.

(g) Lattice Squares

The outstanding disadvantages of the Balanced Incomplete Blocks is that to obtain balance the number of replications necessary becomes rather high as the number of treatments increases. Generally, p^2 treatments require $(p + 1)$ replications, e.g. 36 treatments require 7 replications, and this we may consider to be more than is justified.

The Lattice Square is probably the most suitable device for this situation. Suppose we have 25 treatments which we wish to compare. We can write them down in the form of a square as in Table 1.7.

Table 1.7

11	12	13	14	15
21	22	23	24	25
31	32	33	34	35
41	42	43	44	45
51	52	53	54	55

These 25 treatments can be tested in blocks of 5 by taking first the rows as blocks and then the columns as blocks. Repeating each set gives a total of 4 replications for each treatment. It will be noted that these designs are not balanced. For example, treatment 11 occurs in the same blocks as treatments 12, 13, 14 and 15 and also 21, 31, 41 and 51, but never with the remaining 16 treatments. Satisfactory comparison are nevertheless possible through intermediates, and with the appropriate algebraic treatment the designs are very efficient.[4]

The chief virtue of these lattice designs is that the number of replications required is independent of the number of treatments. Thus, for example, to test 49 treatments we require only 4 replications, whereas using the Balanced Incomplete Block technique we require 8 replications.

(h) The Nature of "Blocks"

We have been discussing in the previous sections devices for circumventing the difficulties arising through the restricting size of the "blocks" available. The concept of block is an extremely general one, but the following are some examples :

(a) In the science of agriculture, of course, the block is made up of plots of ground immediately adjoining each other, it having been found that plots close together tend to have fertilities more comparable than plots widely separated.

(b) For experiments on the nutrition of animals, it has been found that animals from the same litter resemble each other in their response to a given diet more than animals from other litters.

(c) In experiments on the purification of the products of fermentations, each fermentation may be conceivably different from the others in some slight degree, so may be considered as a block.

(d) If, in any experiment in which the personal idiosyncracies of the operator may effect the result, the total number of treatments to be compared involves the use of more than one operator, then clearly the operator is the block.

(e) There are many other possible sources of inhomogeneity in the experimental background that may be considered as blocks. For example, in a comparison of treatments involving use of a thermostat or incubator it is obviously preferable if possible to place all the units with all the treatments in the same thermostat or incubator at the same time. Errors due to lack of perfection in the equipment will then be at an absolute minimum. It may be, however, that the thermostat is not large enough to take all the treatments at one time. We then either have to use several thermostats, in which case the thermostat is obviously the block, or to use the same thermostat at successive intervals of time, in which case the time is obviously the block.

(g) In any experiment in which a number of treatments are to be compared and in which the material on which they are applied may change slightly with time, and in which only a given number of treatments can be tried out in one day, then the day is the block. Examples are where there might be differential leakage from a gas holder in the case of a mixture of gases, or where a broth, e.g. of penicillin, may be appreciably unstable.

(h) In many cases there are no clear-cut distinctions of the type illustrated above, but nevertheless advantages will result from splitting the experi-

[4] This design will not be discussed in detail as the author has not found instances in industrial work where the comparison of such large numbers of treatments is necessary. It is described here, however, as it is the simplest of a series of such designs. A general description with references is by F. Yates : Empire Journal of Experimental Agriculture VIII, page 223, 1940. Descriptions and methods of computation of several are in C. H. Goulden : "Methods of Statistical Analysis" (John Wiley) 1939.

ment up into blocks. In general experiments done as close together as possible in time and space will resemble each other more than those remote from them. The air temperature, atmospheric pressure, humidity, adjustment of the machines, mood and behaviour of the operators, and many other less tangible factors will all tend to vary less within a short space of time than over a longer period. Accordingly, if the experiment can be so split up into blocks the effective error will be appreciably reduced.

(i) Multiple Factor Experiments

The type of experiment which we have been discussing up to now has had only one "independent variable" or "factor." In much industrial work, of course, there are a relatively large number of independent variables which we wish to investigate, and we therefore require a further set of techniques.

The classical ideal of experimentation is to have all the independent variables but one constant. It is frequently not recognized that this may sometimes be far from the ideal, for in order to get a fair assessment of the effects of varying the particular variable one must allow the others to vary over their full range as well. If they were held constant, they would have inevitably to be held constant at completely arbitrary values. Thus varying factor A from its normal value A_1 to some other value A_2 may produce a given change in the quality of the product when factor B is at a value of B_1 but a different change in the quality of the product when factor B is at a value B_2. The factorial design of experiment is designed to detect this type of effect, and at the same time gives maximum efficiency, i.e. gives the maximum amount of information about the system being experimented upon for a given amount of work.

The technique of factorial experimentation was developed in the science of agriculture in the twenties and thirties largely at the Rothamsted Experiment Station by R. A. Fisher and his colleagues.

Fisher's approach to experimentation differs in two fundamental aspects from the classical one-variable-at-a-time ideology. Firstly, he stresses the importance of obtaining an accurate estimate of the magnitude of the error variation, rather than its minimisation. The accurate estimate of the error variation is necessary in order to apply an exact test of significance.

Secondly, Fisher emphasises the advantages to be gained from including in the same experiment as many as possible of the factors whose effects are to be determined. The advantages of this are—

(a) much greater efficiency ; estimates of a given standard of accuracy for the effects can be obtained in a much smaller total number of observations. When the experiments are on the full industrial scale this may represent a very considerable reduction in their cost ;

(b) information is given on the extent to which the factors interact, i.e. the way in which the effect of one factor is affected by the other factors ; the experiments will therefore give a wider inductive basis for any conclusions that may be reached. To give an illustration of this, imagine one man carrying out a comparison of two catalysts for a contact oleum plant, the conversion efficiency being the dependent variable of interest. He would hold constant all his other factors, e.g. in particular gas inlet temperature and rate of loading. He might conclude from his experiments that catalyst A was better than catalyst B. Meanwhile a second experimenter could conclude from experiments on inlet gas temperature that 420°C. was the best ; the experiments on catalyst may have been made with a temperature of 450°C., and hence were invalid. The first experimenter could point out that the second experimenter's work was made with catalyst B and hence his conclusions are not valid. Similarly, a third set of experiments on rate of loading might show that the rates chosen for the first two sets of experiments were incorrect, and hence the conclusions drawn therefrom are invalid. However, the loading experiments might have been carried out at the wrong temperature and with the wrong catalyst, and hence would not be valid. It is possible, of course, that 420°C. is the best temperature irrespective of which catalyst and loading rate was employed, and that catalyst A is the best catalyst irrespective of which temperature and loading rates were employed, and that the best rate of loading remains the best irrespective of which catalyst and temperature are employed. To make these assumptions without demonstrating their validity is quite unjustified, however. This type of effect, namely the effect of one factor being dependent upon the value of another factor, is known as an "interaction."

(j) The Three Factor Experiment

(i) *Classical*

Let us consider a hypothetical experiment, in which we wish to investigate the effects of three independent variables P, Q and R (which may be temperatures, pressures, flow rates, concentrations, etc.) upon a dependent variable x (which may be yield, purity, etc.).

Suppose that in the first instance it will be adequate to investigate them each at only two levels. Thus suppose the normal values for the process are P_1, Q_1, and R_1, and we wish to find the effects of increasing them to P_2, Q_2 and R_2 respectively. How would we carry out this experiment in the classical style ?

We would first do an experimental control with values $P_1\ Q_1\ R_1$. A value of x would be obtained which we denote by $(P_1\ Q_1\ R_1)_x$.

To obtain the effect on x of changing P from P_1 to P_2 (which we will symbolically denote by $(P_1 - P_2)_x$ we do an experiment with values $P_2\ Q_1\ R_1$. A value of x will be obtained which we denote by $(P_2\ Q_1\ R_1)_x$. It is then clear that

$$(P_1 - P_2)_x = (P_1\ Q_1\ R_1)_x - (P_2\ Q_1\ R_1)_x$$

Similarly, experiments at $P_1\ Q_2\ R_1$ and $P_1\ Q_1\ R_2$ give us

$$(Q_1 - Q_2)_x = (P_1\ Q_1\ R_1)_x - (P_1\ Q_2\ R_1)_x$$

and $(R_1 - R_2)_x = (P_1\ Q_1\ R_1)_x - (P_1\ Q_1\ R_2)_x$

Now a very important point is that each of these experiments would have to be repeated not less than once, for without not less than two observations it is quite impossible to make any estimate of experimental error. Without such an estimate it is quite impossible to say whether any apparent difference between, say, $(P_1\ Q_1\ R_1)_x$ and $(P_2\ Q_1\ R_1)_x$ is real or is due to the errors of measurement and sampling, etc. We therefore require our four experiments to be repeated once, making eight observations in all. Each level of each effect will be given by two observations, i.e. we will be comparing the mean of two observations with the mean of two observations.

No information is given by this experiment as to any possible interactions between the factors. Thus for example, $(R_1 - R_2)_x$ with P at P_1 may well be different from $(R_1 - R_{2x})$ with P at P_2, but our experiment is quite unable to detect such an effect.

(ii) *Factorial*

With the factorial design we should carry out experiments at all combinations of P, Q, and R, namely $(P_1\ Q_1\ R_1)$, $(P_2\ Q_1\ R_1)$, $(P_1\ Q_2\ R_1)$, $(P_2\ Q_2\ R_1)$, $(P_1\ Q_1\ R_2)$, $(P_2\ Q_1\ R_2)$, $(P_1\ Q_2\ R_2)$, and $(P_2\ Q_2\ R_2)$, making a total of eight observations, the same total as in the classical design.

It may make it easier to grasp the significance of the above set of combinations if we realize that they are the co-ordinates of eight corners of a cube whose axes are P, Q, and R (Figure 1).

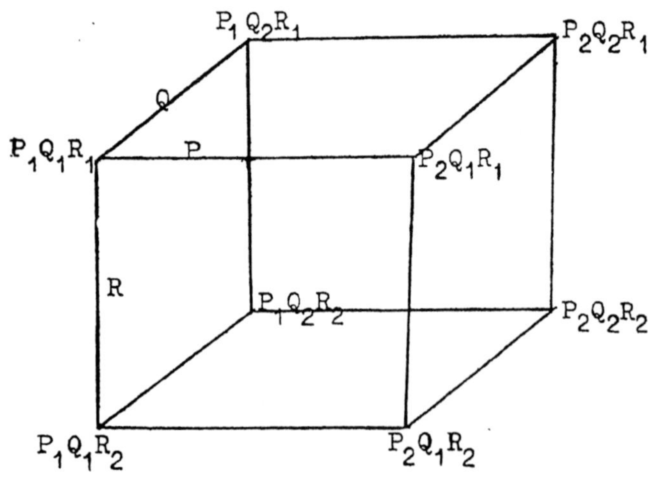

Figure 1.

Having such a picture we can now visualise how we obtain our estimates of the three main effects. We obtain our estimate of $(P_1 - P_2)_x$ by comparing the average of the P_1 plane with the average of the P_2 plane; in detail, the average of $(P_1\ Q_1\ R_1)_x$, $(P_1\ Q_2\ R_1)_x$, $(P_1\ Q_2\ R_2)_x$, $(P_1\ Q_1\ R_2)_x$ with the corresponding set $(P_2\ Q_1\ R_1)_x$, $(P_2\ Q_2\ R_1)_x$, $(P_2\ Q_2\ R_2)_x$, $(P_2\ Q_1\ R_2)_x$. Although the other two variables Q and R are varying, they are varying in such a way that they correspond in the two sets, and thus to a first approximation their disturbing effects cancel out. The other main effects $(Q_1 - Q_2)_x$ and $(R_1 - R_2)_x$ are obtained similarly.

The first advantage of our factorial design is that our main effects are obtained as the difference between the mean of one set of four observations and the mean of another set of four observations. In the classical design our main effects were the differences between means of two observations. We have thus obtained double the accuracy for the same number of experiments. If this experiment is being carried out on the full industrial scale at considerable cost and trouble, this factor can be of the greatest economic importance.

The second advantage of the factorial design is that it provides us with an estimate of the possible interactions between the main effects.

Consider our cube again. To obtain the interaction between P and R, average the front plane with the back plane, i.e. we average our Q. This gives us a table as below, the superscript $\bar{Q}$ indicating that figures are averaged over Q.

$(P_1\ R_1)_x^{\bar{Q}}$	$(P_2\ R_1)_x^{\bar{Q}}$
$(P_1\ R_2)_x^{\bar{Q}}$	$(P_2\ R_2)_x^{\bar{Q}}$

The top line gives us $(P_1 - P_2)_x$ at $R = R_1$ and the bottom line gives us $(P_1 - P_2)_x$ at $R = R_2$. Since each figure in the table is the average of two results, we have a valid estimate of error, and can determine whether $(P_1 - P_2)_x^{R_1}$, the superscript indicating that the figure is obtained with R at R_1, is significantly not equal to $(P_1 - P_2)_x^{R_2}$. If they do differ significantly, then there is an interaction between P and R. The other interactions can be derived similarly.

The computation of the three factor experiment is discussed in Chapter XI (d).

(k) Higher Factorial Experiments

We have been discussing a three factor experiment, all factors being at two levels. We can represent this symbolically as $2 \times 2 \times 2$, or 2^3. The extension to a fourth factor is obvious, though not capable of a geometrical representation. If the fourth factor is represented by S, then we can regard the eight experiments so far mentioned as having been carried out with S at its lower value, S_1, and to introduce the fourth factor S we carry out a similar eight experiments with S now at its upper level S_2. The estimate of the main effect of S is then given by the difference between the average of the first eight with $S = S_1$ and the average of the second eight with $S = S_2$. The main effects of the other three factors are obtained similarly. There are now six possible first order interactions, taking the factors in pairs, namely PQ, QR, PR, PS, QS, RS, and to obtain each of these we average over the two factors not mentioned in the interaction, e.g. for PQ we average over R and S.

It will be apparent that the introduction of the fourth factor has improved the experiment appreciably. The main effects are given as a result of the comparison of averages of eight results (instead of four): the first order interactions are given as a result of the comparison of averages of four results (instead of two). Further, it is now possible to check on the possible existence of what are known as second order interactions. As an example of one of these, consider the interaction PQ: it is possible that its magnitude may depend on the value of R, being different when $R = R_1$ from what it is when $R = R_2$. Such an effect we call a second order interaction and denote as PQR or $P \times Q \times R$. Actually it is found that such interactions are symmetrical with respect to three factors. PQR can be regarded as the interaction of PQ with R, QR with P, or RP with Q. With four factors there are four possible second order interactions, PQR, QRS, RSP and PQS. Our four factor experiment will estimate the existence of all these possible effects (the procedure is given in Chapter XI (e)).

It will be noted that the four factor experiment is even more efficient relative to the classical design than the three factor experiment, which achieved double the accuracy for the main effects.

The four factor experiment requires $2^4 = 16$ runs, and its main effects are given as the comparison of the average of 8 runs with the average of 8. The nearest equivalent classical experiment is to carry out the five combinations

$$\begin{array}{ll} P_1\ Q_1\ R_1\ S_1 & P_2\ Q_1\ R_1\ S_1 \\ & P_1\ Q_2\ R_1\ S_1 \\ & P_1\ Q_1\ R_2\ S_1 \\ & P_1\ Q_1\ R_1\ S_2 \end{array}$$

each three times which would require a total of 15 runs. The main effects are then given as the comparison of averages of 3 runs, which are markedly inferior to the factorial experiment. The latter of course also checks on the existence of the six possible first order interactions and the four possible second order interactions.

It is clear where the immense superiority of the factorial experiment is arising. In the classical experiment all the 12 observations on the last four combinations are each only being used once, to contribute information on only one effect. Thus the three replications of $P_2Q_1R_1S_1$ contribute information only on the main effect of P and add nothing whatever to our knowledge of the other three factors or to the various possible interactions. Similarly for $P_1Q_2R_1S_1$, $P_1Q_1R_2S_1$ and $R_1Q_1R_1S_2$. Only the combination of $P_1Q_1R_1S_1$ is used several times. In the factorial experiment, on the other hand, every observation is used many times over in a different manner each time.

The extension to more than four factors or to factors at more than two levels follows naturally.

Finally, it will have been noted that the larger factorial experiments require a fair number of experiments, e.g. a 2^4 or $2 \times 2 \times 2 \times 2$ experiment requires $2^4 = 16$ runs. This number may be larger than can be comfortably put into a block. Methods have been worked out which evade these difficulties and enable us to put these 16 runs into 2 blocks of 8 runs or into 4 blocks of 4 runs. These are discussed in Chapter XIV.

CHAPTER II

FUNDAMENTAL STATISTICAL CONCEPTIONS

(a) Statistical Terminology

Statistics, like every other science, has its own words and symbols of special meaning. These may be confusing to the newcomer, but are almost essential for the normal use of its methods.

We apply our statistical methods to sets of numbers obtained by making measurements upon some property of our product or process. The property might be yield, purity, or such qualities as the life in days or in tons throughput of a piece of plant before failure. Or a machine may be making articles whose size, weight, or metallurgical hardness we measure. This variable we refer to as the "dependent variable," and we are frequently interested in the effect upon it of the conditions under which it is obtained. These conditions can generally be specified in terms of a number of "independent variables," which we can refer to as "factors." Thus in many chemical processes the conditions can be determined by specifying values for the temperature, pressure, time of reaction, proportions of reactants. A given value for an independent variable is referred to as a "level." A given observation on a dependent variable is referred to as an "individual."

An important concept is that of "population," broadly speaking a large number of individuals from a particular source. We frequently wish to estimate the mean value of a property of a whole set of individuals from a small number of them: this part withdrawn from the whole we refer to as a "sample."

The use of a bar over a symbol indicates that the average is meant—thus $\bar{x}$ is the average of the set of x's considered. Σ indicates summation, i.e. addition, of the series of terms considered.

An awkward conception is "degrees of freedom." It is closely related to the number of observations, in general the number of observations minus the number of constraints imposed on the system. An accurate definition is difficult, however, and we will be content with giving an explicit account for each particular application. It is interesting to note that rather similar conceptions will be familiar to physical chemists in the application of the phase rule and in the quantum mechanics of molecules.

(b) Probability

Probability is expressed on the scale 0 to 1, the former implying that an event will certainly not occur (or that a hypothesis is not true) and the latter implying that the event is certain to occur (or that the hypothesis is definitely true). On this scale a value of 0.5 implies that the event is as likely to occur as not (or that the hypothesis is as likely to be true as not).

Frequently in practice this scale of fractions is transformed into one of percentages, e.g. a probability of 0.05 is referred to as a 5% probability.

(c) Populations: Tests of Significance

"The idea of an infinite population distributed in a frequency distribution in respect of one or more characteristics is fundamental to all statistical work." From a limited experience of some function or of individuals of a given type "we may obtain some idea of the infinite hypothetical population from which our sample is drawn, and so of the probable nature of future samples to which our conclusions are to be applied. If a second sample belies this expectation we infer that it is, in the language of statistics, drawn from a different population; that the treatment to which the second sample" has been subjected "did make a material difference . . . Critical tests of this kind may be called tests of significance, and when such tests are available we may discover whether a second sample is or is not significantly different from the first" (Fisher, "Statistical Methods for Research Workers").

The most common type of test has the form in which we assume that the means (Student's t test), the variances (Fisher's z test), or the fit of the assumed distribution to the actual data (Use of χ^2) are the same for the two samples and calculate the probability of getting such results as we did get on the basis of this hypothesis being true. So long as the probability is greater than 0.05 (5%) there is no strong reason to doubt the hypothesis. When the probability is 0.05 however, a value as small as this would only be obtained once in 20 times if there were really no difference, and hence it is generally taken that this indicates that the hypothesis is not true. Smaller values of the probability are, of course, an even stronger indication that the hypothesis is incorrect. Thus a small probability corresponds to a high degree of significance.

(d) **Significance Levels**

It is entirely a matter of judgment what probability level we take as being significant. For many purposes the 5% level is accepted, but we must realize that this means that 1 in every 20 times we will assert that an effect exists when it really does not. If this is too frequent an error, then we must adopt a higher significance level, say 1%. The trouble now is that we will be ignoring effects when they really do exist. The best practical compromise is probably to regard results at or even just under the 5% level of significance as well worth following up. For presentation of final results and conclusions, however, one would prefer a higher level. This can be obtained, if the effect really does exist, by obtaining more observations.

Throughout this book we shall use the word "significant" in the sense "statistically significant." "Significant" accordingly will mean merely that the data in question is sufficient to establish that such and such an effect exists with the stated level of significance: it is not meant to imply that the effect is necessarily of great importance from the practical point of view, though of course it might be. The converse also holds: an effect may appear on a given set of data to be non-significant, but this may be merely because the data is inadequate to show it and the effect may be of the greatest practical importance. Our aim generally is to give an estimate of each effect together with the so-called fiducial or confidence limits within which it probably (with a stated level of probability) lies, though in some cases the solution of this problem is by no means simple.

For example, if an effect has to be of magnitude 15% to be of practical importance, and our data gives us as our estimate of it 5% ± 2%, it is clear that the effect is statistically significant but not of practical importance. Alternatively if our result was 5% ± 10%, then it is not statistically significant on our present data but may still be of practical importance.

(e) **Computation**

The application of statistical methods generally involves a certain amount of computation. A large part of this is the summing of numbers and of their squares; this can easily be performed with a table of squares ("Barlow's Tables of Squares, etc." (E. and F. M. Spon) is a very complete set), and with a simple adding machine. For much correlation work on calculating machine (one that will multiply and divide) is almost essential. There are a variety of models available; it can be safely said that the better the machine the more accurately and rapidly can the work be carried out. An electric machine with automatic division and multiplication is really desirable.

(f) Measures of Variability

In statistical work we are largely concerned with the variability in determination of some property of a system, e.g. the variability in yield or in quality of some chemical process.

The variability of a set of observations can be assessed in a variety of ways :—

(a) The "range," i.e. the difference between the largest and the smallest of the set, generally denoted by the symbol w.

(b) The "mean deviation," i.e. the mean of the deviations of the observations from their mean.

(c) The "variance," i.e. the sum of the squares of the deviations of the observations from their mean, divided by one less than the total number of observations, generally denoted by the symbol σ^2.

Thus for the set of observations

9, 11, 14, 11, 13, 12, 10, 13, 12, 15

(a) the range would be $15 - 9 = 6$.

(b) the mean deviation would be obtained by calculating the mean as $(9 + 11 + 14 \ldots + 12 + 15)/10 = 120/10 = 12.0$, the deviations as $(12 - 9) = 3$, $(12 - 11) = 1$, $(14 - 12) = 2$, etc., and taking the mean of these deviations as $(3 + 1 + 2 + \ldots)/10 = 14/10 = 1.4$.

c) the variance denoted by σ^2 would be defined as

$$\sigma^2 = \frac{\Sigma(x - \bar{x})^2}{n - 1}$$

where $\bar{x}$ is the mean of the x's, n is the number of observations, $(x - \bar{x})^2$ represents the square of the deviation of an x from the mean, and the summation sign Σ indicates that $(x - \bar{x})^2$ is to be obtained from all the x's and summed for them. Thus the variance of the set of numbers quoted above would be (the mean $\bar{x}$ is here equal to 12.0)

$$\sigma^2 = \frac{(12 - 9)^2 + (12 - 11)^2 + (14 - 12)^2 + \ldots.}{10 - 1} = \frac{30}{9} = 3.33$$

Of these three measures of variability, the range is much used for small samples (n not greater than 10) in process control work (the quality control chart, discussed in Chapter VIII) on account of its arithmetical simplicity. It is clear that it does not utilise the whole of the information from the data, for the detail of the intermediate results does not enter into the determination.

The mean deviation has the virtue of arithmetical simplicity, but its properties are such that it is difficult to employ mathematically, and it must be considered obsolete.

The variance is generally greatly to be preferred as a measure of variability, for its properties are well known and tests of significance based upon it are available. It also has the valuable property of being additive, i.e. if a process is subject to a number of separate variances σ_1^2, σ_2^2, ... due to several independent causes, then the total variance σ_T^2 is numerically equal to their sum, i.e. $\sigma_T^2 = \sigma_1^2 + \sigma_2^2 + \sigma_3^2 + \ldots.$. The converse of this is of particular importance, where we analyse the total variance of a system into components attributable to various parts of the process. This is discussed at length in Chapter VII. A further advantage of the variance as a measure of variability is that it has the maximum efficiency, i.e. it extracts more information about the variability from the data than the other measures.

The square root of the variance is termed the "standard deviation" and denoted by the symbol σ.

The relation between range and standard deviation is discussed in Chapter VIII (e).

(g) The Calculation of Variances

It is often troublesome to calculate the mean $\bar{x}$ and then find the deviation of each observation x from it before squaring and summing these deviations.

We therefore use the algebraically equivalent formula

$$\sigma^2 = \left[\Sigma(x^2) - \frac{(\Sigma x)^2}{n}\right]/(n-1)$$

For the above set of numbers

$$\sigma^2 = \left[9^2 + 11^2 + 14^2 + \ldots + 15^2 - \frac{(9 + 11 + \ldots + 15)^2}{10}\right]/(10-1)$$

$$= (1470 - \frac{120^2}{10})/9 = (1470 - 1440)/9 = 30/9 = 3.33$$

To lighten the arithmetic in calculating variances, it is frequently worth while to take an arbitrary zero and transform all the numbers on to the new scale. Thus with the above set of numbers we might shift the axis by 9 units so that they now become

0, 2, 5, 2, 4, 3, 1, 4, 3, 6.

The variance of these observations is then

$$\sigma^2 = \left[(0^2 + 2^2 + 5^2 + \ldots + 6^2 - \frac{(0 + 2 + 5 + \ldots + 6)^2)}{10}\right]/(10-1)$$

$$= (120 - \frac{30^2)}{10}/9 = (120 - 90)/9 = 30/9 = 3.33$$

as before. Thus shifting the zero has not affected the estimate of the variance. It should be clear that this should be so : we are measuring the variabilityabout the *mean*, and even if we added 100 to all the observations the variability remains the same.

If the numbers had all been 100 larger, then the sum of squares would have been of the order of 100,000, i.e. the arithmetic would have been rather unpleasant, and would have been very much lightened by shifting the zero by 100 units, giving us our first calculation in which the sum of squares was 1470, or by 109 units, giving us our second calculation in which the sum of squares was only 120.

The business of shifting the origin is largely a matter of personal taste. It has to be done carefully, but when done the subsequent arithmetic is much lighter. It has two advantages. Firstly, one will then be working with numbers less than 100, and with a little practice it is easy to carry the squares of these numbers in one's head. Secondly, the squares of two figure numbers cannot have more than four figures, and since one has only four fingers on one's hand this makes entering them on an adding machine easier.

(h) The Definition of Variance

The definition of variance is formally not $\Sigma(x - \bar{x})^2/(n-1)$, as quoted above, but $\Sigma(x - \bar{x})^2/n$, and it is quoted as the latter in many statistical texts. In any practical application, however, we should use the formula with $(n-1)$ as the denominator.

The reason for this apparent confusion is as follows :—

In calculating $\Sigma(x - \bar{x})^2$ we should be calculating the sum of squares of the deviations from the true mean of the population from which the sample is drawn. We have only an estimate of the mean, the mean of our sample, which will not in general be identical with the true mean of the whole population. The sum of squares of the deviations from the mean of the sample will be smaller than the sum of the squares of the deviations from the true mean. To see this, suppose we have two observations 1 and 3, and that the true population mean is actually 1. The sum of the squares of the deviations from the true mean is $(1-1)^2 + (3-1)^2 = 4$: working from the true mean we would use n as the divisor to get the estimate of the variance as $4/2 = 2$. The sum of the squares of the deviations from the sample mean is $(2-1)^2 + (3-2)^2 = 2$: if we used n as the divisor the estimate of the variance is $2/2 = 1$, whereas if we use $(n-1)$ as the divisor we get $2/(2-1) = 2$ as our estimate of the variance. It is apparent that the use of $(n-1)$ instead of n as the divisor helps to compensate for the use of the sample mean instead of the true mean.

The number (n — 1) is known as the degrees of freedom of the variance, and is used in making tests of significance in comparing one variance with another (Chapter IV).

(i) Distributions

It is a matter of common experience that we cannot manufacture articles identically; successive individuals differ slightly in their size, quality, etc. Similarly, if we make repeat determinations of some physico-chemical quantity, e.g. the yield from some process, the values we obtain will not be exactly similar: this variability would be due not only to the (possible) variability of the process, but also to the errors of measurement.

It can be shown theoretically that if we assume that there is a very large number of very small errors all operating independently, then we get a distribution of the form shown in figure 2, known as the Gaussian distribution.

This Gaussian distribution has the following valuable properties :—

(a) it is completely defined by two statistical parameters, (i) the mean (fixing its position along the x-axis) and (ii) the standard deviation (fixing its width or spread).

(b) There is a relation, for which tables are already calculated, between the deviation from the mean, expressed as a multiple of σ, and the frequency with which these deviations occur. Thus to particularise, 95% of the individuals should lie between $-1.96\ \sigma$ and $+1.96\ \sigma$ on each side of the mean, and 99.8% between $-3.09\ \sigma$ and $+3.09\ \sigma$ on each side of the mean. Similarly, if we get a deviation from the mean of d, we calculate the quantity known as Student's t defined by d/σ, and tables are available to show how often a deviation of this size should occur.

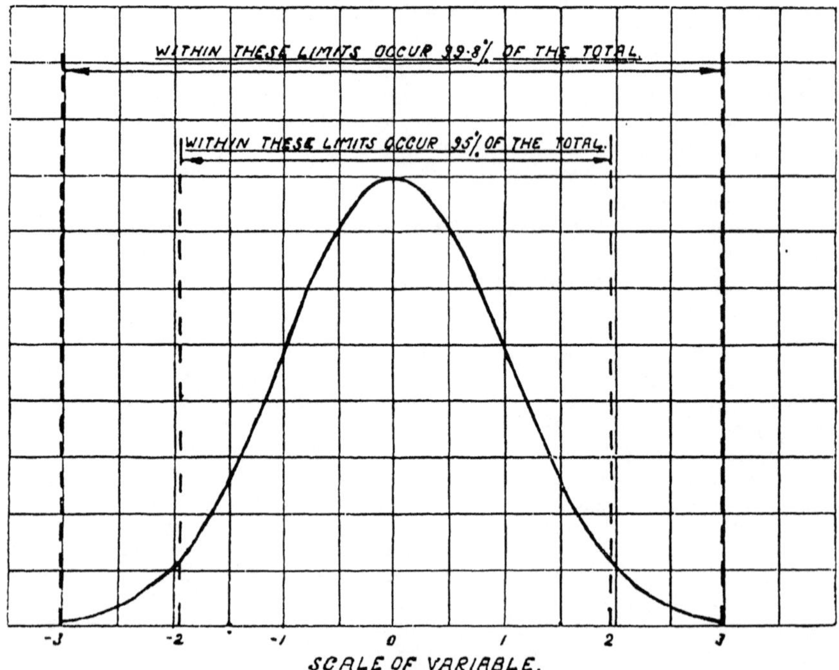

Figure 2.

Figure 3 shows a typical distribution occurring in the chemical industry. It refers to the quantity of one ingredient in a four component mixture. The height of the y-axis at any interval of the x-axis indicates the number of batches

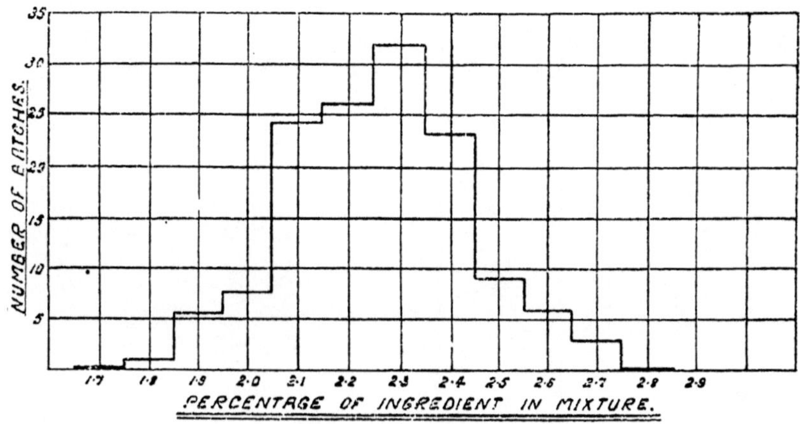

Figure 3

which had their content of this ingredient in that interval. It will be seen that though the experimental distribution does not follow exactly the theoretical Gaussian curve, yet its features are very similar. It must be remembered that we have here only a total of 138 observations: in any given interval the number to be expected is quite small, therefore, and we must expect random fluctuations about the expected value. If the total number of observations was 1000 we would expect the experimental distribution to be a closer approximation to the Gaussian, and with 10,000 observations even closer.

Many of the tests of significance that we make are based on the assumption that our variable is distributed according to the Gaussian form. It is true that distributions found experimentally often are not exactly of the Gaussian form, but they almost invariably approximate reasonably closely to it. It is fortunate that the departure from the Gaussian form has to be very severe indeed before our tests of significance become appreciably inaccurate. The discrepancies for any distribution with a hump somewhere near the middle and tailing off to zero either side are quite negligible.

(j) Grouped Frequency Distributions

If the number of observations whose standard deviation is to be calculated is large, say 40 or more, the labour involved can be reduced by using what is called a grouped frequency distribution.

We will use the data of the previous section as an illustration (see Table 2.1).

We divide the variable (here percentage of the component) into about 10 to 20 equal sized groups (column headed X). We count up the number of observations occurring in each of these groups (column headed f). This column f is the vertical axis in figure 2. We select a new origin somewhere near the middle of the range, and lay out a new scale as shown in the column headed x. The remainder of the arithmetic should be clear. We obtain σ_x in our x units. Since 1 x-unit equal 0.1 X-unit, $\sigma X = 0.182$. Since $\bar{x} = 0.59$ this means that the mean is 0.59 units up from the x-origin, or $0.59 = 0.06$ units up from the X-origin. The X-origin was at 2.20, hence the mean is at $2.20 + 0.06 = 2.26$ X-units.

Table 2.1

X	f	x	fx	fx^2
1.75—1.84	1	—4	—4	16
1.85—1.94	6	—3	—18	54
1.95—2.04	8	—2	—16	32
2.05—2.14	24	—1	—24	24
2.15—2.24	26	0	—62	0
2.25—2.34	32	1	32	32
2.35—2.44	23	2	46	92
2.45—2.54	9	3	27	81
2.55—2.64	6	4	24	96
2.65—2.74	3	5	15	75
	138		+144	502
			— 62	
			+ 82	

$$\sigma_x^2 = \left[502 - \frac{(82)^2}{138}\right]/(138-1)$$
$$= (502 - 48.72)/137 = 453.28/137$$
$$= 3.31$$
$$\sigma_x = 1.82$$
$$\sigma_X = 0.182$$
$$\bar{x} = 82/138 = 0.59$$
$$\bar{X} = 2.20 + 0.59/10 = 2.26$$

In our discussion of the properties of the Gaussian distribution it was remarked that 95% of the total number of observations would lie within $\pm$ 1.96 σ of the mean. These limits here are at $2.26 - 1.96 \times 0.18 = 1.91$ and at $2.26 + 1.96 \times 0.18 = 2.61$. Inspecting our table we find that those in the two end intervals are 1 and 3, making a total of 4 out of 138, or 2.9%. However, the 1.85 — 1.94 and 2.55 — 2.64 intervals probably contain some outside the limits less than 1.91 and greater than 2.61, so the actual agreement is reasonable.

Similarly, we would expect very few (of the order of 2 out of 1000) observations outside the limits $2.26 - 3.09 \times 0.18 = 1.70$ and $2.26 + 3.09 \times 0.18 = 2.82$. Inspecting our table we find none of our 138 outside these limits, in good accord with this prediction based on the Gaussian distribution.

(k) **Lognormal Distributions**

For certain types of data there are sometimes good reasons for considering the use of the logarithm of the variable rather than the variable itself. Thus in some cases the larger the value of the variable the more erratic will it become, e.g. in corrosion experiments the larger the corrosion the less the agreement there is between duplicates. Under these circumstances we would expect a skewed distribution with a long tail to the upper end. However, any deviation which is proportional to the mean of the unlogged data when expressed logarithmically becomes constant. Figure 4 gives the distribution of throughputs before failure in thousands of tons of a piece of acid plant. Figure 5 is the same data grouped according to the logarithm of the throughput. One individual tends to give the impression of a tail at the lower end, but taking an overall view it is doubtful if the logarithmic distribution departs significantly from normality.

When we have a variable which clearly has a lognormal distribution and we wish to make a test of significance, e.g. compare two means, then it is probably advisable to carry out the test on the logarithms of the variable. An example of this is given in Chapter XII (k).

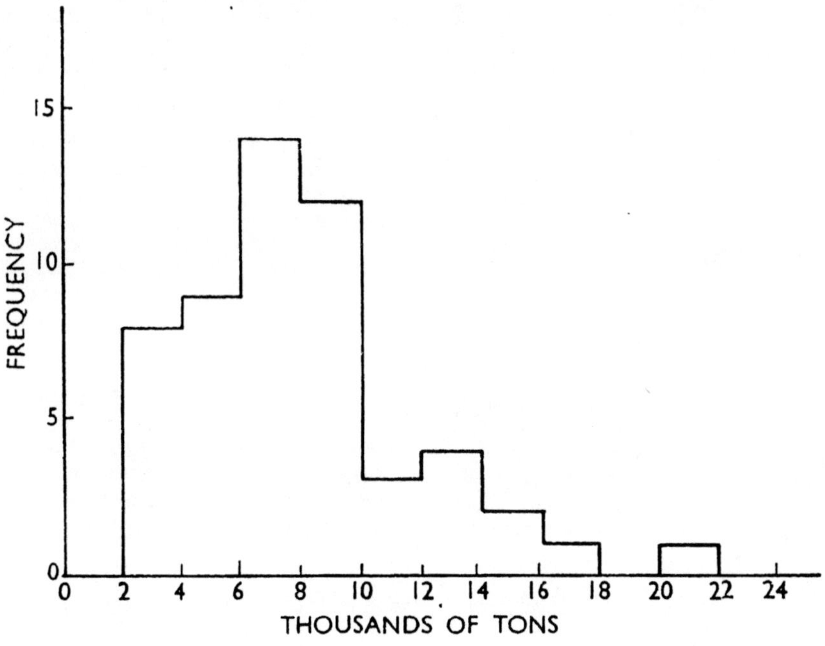

Figure 4.

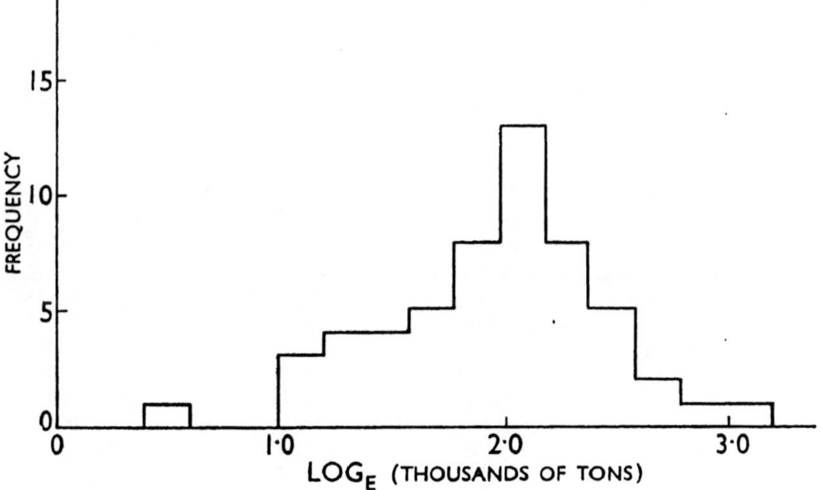

Figure 5.

CHAPTER III

SIGNIFICANCE OF MEANS

(a) Significance of a Single Mean

Suppose we have a population distributed with standard deviation σ about its mean $\bar{X}$. Suppose we take samples of n individuals at a time. The first sample will have a mean $\bar{x}_1$, the second sample will have a mean $\bar{x}_2$ not necessarily the same as $\bar{x}_1$, and so on. It is a valuable property of these sample means that they are distributed about the population mean $\bar{X}$ with standard deviation $(\sigma/\sqrt{n})$.

Now if we take an individual at random and find that it lies further from the population mean $\bar{X}$ than 1.96 σ then we conclude that this individual is not very likely to belong to the population we are considering. In exactly the same way if we take a sample of n individuals and find that its mean is more than $1.96\,\sigma/\sqrt{n}$ from the population mean $\bar{X}$ then we conclude that it is not very likely that this sample of n individuals was drawn from the population we are considering.

The ratio of the deviation of the mean $\bar{x}$ of a particular sample of n individuals from an expected value E to its standard deviation $\sigma/\sqrt{n}$ is known as Student's t, i.e.

$$t = \frac{\bar{x} - E}{\sigma/\sqrt{n}}$$

We will deal with a specific example. Two analysts A and B analysed a series of chemical mixtures, and obtained the results below for the percentage of one ingredient. We would expect the differences between the operators for each mixture to average zero if there was no systematic difference between the operators.

The essential point about this example is that we have ten numbers (the last row in Table 3.1) and we wish to test whether their mean differs significantly from zero.

Table 3.1

Mixture	1	2	3	4	5	6	7	8	9	10
Analyst A	7	9	8	10	8	11	9	8	9	8
Analyst B	11	7	10	10	9	10	10	9	11	11
A — B = x	—4	2	—2	0	—1	1	—1	—1	—2	—3

The average value $\bar{x}$ for A — B is —1.10, and the expected value E is 0.

We calculate the standard deviation of these individuals as

$$\sqrt{[[(-4)^2 + 2^2 + \ldots + (-3)^2 - (-4 + 2 + \ldots -3)^2/10]/(10-1)]} = 1.79.$$

The standard deviation of the mean $\bar{x}$ is given by $\sigma/\sqrt{n} = 1.79/\sqrt{10} = 0.565$. We then calculate t as $1.10/0.565 = 1.95$.

Now the value we used for σ is of course only an estimate of the population value. Being based on ten individuals it is not as accurate as if it were based on one hundred or one thousand individuals. The table of the significant values of t takes this into account (Table I in the Appendix). Examining this Table, we see that for infinite degrees of freedom (the degrees of freedom here are numerically one less than the numbers of observations) a value of t as large as 1.96 should only occur 1 in 20 times (P = 0.05) if the hypothesis being tested is true. Here the number of observations is 10, so the degrees of freedom are 9. For the 5% level of significance we would need a value of t of 2.26. Our present value is 1.95 and this is less than the value for the 5% level but is greater than the value

1.83 for the 10% level. The significance of the present result is thus between 10% and 5%, i.e. our hypothesis that there is no difference between the two analysts is in reasonable accord with the data. If our values of t had been a little larger, however, we would have had to regard the hypothesis as incorrect and had to accept the conclusion that there almost certainly was a genuine difference between the analysts.

(b) Confidence Limits for a Single Mean

We have shown that the difference of the mean of this quantity (A—B) is not significantly different from zero. This attainment of non-significance might be due to the quantity not differing from zero, but alternatively it might be due to the inadequacy of our data, i.e. our data may be insufficient to give us a reasonably accurate estimate of the quantity. We can estimate which of these two alternatives is operating as follows.

We are going to determine the limits between which we can be reasonably confident that the true value of the mean, as determined from our sample, lies.

The first requirement is to decide what we mean by "reasonably confident." We might consider that if we are right 19 out of 20 times (equivalent to 95%) we would be satisfied.

We would then look up in the table of t for 9 degrees of freedom its value for the 5% level (95% chance of being right is equivalent to a 5% chance of being wrong). Here t is 2.26. Then the limits $\pm L$ on either side of the sample mean, where $\sigma =$ the standard deviation of the population and n is the number of individuals in the sample, are

$$\begin{aligned} \pm L &= \pm t(\sigma/\sqrt{n}) \\ &= \pm 2.26 \times 0.565 = \pm 1.28. \end{aligned}$$

Thus it is reasonably certain (within that chosen probability level) that the true value of the mean lies between $-1.10 + 1.28 = 0.18$ and $-1.10 - 1.28 = -2.38$. These limits are known as 95% confidence limits.[1]

If 19 out of 20 was not sufficiently certain for us, we might choose 999 out of 1000 (99.9%) and find from the table for t the value for 9 degrees of freedom and the 0.001 level as 4.78. The limits would then be $-1.10 \pm 4.78 \times 0.565$ or from —3.80 to 1.60.

We now consider the actual width of these limits (the 95% or 99.9%, or whatever level we have chosen). They fix the accuracy with which we have determined the mean. If the limits are narrow our determination is accurate, if they are wide the determination is not very accurate. These considerations should indicate whether the non-significant result we obtained was due to the real equality of the mean with the expected value or due to the inadequacy of the data. Here, where the mean has a 95% chance of lying anywhere between 0.18 and —2.38, it would seem that our determination is rather inaccurate.[2]

Greater accuracy in a mean can be obtained by taking more observations, i.e. by increasing n, since the standard deviation of the mean (or standard error) is $\sigma/\sqrt{n}$. Doubling the number of observations will give limits approximately $\frac{1}{\sqrt{2}} = 0.707$ of the present ones. Quadrupling the numbers would give limits $\frac{1}{\sqrt{4}} = 0.500$ of the present ones.

(1) Strictly speaking, these are "fiducial limits" and not confidence limits. For practical purposes the distinction is so slight as to be not worth making, and because of its greater intelligibility the term confidence limit is used here.

(2) A more accurate statement would be "If we say that the true population mean lies between 0.18 and —2.38, then the probability of our being correct is 0.95."

(c) **Comparison of Two Means**

We obtain two sets of numbers, and wish to test whether the mean of one set is significantly different from the mean of the other set, or whether the two sets can be regarded as drawn from one population.

Let $x_1, x_2 \cdots\cdots x_{n_1}$, and $x_1', x_2', \cdots\cdots x'_{n_2}$ be the two samples. The method of treatment depends upon the size of sample. Large samples can be considered to be those in which the total number of individuals $(n_1 + n_2)$ is greater than 30.

(i) *Small Samples*

We calculate the following terms. Σ denotes summation.

$$\bar{x} = \frac{\Sigma(x)}{n_1}, \bar{x}' = \frac{\Sigma(x')}{n_2}$$

$$\sigma^2 = \left[\Sigma(x'^2) - \frac{(\Sigma(x'))^2}{n_2} + \Sigma(x^2) - \frac{(\Sigma(x))^2}{n_1}\right] / (n_1 + n_2 - 2)$$

$$t = \frac{\bar{x} - \bar{x}'}{\sigma} \sqrt{\frac{n_1 \times n_2}{n_1 + n_2}}$$

Having found the value of t, we enter the table of t with degrees of freedom $(n_1 + n_2 - 2)$. If our value of t exceeds that for the 5% level we may take it with that degree of assurance that the populations are different.

Let us consider a specific example. The numbers below represent the throughputs in hundreds of tons of acid before failure for two sets of pots, one from Foundry A, the other from Foundry B, used in sulphuric acid pot concentration. Is there any reason to suppose that one foundry is better than the other ?

Foundry A.	71, 67, 33, 79, 42
Foundry B.	73, 80

$$\bar{x}_A = (71 + 67 + 33 + 79 + 42) / 5 = \frac{292}{5} = 58.4$$

$$\bar{x}_B = (73 + 80)/2 = \frac{153}{2} = 76.5$$

$$\sigma^2 = \left[(71^2 + 67^2 + \ldots + 42^2 - \frac{292^2}{5} + 73^2 + 80^2 - \frac{153^2)}{2}\right] / (5 + 2 - 2)$$

$$= 1596/5 = 319.2$$

$$\sigma = 17.9$$

$$t = \frac{76.5 - 58.4}{17.9} \sqrt{\frac{5 \times 2}{5 + 2}}$$

$$= 1.21 \text{ for } (5 + 2 - 2) = 5 \text{ degrees of freedom.}$$

Consulting the table of t, we find that for 5 degrees of freedom t must be not less than 2.57 to be significant at the 5% level. Accordingly there is no evidence that here the populations are different.

Looking up this value of t in a more complete table of t than the one in the Appendix, we find it corresponds to a level of significance of approximately 25%. That is to say, in the absence of any difference between the two foundries, if we repeatedly sampled from them we would get as large an apparent difference between them as we did here 1 out of every 4 times. The present result, therefore, is only a very slight indication of the possible superiority of Foundry B.

We have shown that the difference in these means is not significantly greater than zero. We can further lay down the confidence limits within which the difference will have a chosen probability of lying. We proceed on the same lines as before.

We have that the standard error of the difference in the means of the two samples, denoted by σ_m, is

$$\sigma_m = \sigma \sqrt{\frac{n_1 + n_2}{n_1 \times n_2}} = 17.9 \times \sqrt{\frac{5 + 2}{5 \times 2}} = 14.9$$

We also have t = its value in the table of t corresponding to $(n_1 + n_2 - 2) = (5 + 2 - 2) = 5$ degrees of freedom and to the significance level chosen. If we select the 5% level of significance (95% chance of being correct in the prediction that the true value of the difference in the means of the two samples lies between the limits stated) then for 5 degrees of freedom, $t = 2.57$.

Then if $\pm$ L is the maximum deviation likely (at this significance level) we have

$$L = t\,\sigma_m = 2.57 \times 14.9 = 38.3$$

The actual mean value obtained for the difference between the two types of pot was 18.1 The true value will lie 95% of cases $\pm$ 38.3 on either side of this, i.e. from -20.2 to $+ 56.4$ We thus see what a poor comparison is afforded by the data cited. There may well be marked differences between the foundries, but the present data is quite inadequate to answer these queries.

(ii) *Large Samples*

For large samples the same treatment as for small samples holds, but it can be simplified since we do not need to stick to the use of $(n - 1)$ instead of n.

We calculate the means of the two samples.

$$\bar{x} = \frac{\Sigma(x)}{n_1},\quad \bar{x}' = \frac{\Sigma(x')}{n_2}$$

We further calculate the standard deviations σ_1 and σ_2 of the individuals of the two samples. The standard error of the difference in the means of the two samples $\bar{x} - \bar{x}'$ is then given by

$$\sigma_D^2 = \frac{\sigma_1^2}{n_1} + \frac{\sigma_2^2}{n_2}$$

As before, we find t as

$$t = (\bar{x} - \bar{x}')/\sigma_D$$

and enter the table of t with infinite degrees of freedom (the last row in the table).

Thus if $\bar{x} = 100,\ n_1 = 40,\ \sigma_1^2 = 120$

$\bar{x} = 110,\ n_2 = 30,\ \sigma_2^2 = 60$

$$\text{then } \sigma_D = \sqrt{\frac{120}{40} + \frac{60}{30}} = \sqrt{5} = 2.236$$

$$\text{and } t = (110 - 100)/2.236 = 4.47$$

This is very much more significant than the 0.1% level of significance, so it may be taken as certain that the two means do differ.

To lay down the confidence limits $\pm$ L between which the true value of the difference between the two means has, say, a 95% chance of lying, we look up t for infinite degrees of freedom for this level, and the limits are $(\bar{x} - \bar{x}') \pm t\,\sigma_D$, or here $10 \pm 1.96 \times 2.24$ or between 5.6 and 14.4.

(d) Conclusions

In general, therefore, in any account of experimental work involving the determination of a mean in addition to the value obtained, its standard deviation and the number of observations upon which it is based should also be given. This will enable readers to assess the level of significance of the result.

An important proviso in the calculation of a standard deviation is that the individuals should be independent. Thus if we made 10 batches of some material, and took duplicate samples from each batch, we could not calculate the standard deviation on the assumption that we made 20 observations. Clearly the duplicate observations on each batch are not independent of each other. The methods of dealing with this type of situation are discussed later (Chapter XII (j)).

CHAPTER IV

COMPARISON OF VARIANCES

(a) Comparison of Two Variances

When we wish to compare the means of two groups of numbers we use the Student t test. It is sometimes the case, however, that what we wish to compare is the spreads or variabilities of the two sets of figures, and this is a different problem.

The test of significance for this type of problem is due to Fisher (Fisher actually dealt with the natural logarithm of the ratio of the square roots of the variances, which he called z, but here we will use the simple variance ratio which is denoted by F).

To deal with an example, suppose we have two alternative methods of technical chemical analysis. One or both of the methods may have a *systematic* bias, but that does not matter, for all we require is a method that will give a *reproducible* result.

Table 4.1 gives the results of 6 analyses by Method A on a sample and 7 analyses by Method B on the same sample.

Table 4.1

Method A.	95.6	94.9	96.2	95.1	95.8	96.3	
Method B.	93.3	92.1	94.7	90.1	95.6	90.0	94.7

The averages for Methods A and B are 95.65 and 92.93 respectively. If we wished to test the significance of this apparent difference we would use the Student t test. Here we are comparing the variances, which we proceed to calculate.

$$\sigma_a^2 = \left[(5.6^2 + 4.9^2 + \ldots + 6.3^2) - \frac{(5.6 + 4.9 + \ldots + 6.3)^2}{6}\right]/(6-1)$$

$$= (193.15 - 191.53)/5 = 0.324$$

$$\sigma_b^2 = \left[(3.3^2 + 2.1^2 + \ldots + 4.7^2) - \frac{(3.3 + 2.1 + \ldots + 4.7)^2}{7}\right]/(7-1).$$

$$= (90.85 - 60.04)/6 = 5.14.$$

We now calculate the ratio of the larger variance to the smaller, termed the variance ratio or F. Attached to the variance ratio are two sets of degrees of freedom, n_1 for the larger variance and n_2 for the smaller.

Here the variance ratio is $5.14/0.324 = 15.9$ for degrees of freedom $n_1 = 6$, $n_2 = 5$. In the Appendix are tables for the variance ratio for a comprehensive series of values of n_1 and n_2 for the 20%, 5%, 1% and 0.1% levels of significance. If our value of the variance ratio is greater than that given in a particular table for the corresponding degrees of freedom, then our result is more significant than the significance level for the table.

Thus for degrees of freedom $n_1 = 6$, $n_2 = 5$, for the 20%, 5%, 1% and 0.1% levels of significance the values of the variance ratio are 2.2, 5.0, 10.7 and 28.8 respectively. Our value of the variance ratio was 15.9: its significance thus lies between the 1% and the 0.1% levels (but see below).

That is to say, assuming our hypothesis to be correct we would be very unlikely to get the result we did. Accordingly it is very probable that our hypothesis is incorrect. Our hypothesis was that the two sets of figures were drawn from the same population, i.e. the variabilities of the two methods were the same. Our hypothesis having been proved incorrect, we can assert that the variabilities of the two methods do differ significantly.

A point of some subtlety arises here. The variance tables were constructed for the purpose of testing whether a variance A was greater than a variance B, A being known beforehand as derived in a particular way which distinguished it from B. Here we are testing whether a variance A is greater than a variance A^1, and until we have calculated them we do not know which is A and which is A^1: A is that one which turns out to be the larger. The effect of this distinction is to alter the level of significance of the 20%, 5%, 1%, and 0.1% tables to 40%, 10%, 2%, and 0.2% respectively.

(b) Averaging of Several Variances

Suppose, extending our previous example, we had a number of determinations of variability for each method on a number of different samples. Suppose a second sample analysed by Method B gave results 93.1, 91.2 and 92.6. Its variance would then (using the revised zero by subtracting 90 from every observation) be $[3.1^2 + 1.2^2 + 2.6^2 - (3.1 + 1.2 + 2.6)^2/3]/(3 - 1) = (17.81 - 6.9^2/3)/2 = 1.94/2 = 0.97$.

To form the average of the two variances, we weight them in accordance with their degrees of freedom. Thus the average would be

$$\frac{2 \times 0.97 + 6 \times 5.14}{2 + 6}$$

This average is the same as obtained by pooling the sums of squares and degrees of freedom for the two samples, i.e. $(30.82 + 1.94)/(6 + 2)$.

This is the correct method for obtaining an average variance. It is incorrect

(a) to take the average of the variances without regard for the degrees of freedom;

(b) to take the average of the standard deviations.

If we have the variances expressed as standard deviations, we should square them to convert them to variances, and take the average as indicated.

The average variance, correctly obtained, can be regarded as having as its degrees of freedom the sum of the degrees of freedom of the separate variances going to make up that average. Thus in the present example the degrees of freedom of the average variance are $(6 + 2) = 8$.

In parenthesis, it might be pointed out that in the calculation of the average variance of the two samples, the two variances must be calculated separately and then pooled. It would be incorrect to pool all the $7 + 3 = 10$ observations together and calculate their variance, because the variance so obtained includes not only the variance of repeat measurements on the same sample (which is what we require) but also the variance between samples, which is quite irrelevant.

(c) Comparison of Several Variances

The Fisher variance ratio test will compare two variances, but not more than two. Suppose we have a group of ten machines turning out batches of some product, and we measure some quality x on each batch. Suppose we suspect that some machines manufacture the product more regularly than others, i.e. that there is less variability in their product. The test of significance for this type of problem is generally known as Bartlett's test.

Column 2 in the table below represents the value of the property x of six consecutive batches off machines 1 to 10. The figures in column 2 actually are transformed by shifting the zero to simplify the arithmetic: originally each had 2200 added on to them.

Machine	Data	$\Sigma(x)$	$\Sigma(x^2)$	$(\Sigma(x))^2/6$	$\Sigma(x-\bar{x})^2$	σ_i^2	$\log_e(\sigma_i^2)$
1	28, 14, 15, 2, 9, 2,	70	1294	816.7	477.3	95.46	4.5587
2	11, 3, 0, 9, 2, 12	37	359	228.2	130.8	26.16	3.2642
3	7, 0, —1, —1, 0, 1	6	52	6.0	46.0	9.20	2.2192
4	8, 0, 3, —1, 6, —1	15	111	37.5	73.5	14.70	2.6878
5	10, 5, 3, 0, 0, 1	19	135	60.2	74.8	14.96	2.7054
6	4, 8, 7, 0, —1, 1	19	131	60.2	70.8	14.16	2.6502
7	11, 2, 3, 11, 10, 0	37	355	228.2	126.8	25.36	3.2331
8	15, 10, 0, 8, 10, 10	53	589	468.2	120.8	24.16	3.1847
9	7, 7, 4, 9, 5, 6	38	256	240.7	15.3	3.06	1.1184
10	10, 2, —1, 10, —1, 7	27	255	121.5	133.5	26.70	3.2847
						253.92	28.8906

The columns headed $\Sigma(x)$, $\Sigma(x^2)$, $(\Sigma(x))^2/6$ and $\Sigma(x-\bar{x})^2$ where Σ denotes summation, are merely the steps in calculating the variances for the ten machines. The latter are given in the column headed σ_i^2.

We now wish to test the hypothesis that these ten variances could reasonably have been obtained from the same population, i.e. that the batches from the ten machines are of the same variability.

We proceed by obtaining (from tables) the natural logarithm of each variance (last column), and summing these. Let us denote this sum by $\Sigma(\log_e\sigma_i^2)$. We take the mean of the variances as 253.92/10 = 25.392: we can denote this mean variance as S^2. We take its natural logarithm $\log_e S^2$, here 3.2343. Let k equal the number of variances being compared (here 10) and n equal the degrees of freedom of these individual variances (here 5). Then we calculate two terms B and C as

$$B = k\,n\log_e S^2 - n\ \Sigma(\log_e\sigma_i^2)$$
$$= 10 \times 5 \times 3.2343 - 5 \times 28.8906 = 17.18$$

$$\text{and } C = 1 + \frac{k+1}{3\,n\,k}$$

$$= 1 + \frac{10+1}{3 \times 10 \times 5} = 1.073$$

If B/C is greater than χ^2 at the 5% level of significance for (k — 1) degrees of freedom, then there is an indication of that level of significance that the variances are not drawn from a homogeneous population.

Here B/C = 17.18/1.073 = 16.0 with (10 — 1) = 9 degrees of freedom. For 9 degrees of freedom for the 10%, 5% and 2% levels of significance χ^2, or here B/C, needs to reach values of 14.68, 16.92 and 19.68 respectively. Here our present value does not reach the 5% level, but is near it, and there is some indication that the machines do differ significantly in the variability of their product.

It should be clear that if the largest and smallest variances of a set do not differ significantly as tested by the variance ratio test, then clearly those lying between cannot differ significantly either, and the whole set can be reasonably regarded as coming from a single population. In these circumstances there would be no need to employ the Bartlett Test.

A more general form of Bartlett's test, for the case where the several variances being compared have different degrees of freedom, is available, but will not be discussed here.

(d) Confidence Limits for Variances

In the same way as we laid down confidence limits for means, we can lay down confidence limits for variances.

(i) *Small Samples*

If we wish to calculate the probable upper limit for the true variance (say φ), at say the 5% level of significance, we calculate

$$\varphi = \frac{n}{\chi^2}\sigma^2$$

where σ^2 is the variance as calculated from our sample with n degrees of freedom, and χ^2 has its value corresponding to n degrees of freedom and the 5% level of significance.

Thus suppose we have a variance σ^2 of 10.0 units, based on a sample of ten individuals (nine degrees of freedom), then for the 5% level of significance

$$\chi^2 = 16.92 \text{ and}$$

$$\varphi = \frac{9}{16.92} \times 10.0 = 5.31$$

This is the lower limit. The corresponding upper limit is given by the 95% level of χ^2, for which χ^2 for 9 degrees of freedom is 3.32, whence

$$\varphi = \frac{9}{3.32} \times 10.0 = 27.1$$

Regarding these limits together, we have a 5% probability of the true population variance being less than 5.31 and a 5% probability of its exceeding 27.1 The total probability of the true value being outside these limits is thus (5% + 5%) = 10%.

Speaking generally, therefore, our confidence limits should be regarded as 10% and not 5% ; if we wish to have limits nearer 5% we can use the 98% and 2% levels of χ^2 giving us confidence limits of 4%.

(ii) *Large Samples*

For larger sample (greater than 30 individuals) we can use the fact that the standard deviation σ_σ of a standard deviation σ is $\frac{\sigma,}{\sqrt{2n}}$ where n is the number of observations.

Thus if we have a sample of 50 individuals whose standard deviation is 10.0, the standard deviation of the sample standard deviation is $10.0/\sqrt{2 \times 50} = 1.0$. The 95% confidence limits are thus $10.0 \pm 2.01 \times 1.0$ (2.01 is the value of t for the 5% level of significance and 50 degrees of freedom).

CHAPTER V

THE χ^2 TEST

(a) Introduction

We now turn to a different type of problem which requires a technique different from those previously discussed. The χ^2 test is applied in general to those problems in which we wish to determine whether the frequency with which a given event has occurred is significantly different from that which we expected.

The technique is applied, therefore, to such phenomena as the occurrence of heads or tails in the spinning of a coin: the frequency of bursting of drums in transit: the numbers of accidents on different shifts: the number of defective castings made by different methods.

To apply the method we calculate the expected frequencies of the events on the basis of the theory we are testing, and we then test whether the observed frequency differs significantly from the expected. If it does, of course, then our theory is unlikely to be correct: if it does not, then our theory is in reasonable accordance with the data, and the differences can be due to random error.

The statistic χ^2 is defined as

$$\chi^2 = \Sigma\left[\frac{(O - E)^2}{E}\right]$$

where O is the observed class frequency, E is the expected class frequency, and Σ denotes summation over all the classes.

In general, it is inadvisable to use the χ^2 test where any expected class frequency is less than 5. This point is discussed later in Chapter V (h).

We will now discuss a series of examples.

(b) The 1 × 2 Table

Suppose we tossed a coin 100 times, and we obtained 60 heads and 40 tails. Could we say that the coin was definitely biassed?

Here we have two classes, heads and tails, and on the hypothesis which we are testing the expectation E in each class is 50.

We have to make a correction for the fact that our actual distribution is discontinuous whereas χ^2 is a continuous variable. This correction for continuity, as it is called, consists in reducing by 0.5 the values which are greater than expectation and increasing by 0.5 those which are less. We thus have

$$\chi^2 = \frac{(59.5 - 50)^2}{50} + \frac{(40.5 - 50)^2}{50}$$
$$= 3.61$$

The appropriate number of degrees of freedom is found as the number of classes to which values can be assigned arbitrarily. Here, given the total, we can only fill one class arbitrarily, because when that is done the second class is automatically determined, i.e. if we make 100 tosses and obtain 60 heads, then the number of tails must be 40. Accordingly, entering the table of χ^2 with one degree of freedom, we see that to reach the 5% level of signifiance χ^2 would have to be equal to or greater than 3.84. Hence our result does not reach significance at the 5% level, and so we cannot assert that the coin is definitely biassed.

It might perhaps be stressed that the probability we have derived is not that of getting 60 heads exactly, but that of getting either 60 or more heads or 60 or more tails. The probability of getting exactly 60 heads with an unbiassed coin is

$$\frac{100\,!}{60\,!\;40\,!} \cdot \frac{1}{2^{100}} = 0.010843\ 867$$

(this at first sight rather formidable calculation is made easy by the tables of powers and of factorials contained in Barlow's Tables of Squares, etc. (E. & F. N. Spon)). The probability of getting exactly 61 heads is

$$\frac{100\,!}{61\,!\;\;39\,!}\cdot\frac{1}{2^{100}}=0.007110\,733.$$

Proceeding in this manner, we can get the series for 62, 63, etc., heads, and summing this series we get for the sum of probabilities 0.028 443 968. This is the probability of getting 60 or more heads. Adding the similar probability of getting 60 or more tails, the total probabiilty is 0.056 887 436, or 5.69%.

The χ^2 test gives as the probability, using a detailed table of χ^2 for 1 degree of freedom[1], as 5.8%. The two methods are thus in close agreement.

(c) The χ^2 Table

It will be noted that the χ^2 Table (Table II in the Appendix) is given for values of P greater than 0.10, namely 0.50, and 0.90, 0.95, 0.98, and 0.99.

The latter values are those which occur when a fit is better than it should be. It may seem surprising that this could be so. However, consider the case of a trial of 1,000 tosses to decide whether a coin is biassed. Our expectation for each of the two classes are 500. If we got exactly 500 of each in our trial, this agreement would be remarkable. Thus suppose we repeated the experiment a large number of times, then in general we should expect to get observed values of the frequencies corresponding to values of χ^2 corresponding to values of P scattered over the range 0.95 to 0.05, with 1 out of 40 outside the upper limit and 1 out of 40 outside the lower limit. The value of χ^2 which turns up most frequently is that corresponding to $P = 0.50$. Close fits should only occur with that frequency given the χ^2 test, and if they occurred more frequently we might reasonably suspect that the data was being "cooked."

(d) The $1 \times n$ Table

An example of a $1 \times n$ table, in which $n = 3$, is below.

Shift	Accidents in a particular period
A	1
B	7
C	7

We formulate the hypothesis that there is no association of number of accidents with shift, and proceed to test it with the χ^2 test. On our hypothesis the expectations for the three classes are 5, 5, and 5 respectively.

$$\chi^2 = \frac{(5-1)^2}{5} + \frac{(7-5)^2}{5} + \frac{(7-5)^2}{5}$$
$$= 4.80$$

The degrees of freedom are two (given the total, we can fill in two classes arbitrarily but then the third class is uniquely determined). Entering the χ^2 table, we find that for 2 degrees of freedom, to reach the 5% level of significance χ^2 has to be equal to or greater than 5.99. Since our value of χ^2 is less than that, our hypothesis is reasonable, i.e. there are insufficient grounds for asserting that the three shifts differ in their liability to accidents.

This result will probably be surprising to the non-statistician, who almost certainly would have assumed that it was quite certain that the three shifts did differ. It is important to note that the statistician does not assert that the three shifts do not differ: he merely states that the evidence that they differ is inadequate.

(1) Such as that in "An Introduction to the Theory of Statistics": G. U. Yule and M. G. Kendall (Charles Griffin), Appendix Table 4A.

Of course, we might formulate the hypothesis that the accidents are in the ratio 1 : 7 : 7 ; χ^2 would then be zero, i.e. there is no evidence that the accidents depart from the ratio 1 : 7 : 7. It is thus apparent that the data is simply inadequate to draw any conclusion.

Suppose we waited for a further period, and the accidents in the total period were 2, 14, and 14 respectively. The table would then become

Shift	Accidents in total period
A	2
B	14
C	14

Again testing our hypothesis that there is no association of accidents with shift, the total number of accidents is 30, and on this hypothesis the expectation E for each category is 10.

Accordingly

$$\chi^2 = \frac{(2-10)^2}{10} + \frac{(14-10)^2}{10} + \frac{(14-10)^2}{10}$$
$$= 9.60$$

Such a value of χ^2 with 2 degrees of freedom is more significant than the 1% level, i.e. on our hypothesis such a value would have been obtained less than 1 in 100 times. Thus the additional evidence has now made it very probable that the shifts do differ in their liability to accident.

Table 5.1 gives some data obtained on a process for beating paper in a beater. Four alternative methods of loading the beater were tried, the numbers of cycles carried out for the four cycles being given by the first row in Table 5.1. The second row gives the number of chokes of paper between the bed-plate and the roll that occurred.

Table 5.1

Method of Loading	A	B	C	D	Total
Number of cycles	8	10	9	13	40
Chokes occurring	5	8	9	10	32
Chokes expected	6.4	8.0	7.2	10.4	32

We wish to test the hypothesis that there is no association of frequency of choking with method of loading, i.e that frequency of choking is independent of method of loading. On this hypothesis the expectation of a choke, the same for all methods, is given by 32/40 = 0.80 chokes per cycle. The third row in Table 5.1 gives the expectation for the four methods. We have therefore

$$\chi^2 = \frac{1.4^2}{6.4} + \frac{0^2}{8.0} + \frac{1.8^2}{7.2} + \frac{0.4^2}{10.4}$$
$$= 0.77$$

We have used one degree of freedom in making the restriction that our expected total is equal to the actual total. (If we had an *a priori* expectation, e.g. if we had the hypothesis that there was one choke per cycle, then we wouldn't have lost this degree of freedom). Entering the table for χ^2 with 3 degrees of freedom, we see that to reach the 5% level of significance we would have to have a χ^2 of

7.82. It is clear that the present data is in excellent accord with the hypothesis that the frequency of choking is independent of the method of loading.

It will be noted that Table 4 at first sight is a 2 × n table (see Section (d)). In a 2 × n table the frequencies being compared relate to the same general class of events. Here, however, the occurrence of a cycle is not of the same class as the occurrence of a choke. Accordingly we are concerned with the 1 × n table of chokes occurring and only use the other row to derive our expected frequencies.

(e) The 2 × 2 Table

A problem frequently occurring can be reduced to the following form :—

One type of process produces (a) defectives in a sample of (a + b) individuals : another type of process produces (c) defectives in a sample of (c + d) individuals. Are the two populations the same or different ?

This type of problem can occur, for example, in cordite manufacture, where the detectives might be sticks rejected for e.g. surface blemishes, and we are interested in whether e.g., one method of packing the press cylinder gives less rejects than another.

The problem is formally exactly the same when articles are being tested with go-not go gauges instead of continuously measuring gauges ; if an article fails to pass on one or the other of the gauges it is a defective, if it passes the gauges it is a non-defective.

To take an example, suppose that in our first sample of 1000 there were 100 defectives (fraction defective 10%) and in the second sample of 500 there were 60 defectives (fraction defective 12%). Are we justified in taking it as reasonably certain that the populations represented by these two samples are different ?

Our contingency table then has the form

	Defective	Non-Defective	Totals
Process A Process B	a = 100 c = 60	b = 900 d = 440	a + b = 1000 c + d = 500
Totals	a + c = 160	b + d = 1340	1500

We must calculate the expectation for each cell : it is directly proportional to the appropriate row and column totals, and inversely proportional to the grand total, i.e. the expectations for a, b, c and d are

$$\frac{160 \times 1000}{1500} = 106.7,$$

$$\frac{1340 \times 1000}{1500} = 893.3, \frac{160 \times 500}{1500} = 53.3, \text{ and } \frac{1340 \times 500}{1500} = 446.7$$

Accordingly

$$\chi^2 = \frac{6.7^2}{106.7} + \frac{6.7^2}{893.3} + \frac{6.7^2}{53.3} + \frac{6.7^2}{446.7}$$
$$= 1.4$$

For one degree of freedom (given the marginal totals, we can only fill in one cell arbitrarily, for then the others are uniquely determined) this is about the 20% level of significance, i.e. the apparent superiority of process A is not established by this experiment.

We omitted in the above example to apply the correction for continuity : with large numbers such as are in the above example this is permissible, for the resulting difference is only slight.

In the above example we calculated the cell expectations separately, and summed the series of terms for χ^2. There is, however, a convenient mechanical method, which merely involves calculating

$$\chi^2 = \frac{(ad - bc)^2 \times N}{(a + b)(b + d)(c + d)(a + c)}$$

where a, b, c, and d have the meanings as in the contingency table quoted above and $N = a + b + c + d$. Thus in the above example

$$\chi^2 = \frac{(100 \times 440 - 900 \times 60)^2 \times 1500}{160 \times 1340 \times 500 \times 1000}$$

$$= 1.4$$

as before.

With small sample sizes it is essential to apply the correction for continuity, as in the following example.

A pressing process using one batch of powder gave 9 defective pellets out of 45 pressed (20% defective) and with a second batch of powder 29 defectives out of 87 pressed (33% defective).

	Batch A	Batch B	Totals
Non-Defective Defective	58 = a 29 = c	36 = b 9 = d	94 38
Totals	87	45	132

As before, the method of correcting for continuity is to add ½ to the observation in those cells which are below expectation and subtract ½ from those above expectation. The marginal totals are, of course, unchanged by this operation.

$$\chi^2 = \frac{(58.5 \times 9.5 - 28.5 \times 35.5)^2 \times 132}{94 \times 45 \times 38 \times 87} = 1.96$$

For 1 degree of freedom this is quite non-significant. If we had neglected to apply the correction for continuity we would have obtained a value for χ^2 of 2.57, in this case still non-significant. In borderline cases, however, the difference may be important[2].

(f) The 2 × n Table

The data in Table 5.2 below refers to two types of incident, two certain types of breakdown, A and B, which can occur in a certain process. The process can be run on three grades of raw material, L, M, and N.

Table 5.2

	L	M	N	Totals
A B	42 20	13 8	33 25	88 53
Totals	62	21	58	141

(2) An interesting discussion of how faulty conclusions can easily be reached from 2 x 2 table is by J. Berkson on hospital data: Biometrics Bulletin, Vol. 2, No. 3, page 47, 1946.

We form the hypothesis that there is no association of type of incident with raw material. In other words, that the relative likelihood of incidents is the same for the three types of raw material. We proceed to test this hypothesis with the χ^2 test.

The expectation for the cell L A is $62 \times 88/141 = 38.7$ and the contribution to χ^2 is $(42 - 38.7)^2/38.7 = 0.28$. Similarly, the expectation for the cell M A is $21 \times 88/141$, etc.

The degrees of freedom for $n_1 \times n_2$ tables are $(n_1 - 1) \times (n_2 - 1)$, or here $(2 - 1)(3 - 1) = 2$. The value of χ^2 comes out, summing for all six cells, as 1.5, which is very much less significant than the 5% level. Accordingly we can conclude that the data is in excellent accord with our hypothesis.

Non-statistically, we would have calculated the ratios A/B for raw material classes L, M, and N as $42/20 = 2.10$, $13/8 = 1.63$, and $33/25 = 1.32$. We would probably have concluded that these ratios were significantly different. The use of the χ^2 test, however, shows that such a conclusion would be unwarranted.

As for a 2×2 table, so for a $2 \times n$ there is a convenient mechanical method for computing χ^2. Suppose the frequencies in pairs of cells are a and A, b and B, etc., and the corresponding totals n and N. Then we calculate for each pair

$$p = a/(a + A) \text{ and}$$
$$ap = a^2/(a + A)$$

and from the totals

$$P = n/(n + N)$$

and then

$$\chi^2 = \frac{1}{P(P - 1)} [\Sigma (ap) - nP]$$

Our three pairs give as values of ap

$$42^2/62 = 28.452, \; 13^2/21 = 8.048, \text{ and } 33^2/58 = 18.776$$

Σ (ap) is then 55.276

$$\text{and } P = 88/141 = 0.624$$
$$\text{and } nP = 88^2/141 = 54.972$$

Whence $\chi^2 = (55.276 - 54.972)/0.624 \times 0.376 = 1.51$ as before.

(g) The $n_1 \times n_2$ Table

An $n_1 \times n_2$ table, with $n_1 = 3$, $n_2 = 6$ is given below.

	a	b	c	d	e	f	Total
A	11	23	8	5	18	18	83
B	17	29	10	17	7	15	95
C	6	21	8	24	15	9	83
Totals	34	73	26	46	40	42	261

A product was being produced on three shifts, A, B, and C and was classified into six grades, the order of quality being a to f.

On the average each of the three shifts would be supplied with raw material of the same average quality. The question arose as to whether any shift was tending to produce better quality material than the others, i.e. was there a relative excess of particular qualities on any one shift.

To test the hypothesis that there is no association of quality with shift, we calculate χ^2 for this table. The expectation of the cell Aa is $83 \times 34/261 = 10.8$, and the contribution to χ^2 is $(11 - 10.8)^2/10.8 = 0.004$. Similarly the expectation for the cell Ba is $95 \times 34/261 = 12.38$, and the contribution to χ^2 is $(17 - 12.38)^2/12.38 = 1.72$.

Performing the operation for all the cells and summing all the contributions, we get for χ^2 the value 26.3. The degrees of freedom with which we enter the χ^2 table is given by the number of independent ways the contingency table can be filled up, given the marginal totals. For an $n_1 \times n_2$ contingency table this is $(n_1 - 1)(n_2 - 1)$, here $5 \times 2 = 10$. Entering the χ^2 table for 10 degrees of freedom with the value 26.3 for χ^2 we have the probability of getting so large a value as less than 0.01 (i.e. 1%). Accordingly the hypothesis that there is no association of grade with shift would seem to be incorrect, i.e. there is an association of quality and shift.

The χ^2 test, should it give significance to the association between the two variables, does not give any information as to the type of association. This can only be found by inspection of the original contingency table. To assist in this it is convenient to enter in each cell, alongside the observed frequency, the expected frequency. Doing this for the present example, we find that A shift were producing a relative excess of e and f, B shift of a and C shift of d.

(h) Restriction of Expected Cell Frequency to be not less than 5

As mentioned at the beginning of this discussion of χ^2, it is not safe to use the χ^2 test where any expected class frequency is less than 5. Sometimes this means that the test cannot be applied. On other occasions the difficulty can be evaded.

Consider the table below:

	L_1	L_2	M	N_1	N_2	Total
A	5	37	13	28	5	88
B	3	17	8	20	5	53
Totals	8	54	21	48	10	141

It represents the data from which Table 5 in section (f) was built up. The expectations for cells L_1B, and N_2B are both less than 5. As the table stands, therefore, the χ^2 test cannot be applied. However, if we pool the data in columns L_1 and L_2 and in columns N_1 and N_2, we get the 2×3 table quoted in section (f), Table 5.2, which is perfectly satisfactory.

CHAPTER VI

THE POISSON DISTRIBUTION

(a) Introduction

Consider a manufacturing process in which an operation is being repeated a great many times each day, and occasionally an inflammation occurs. If we set out in time sequence the daily number of inflammations we may get such a set of figures as

0 0 1 0 0 2 0 3 0 0 0 1 3 0 1 4 0 0 0 2 ... ...

Some days will be without any, others will have a relatively large number. The question we will discuss is whether the probability of obtaining an inflammation is constant throughout. *Prime facie* we might consider that the days with 0 or 1 incidents have low probabilities of obtaining an inflammation and the days with 3, 4 or more high probabilities. If this were the case, then we could look for assignable causes of variation in the probability, i.e. find out in what way the days with high numbers of inflammations differed from days with low numbers, with a view to correcting the manufacturing practice. On the other hand, if the probability were really constant throughout we should be wasting our time trying to find out in what ways the days differed.

If we assume that the probability of obtaining an incident at any one instant is small but finite and constant, then over a finite period the chance of obtaining an incident will be appreciable. The incident can be of any type (we are considering spontaneous ignitions in a manufacturing process) and can include the occurrence of defective articles in their mass production. In this latter case we must pay due regard to the proviso that the probability of obtaining an incident at any one instant (in the terminology of this example of obtaining a defective on selecting any particular article) is small. In practice the approximation is good enough if the percentage defective is less than 10%.

(b) Number of Incidents per Interval

To revert to our example of spontaneous inflammation, let us count up the number of days on which no incident occurs, on which 1 incident occurs, on which 2 incidents occur, etc. Then if our hypothesis is correct, the relative frequencies will be as in Table 6.1 below (the e is the base of natural logarithms, m is the average frequency, and e.g. 4 ! is factorial 4, i.e. 4 × 3 × 2 × 1).

Table 6.1

Number of Incidents in one day	Relative Frequency
0	e^{-m}
1	$me^{-m}/1!$
2	$m^2e^{-m}/2!$
3	$m^3e^{-m}/3!$
4	$m^4e^{-m}/4!$
etc.	etc.

This series of terms is known as the Poisson series.

The sum of the Relative Frequencies is unity, for it is

$$e^{-m} + m\,e^{-m}/1! + m^2e^{-m}/2! + m^3e^{-m}/3! + \ldots\ldots$$
$$= e^{-m}[1 + m/1! + m^2/2! + m^3/3! + \ldots\ldots]$$
$$= e^{-m} \times e^{m} = 1$$

The first two columns in Table 6.2 summarises the results observed on 201 days working of an industrial process. The incident was an inflammation that would occur in a repetition process that was being repeated a large number of times each day. Over this period of 201 days there were 150 incidents, and they were distributed as in Table 6.2 Thus there were 102 days without any incidents, 59 days with 1 incident, 31 days with 2 incidents. etc. The total number of days is given by

$$102 + 59 + 31 + 8 + 0 + 1 = 201$$

and the total number of incidents is given by

$$102 \times 0 + 59 \times 1 + 31 \times 2 + 8 \times 3 + 0 \times 4 + 1 \times 5 \doteq 150$$

Table 6.2

Number of Incidents on one Day	Number of Occurrences of this type	Expectation of Occurrences
0	102	95.3
1	59	71.1
2	31	26.5
3	8 } 9	6.6 } 8.1
4	0	1.3
5	1	0.2
6	0	0
Total	201	201.0

We have 150 incidents in 201 days, so the daily average frequency m is 0.7463. A table of natural logarithms gives us e^m as 2.109 : e^{-m} is the reciprocal of this, namely 0.4742. The initial term of the series, corresponding to 0 incidents in a day, is $Ne^{-m} = 201 \times 0.474 = 95.3$. The next term is $mNe^{-m}/1\,! = 0.7463 \times 95.3 = 71.1$. The next term is $m^2Ne^{-m}/2\,! = 0.7463 \times 71.1/2 = 26.5$, and so on. These Poissonian expectations are given in the last column of Table 6.2.

To test the significance of the departure of the observed frequencies from the expected frequencies we use the χ^2 test in the usual way, as for a $1 \times n$ table. Thus the first cell's contribution to χ^2 is

$$\frac{(102 - 95.3)^2}{95.3} = 0.47$$

and similarly for the other cells. In applying the χ^2 test it is essential to pool sufficient cells at the bottom end of the table to satisfy the condition that the expected frequency in any cell should not be less than 5.

A further essential condition in applying the χ^2 test is that we should take as the degrees of freedom $(n - 2)$. The reason for losing 2 degrees of freedom as compared with 1 as in the usual $n \times 1$ table is that we have not only made the totals agree (as in the $1 \times n$ table, this taking up 1 degree of freedom) but also used one constant in fitting the shape of the distribution, this latter taking the second degree of freedom.

In the above example we obtain a value of 3.4 for χ^2 with 2 degrees of freedom. This corresponds to a probabiilty of 15%, so the fit can be considered satisfactory (P would have to be 5% or less before we could consider the hypothesis of agreement between the observed and expected distribution disproved).

It will be noted that the shape of the Poisson distribution depends on the value of m, the average frequency. If m is less than 1, as in the previous example, then each term must be less than the preceding one, and the first term will be the largest.

If m is greater than 1 but less than 2, then the second term is larger than the first, since it is equal to the first multiplied by m and divided by 1. It will also be greater than the third, so it is the maximum term of the series. If m is greater than 2, but less than 3, then the third term will be larger than the second and larger than the fourth.

Table 6.3 below is derived from the same data as the previous example. The interval taken was 3 days, so the average frequency is now 2.2537.

Table 6.3

Number of Incidents in periods of three days.	Number of Occurrences of this type.		Expectation of Occurrences.	
0	8		7.04	
1	20		15.86	
2	13		17.87	
3	12		13.42	
4	6		7.56	
5	5	} 8.0	3.41	} 5.24
6	2		1.28	
7	0		0.41	
8	1		0.11	
9			0.03	

It will be observed that the expected frequencies correspond closely to the observed frequencies. $\chi^2 = 4.49$ for 4 degrees of freedom, this corresponding to a probability of 40%.

(c) Distribution of Time Intervals

We have considered the number of incidents per time interval. A slightly different way of looking at the matter is to consider the size of interval between each incident. The interval can range from zero up to ten days or more. If we assume that the probability of obtaining an incident is constant throughout, we can predict the relative frequencies of the various sizes of intervals. Let m be the reciprocal of the average interval, and N the total number of intervals observed. Then the number of intervals laying between t_1 and t_2, would be given by

$$N\,(e^{-mt_1} - e^{-mt_2})$$

where e is the base of natural logarithms.

Table 6.4 gives the distribution of time intervals, derived from the same data as the previous table.

Table 6.4

Intervals (hours)	Number Observed.	Number Expected.
0— 7.9	48	44.46
8—15.9	36	34.63
16—23.9	27	26.95
24—31.9	24	21.00
32—39.9	10	16.44
40—47.9	13	12.64
48—55.9	10	10.01
56—63.9	8	7.64
64—71.9	9	6.03
72—79.9	3	4.76
80 to infinity	13	16.45
Total	201	201.01

The computation for this table is easier if we take 8 hours as a unit of time. Using a finer distribution of intervals than is shown in Table 6.4, the average interval is 3.9950 units and m its reciprocal was found to be 0.2503.

The expectation for the first interval is then

$$N(e^{-mt_1} - e^{-mt_2})$$
$$= 201\,(e^{-0.2503 \times 0} - e^{-0.2503 \times 1})$$
$$= 201\,(1 - 0.7788)$$
$$= 44.46$$

The expectation for the second interval is then

$$N(e^{-mt_2} - e^{-mt_3})$$
$$= 201\,(e^{-0.2503 \times 1} - e^{-0.2503 \times 2})$$
$$= 201\,(0.7788 - 0.6065)$$
$$= 34.63$$

The complete expectations are given in the last column of Table 6.4.

The closeness of fit can be tested with the χ^2 test. Here a value of 6.13 is obtained which with $(11 - 2) = 9$ degrees of freedom corresponds to a probability to 75%. The fit is thus excellent.

The time distribution of incidents when expressed in the present form is rather curious in that the commonest interval is the shortest.

It is interesting to note that the two methods test rather different aspects of the distribution. A large number of long periods (say 4 days or more) would show up in the present method as an excessive number in the last category, and since the expected number in this category is small it would not require many to give a significantly large contribution to χ^2. The first method described, however, would record this in the category of days with zero incidents, and since this is frequently a large class the additional number would have to be very large to make this cell give a significantly large contribution to χ^2. Clearly a number of days with zero incidents is more remarkable if they occur as a series consecutively than if they are interspersed with days with incidents, and the latter treatment is more sensitive to this form of departure from the Poisson distribution. On the other hand, the former treatment is more sensitive to the occurrence of a large number of incidents in a short time.

CHAPTER VII

THE ANALYSIS OF VARIANCE

(a) Introduction

It is a valuable property of variance that if a process has a number of factors each making a contribution to the variance of the final product, then this total variance is equal to the sum of the component variances[1].

This statement is less obvious than it may seem. Thus, if we were using standard deviations as our measure of variability, it would not be true to say that the standard deviation of the final product was equal to the sum of the standard deviations produced by the several factors.

This property of additiveness of variance makes possible the technique known as the "Analysis of Variance," whereby the total variance of a process can be analysed into its component factors, the relative importance of which can then be assessed.

The Analysis of Variance can take many forms according to the structure of the process being analysed, and one of the principal difficulties usually found in its application is deciding which is the appropriate form. In the present chapter only the two simplest forms will be discussed, and in the succeeding chapter a more general treatment for dealing with the more complex cases frequently met in practice will be attempted.

[1] Assuming the Factors are acting independently.

(b) **Analysis of Variance Between and Within Batches**

Suppose that we have a two stage process. Stage A takes the raw material in batches of 300 lb. at a time and performs operation A on it. This operation is not perfectly reproducible and gives rise to a variance σ_A^2 in the final product. For stage B of the process, each 300 lb. batch is split into three 100 lb. units and operation B performed on these units. Operation B is also not perfectly reproducible and gives rise to a variance σ_B^2 in the final product. The problem consists of observing the total variance in the final product and analysing it into its two components σ_A^2 and σ_B^2. Having done this, we will then be able to decide which is the part of the process which requires the more careful control in order to reduce the total variability.

In evaluating σ_A^2 and σ_B^2 we proceed by first calculating $(n\,\sigma_A^2 + \sigma_B^2)$ and σ_B^2 (in the general case where there are n units per batch). The reason for this is that it makes the estimation of the significance of σ_B^2 practicable. The function $(n\,\sigma_A^2 + \sigma_B^2)$ has $(m - 1)$ degrees of freedom, where m is the number of batches, and σ_B^2 has $m\,(n - 1)$ degrees of freedom. For σ_A^2 to exist, therefore, $(n\,\sigma_A^2 + \sigma_B^2)$ must be greater than σ_B^2, and we can readily test this with the variance ratio test.

In Table 7.1, below, the value of the property for each unit has been set down in columns of 3, the three units in each column coming from a single batch.

In order to reduce the numbers to small numbers (for convenience in arithmetical computation) a constant has been subtracted from all of them: it is obvious that this shift in level will in no way affect the relative variability.

Table 7.1

											Grand Total
	—3	—4	—3	—1	4	—2	1	2	—1	—1	
	—2	—3	—1	3	3	3	0	1	—1	1	
	—3	—5	—4	2	6	1	1	1	2	1	
Totals	—8	—12	—8	4	13	2	2	4	0	1	—2

The process of computation is as follows:—

(1) Square the individuals and add, i.e.

$$(-3)^2 + (-4)^2 + (-3)^2 + \ldots + 1^2 + 2^2 + 1^2 = 204$$

(2) Obtain the total for each column, square these totals, sum these squares, and divide this total by the number of individuals in each column, i.e.

$$((-8)^2 + (-12)^2 + (-8)^2 + \ldots + 0^2 + 1^2)/3 = 160.67$$

(3) Obtain the grand total for all individuals, square this grand total, and divide by the grand total number of individuals, i.e.

$$(-3 -4 -3 \ldots\ldots\ldots + 1 + 2 + 1)^2/30 = 0.13$$

We then form a table of this analysis of variance:—

Table 7.2

Source of Variance	Sum of Squares	Degrees of Freedom	Mean Squares	Components of Variance
Between columns	(2)—(3) = 160.54	m — 1 = 9	17.84	$n\,\sigma_A^2 + \sigma_B^2$
Within columns	(1)—(2) = 43.33	mn — m = 20	2.17	σ_B^2
Total	(1)—(3) = 203.87	mn — 1 = 29		

m $=$ number of columns.
n $=$ number of individuals in each column.
$\sigma^2_A =$ Variance due to differences between columns.
$\sigma^2_B =$ Variance within columns.

The three Sums of Squares are the differences between the appropriate terms (1), (2) and (3), calculated above. The degrees of freedom are derived as follows :—

(a) *Between Columns.* There are m columns, hence the degrees of freedom for this term is (m —1) (the degrees of freedom in general equal the number of ways the group concerned can be arbitrarily filled in if the total is determined, thus when (m — 1) have been filled in the last one is uniquely determined, i.e. we can only fill (m — 1) classes arbitrarily.)

(b) *Within Columns.* There are n individuals in each column : each column therefore contributes (n — 1) degrees of freedom to this term : there are m columns, hence the total degrees of freedom is m (n — 1) = mn — m.

(c) *Total.* The total degrees of freedom are mn — 1, one less than the total number of observations.

The Mean Squares are the Sums of Squares divided by the degrees of freedom.

The word "Squares" in the column headings in the table refers to Squares of deviations from means, and so the Mean Squares terms have some of the characteristics of variances.

The last column shows that the Between Column Mean Square estimates $(n\,\sigma^2_A + \sigma^2_B)$ and the Within Column Mean Square estimates σ^2_B. Thus if σ^2_A exists significantly, then the Between Column Mean Square must be significantly greater than the Within Column Mean Square.

Accordingly, we wish to test whether the Between Column Mean Square is significantly greater than the Within Column Mean Square. This can be done with the Fisher variance ratio test, discussed earlier in Chapter IV (a).

We merely calculate the ratio of the larger mean square to the smaller, here $17.84/2.17 = 8.22$, and enter the table for F with $n_1 =$ degrees of freedom of the larger variance (here $n_1 = 9$) and $n_2 =$ degrees of freedom of the smaller variance (here $n_2 = 20$). If our value for F is greater than that given in the table, then the result is more significant than the level of the table. Here for example, for $n_1 = 8$ (the table does not give $n_1 = 9$), $n_2 = 20$, F has the values 2.45, 3.56 and 5.44 for the 5%, 1% and 0.1% levels of significance. Accordingly this particular result is more significant than 0.1%.

Having thus established that the Between Columns Mean Square is significantly greater than the Within Column Mean Square, i.e. that the Between Column Variance does exist, we can proceed to calculate its value. We have

$$n\,\sigma^2_A + \sigma^2_B = 17.84$$
$$\sigma^2_B = 2.17$$

where n = number of individuals in each column, here 3.

$$\text{Thus } \sigma^2_A = (17.84 - 2.17)/3$$
$$= 5.22$$
$$\sigma^2_B = 2.17$$

The total variance observed in our original data is thus made up of these two components $\sigma^2_A = 5.22$ due to differences between columns (here columns = batches) and $\sigma^2_B = 2.17$ due to variability within columns (here within batches, that is to say, between units for a given batch).

(c) The Investigation of Multi-Stage Processes

We can thus see that the larger proportion of the total variability in the above process is arising at stage A, and only a minor part at stage B. Thus in any attempt to standardise the process, to reduce the total variability in the final product, almost all the attention should be directed towards stage A.

The total variance as the process is at present is $\sigma_T^2 = \sigma_A^2 + \sigma_B^2 = 5.22 + 2.17 = 7.39$, i.e. its standard deviation is $\sqrt{7.39}$. Our estimate of the spread within which 95% of all individuals should lie is thus $\pm 1.96 \times \sqrt{7.39} = \pm 5.3$, or a total spread of $2 \times 5.3 = 10.6$. From inspection of the original data this is seen to be reasonable: out of the thirty observations the smallest is —5 and the largest is +6, a spread of 11.0.

Suppose we directed our efforts at standardising stage B, and were completely successful, and reduced σ_B^2 to zero. The total variance would now be $\sigma_A^2 = 5.22$, i.e. the standard deviation would be 2.29 and the 95% spread $\pm 1.96 \times 2.29 = \pm 4.5$, or the total spread of 9.0. The total spread originally was 10.6, so the improvement has been comparatively slight.

If, on the other hand, we had directed our efforts at standardising stage A and were completely successful in reducing σ_A^2 to zero, the total variance would now be $\sigma_B^2 = 2.17$ or the standard deviation 1.47. The 95% spread would then be $\pm 1.96 \times 1.47 = \pm 2.9$ and the total spread 5.8.

The improvement effected by standardising stage A is thus very much more substantial than that achieved by standardising stage B. It is clear that effort spent in investigating stage B would have been largely wasted. Before carrying out a detailed physico-chemical investigation on a multi-stage process, it is clearly desirable to find out with such an analysis of variance which are the stages giving rise to the variability, and concentrate upon them. The advantage of this procedure is that the stages subsequently ignored may have contained a large number of variables, each of which would have required investigation. In carrying out these investigations, we could not be confident that we were including the significant variable, and the failure to obtain a significant correlation might be due to the investigation of the wrong variables rather than to the fact that there was no significant variable for this part of the process.

The analysis of variance proceeds by concentrating initially upon the structure of the process, and only subsequently investigating individual variables.

(d) Analysis of Variance of Columns of Unequal Size

It will have been realized that the analysis of variance between and within columns is in effect an extension of the Student t test: instead of comparing two means we are comparing m means, where m is the number of columns. It might be thought that we might make a series of t tests for the column means taken two at a time. This would involve a lot of labour, and in addition involves us in certain complications. Thus if we had 20 comparisons, and we are working to the 5% level of significance, then on the average even if the columns were drawn from the same population we would expect one of them to give us a value of Student's t as large as the 5% value. The use of the analysis of variance evades these difficulties.

It sometimes happens, however, that the number of individuals in each column are not the same, when the treatment given in Section (b) will not be directly applicable.

Consider the data in the table below. It represents the throughputs obtained from units of plant before failure through corrosion. The units are categorised according to the foundry manufacturing them.

Foundry	Throughput obtained	Total	Mean
A	84, 60, 40, 47, 34	265	53.0
B	67, 92, 95, 40, 98, 60, 59, 108, 86	705	78.3
C	46, 93, 100	239	79.7

Prima facie it might be concluded that the pots from Foundry A are giving lower throughputs on the average than those from Foundries B and C.

The analysis proceeds by obtaining the following terms :—

(1) Square the individuals and add, i.e.

$84^2 + 60^2 + 40^2 + \ldots\ldots\ldots\ldots + 93^2 + 100^2 = 95{,}709$

(2) Square each column total, divide by the number of individuals in that column, and sum these terms, i.e.

$265^2/5 + 705^2/9 + 239^2/3 = 88{,}310$

(3) Square the grand total and divide by the total number of individuals, i.e.

$(265 + 705 + 239)^2/17 = 85{,}981$

The analysis of variance is then as below :

Source of Variance	Sums of Squares	Degrees of Freedom	Mean Squares
Between Foundries Within Foundries	(2)—(3) = 2329 (1)—(2) = 7399	2 14	1164 528.5
Total	(1)—(3) = 9728	16	

The degrees of freedom are derived as follows :—

(a) Between Foundries : one less than the number of foundries.

(b) Within Foundries : each foundry contributes one less than the number of observations on that foundry, viz., 4 + 8 + 2 = 14.

(c) Total : one less than the total number of observations.

Testing the Between Foundries Mean Square in the above analysis, it gives a variance ratio of 1164/528.5 = 2.20 for degrees of freedom $n_1 = 2$, $n_2 = 14$. This is considerably less significant than the 5% level of significance, so there is insufficient justification for regarding the Foundry A pots as giving smaller average throughputs than those from the other foundries.

In the present instance we are more interested in the actual averages for the three foundries, and are using the analysis of variance to test the significance of the apparent difference between the averages. In the more general case, of the analysis between and within batches, as discussed in the two previous sections, we probably wish to calculate the two components of variance. The Within Foundries Mean Square as before estimates the Within Foundries variance, i.e. $\sigma_A^2 = 528.5$. The calculation of the Between Foundries variance is more complicated when the batch (column) sizes are unequal.

If N in the total number of observations, and n_i is the number in each batch for i = 1 to k, there being k batches, then the Between Foundries (Between Batches or Columns) Mean Square estimates

$$\frac{N^2 - \Sigma n_i^2}{N(k-1)} \sigma_B^2 + \sigma_A^2$$

It will be noted that in the case where all the batches (columns) are of equal size, i.e. all the n_is are equal to n this reduces to

$$\frac{(n\,k)^2 - k\,n^2}{n\,k\,(k-1)} \sigma_B^2 + \sigma_A^2$$

$$= n\,\sigma_B^2 + \sigma_A^2$$

as quoted in Chapter VIII (b).

In our present example our n_i are respectively 5, 9, 3, $N = 5 + 9 + 3 = 17$, $k = 3$, and thus we get

$$1164.5 = \frac{17^2 - (5^2 + 9^2 + 3^2)}{17\,(3 - 1)}\,\sigma_B^2 + \sigma_A^2$$

$$= 5.118\ \sigma_B^2 + \sigma_A^2$$

Subtracting

$$528.5 = \sigma_A^2$$

We obtain

$$636.0 = 5.118\,\sigma_B^2$$

or $\sigma_B^2 = 124.3$

It might be re-emphasised that the calculation of the component of variance had been given here only to illustrate the method of calculation. In practice with this particular problem it would not be done because firstly we would be more interested in the averages, secondly the effect is so non-significant that its calculation would be meaningless, the component being indistinguishable on the present data from zero. It further would not be desirable practice to estimate the variance between batches (column) from only three batches : a variance so estimated would have a very large error. Finally, this is a case where it might be held that it was unreasonable to suppose that there was an infinite population of foundries from which these three are a sample : this point is commented on further in Chapter XII (b).

(e) Analysis of Variance into Components due to Rows, Columns, and a Residual

It frequently happens that not only can the individuals (units) be categorised according to batches (columns) but also simultaneously according to rows. Thus in the previous example, the first individual in every column (batch) was processed on a particular machine, all the second individuals in every column on another machine, and all the third individuals on a third machine. Each row thus corresponds to one particular machine. There may be a systematic difference between these machines ; we wish to test whether such an effect exists, and if it does exist estimate its contribution to the total variance of the final product.

Formally what we have to deal with here is a twofold classification; every individual belongs to a particular row and to a particular column.

Other examples of twofold categorisation are the output from a shop according to machine and according to the shift operating the machines. Or, in an experiment on conditions of nitration of cellulose, we could have n_1 different acid concentrations, corresponding to rows, and n_2 different acid temperatures, corresponding to columns, where n_1 and n_2 could be any convenient numbers.

To revert to our example of batches split into three units, we proceed by calculating the following terms :—

(1) Square the individuals and add (we have done this already—term (1) of the previous analysis).

(2) Obtain the total for each row, square these totals, sum these squares, and divide this total by the number of individuals in each row (this is the new term, here equal to 8.40).

(3) Obtain the total for each column, square these totals, sum these squares, and divide this total by the number of individuals in each column (term (2) of the previous analysis).

(4) Obtain the grand total for all individuals, square this grand total and divide by the grand total number of individuals (term (3) of the previous analysis).

We then form a table of this analysis of variance.

Source of Variance	Sum of Squares	Degrees of Freedom	Mean Square	Components of Variance
Between Rows	(2) — (4) = 8.40 — 0.13	$n_1 - 1 = 2$	4.13	$n_2 \sigma_1^2 + \sigma_0^2$
Between Columns	(3) — (4) = 160.67 — 0.13	$n_2 - 1 = 9$	17.84	$n_1 \sigma_2^2 + \sigma_0^2$
Residual	(1) + (4) —(2) — (3)	$(n_1 - 1)(n_2 - 1) = 18$	1.94	σ_0^2
Total	(1) — (4) = 203.87	$n_1 n_2 - 1 = 29$		

n_1 = number of rows = 3

n_2 = number of columns = 10

σ_1^2 = variance due to differences between rows

σ_2^2 = variance due to differences between columns

σ_0^2 = residual variance

The Residual Sum of Squares can be obtained as that combination of terms indicated, but in practice it is easier to calculate the Row and Column Sums of Squares, and find the Residual as the difference between their sum and the Total Sum of Squares.

To test for the significance of the Between Rows Mean Square we compare it with the Residual using the variance ratio test. Here the variance ratio is $4.13/1.94 = 2.12$ for degrees of freedom $n_1 = 2$, $n_2 = 18$. Referring to the tables in the Appendix we see that this is not significant. Thus our hypothesis, that there was no systematic difference between the rows (machines), is in reasonable accord with this data. If the Between Rows Mean Square had proved significant, we could have proceeded to estimate the magnitude of σ_1^2, the variance due to differences between rows (machines) from the pair of equations $n_2 \sigma_1^2 + \sigma_0^2 = 4.13$, $\sigma_0^2 = 1.94$, whence $\sigma_1^2 = (4.13 - 1.94)/n_2$.

CHAPTER VIII

THE QUALITY CONTROL CHART

(a) Introduction

The Quality Control Chart has been much used in recent years as a means of control of quality of production, particularly in light engineering processes such as the use of automatic lathes, presses, etc. It has not been used much hitherto in the chemical industry though certain types of process seem suitable for its application. Here it will only be discussed with reference to investigational work.[1]

[1] The literature of industrial quality control is now very great. The standard work is W. A. Shewhart's "Economic Control of Quality of Manufactured Product" (Macmillan : 1931). Short accounts are British Standard 600R "Quality Control Charts," B. P. Dudding and W. J. Jennett, 1942 ; British Standard 1008 "Quality Control" : "A First Guide to Quality Control for Engineers," E. H. Sealy, H.M.S.O., 1946. A fuller account is L. E. Simon's "An Engineer's Manual of Statistical Methods" (Chapman & Hall, 1941).

A discussion of quality control applied to routine chemical analysis is by H. E. MacColl : Chemistry and Industry, December 9th, 1944, page 418.

The quality control chart is designed to detect the presence of "assignable causes of variation" in a sequence of individuals. In effect it takes "rational sub-groups" (that is, a group of individuals more likely to be similar than the general population, e.g. individuals from a particular machine, operator, day, consignment of raw material, etc.), obtains from these rational sub-groups a measure of the population variance, and then checks that the sub-group means do not vary more than they should do on the assumption that all individuals are drawn from the same population, i.e. that there is no significant difference between the sub-group means. It will be apparent that the result of this test is the same as the analysis of variance for between and within batches.

The quality control chart as used in practice almost invariably derives its estimate of variance within the sub-groups not from the variance but from the mean range within the sub-groups, there being available factors for converting mean range to standard deviation (see Section (e)). Having obtained an estimate of σ (the within sub-group standard deviation) we can assert that the means of samples of n will be distributed with standard deviation $\sigma/\sqrt{n}$. Thus 95% will be within $1.96\sigma/\sqrt{n}$ on either side of $\bar{\bar{X}}$ (the grand mean, assumed equal to the population mean. This is the same as 1 in 40 below $\bar{\bar{X}} - 1.96\sigma/\sqrt{n}$ and 1 in 40 above $\bar{\bar{X}} + 1.96\sigma/\sqrt{n}$. The quality control chart normally uses these limits as "inner" limits and also "outer" limits at $3.09\sigma/\sqrt{n}$, these giving 99.8% within the limits, or 1 in 1000 below the lower and 1 in 1000 above the upper limit.

If the mean of a particular sample falls outside the limits, it is probable that the underlying assumptions are not being satisfied. These assumptions are, of course, that the sample is drawn from a population of standard deviation σ and grand mean $\bar{\bar{X}}$. The former point is checked by a control chart on the sub-group ranges (see next section), and therefore it is probable that the sample's mean does differ significantly from the value $\bar{\bar{X}}$.

(b) **Within Batch Variability: the Control Chart for Range**

Consider the data used previously in Table 7.1, Chapter VII (b). We wish now to test the hypothesis that the variabilities within each column (batch) are drawn from a homogeneous population: in other words, that batches do not differ in their internal variability.

Table 8.1

Data	−3	−4	−3	−1	4	−2	1	2	−1	−1
	−2	−3	−1	3	3	3	0	1	−1	1
	−3	−5	−4	2	6	1	1	1	2	1
$\bar{x}$	−2.67	−4.00	−2.67	1.33	4.33	0.67	0.67	1.33	0	0.33
w	1	2	3	4	3	5	1	1	3	2
$\Sigma(x)$	−8	−12	−8	4	13	2	2	4	0	1
$\Sigma(x^2)$	22	50	26	14	61	14	2	6	6	3
$\Sigma(x-\bar{x})^2$	0.67	2.00	4.67	8.67	4.67	12.67	0.67	0.67	6.00	2.67
σ_i^2	0.33	1.00	2.33	4.33	2.33	6.33	0.33	0.33	3.00	1.33

For this purpose we obtain the range w for each batch and plot these consecutively on a chart as in figure 6. We then calculate the mean range $\bar{w}$, here equal to 2.50, and plot on the chart an inner control line at $D'_{0.975}\,\bar{w} = 2.17 \times 2.50 = 5.4$ and an outer control line at $D'_{0.999}\,\bar{w} = 2.98 \times 2.50 = 7.5$. These D factors are obtained from Table V in the Appendix for sample size 3. If the batches are similar in their internal variability, then on the average not more than 1 out of 40 points will lie outside the inner control line, and only 1 out of 1000 points outside the outer control line. The occurrence of two points outside the inner control line within two or three points, or of a single point outside the outer control line, therefore, is strong evidence that we cannot regard the batches as having the same internal variability.

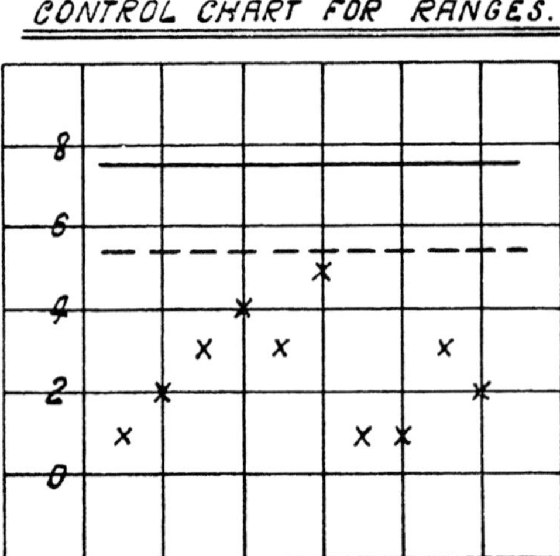

Figure 6.

In the present instance it is clear from figure 6 that there are not points outside either of the control lines, so there is no reason to suppose that the batches differ in their internal variability.

(c) The Control Chart for Ranges compared with Bartlett's Test

To digress from the present theme, it will be noted that the control chart for range is testing exactly the same hypothesis as Bartlett's test (see Chapter IV (c)). To apply the latter, we first calculate the variance of each batch σ_i^2 through the steps indicated, namely by obtaining $\Sigma(x)$, $\Sigma(x^2)$, and thus $\Sigma(x-\bar{x})^2$. The sum of the natural logarithms of the within batch variances σ_i^2 is $\Sigma(\log_e(\sigma_i^2)) = 3.06039$. The degrees of freedom n of the individual variances are 2. The mean of the batch variances, S^2 is 2.164, and k, the number of variances being compared, is 10.

Whence we have

$$B = k\,n \log_e S^2 - n\,\Sigma \log_e(\sigma_i^2)$$
$$= 10 \times 2 \times \log_e 2.164 - 2 \times 3.06039 = 9.31862$$
$$C = 1 + \frac{k+1}{3\,n\,k} = 1 + \frac{10+1}{3 \times 2 \times 10} = 1.183$$

Thus $B/C = 9.319/1.183 = 7.87$ and is distributed as χ^2 with $(k-1) = 9$ degrees of freedom. This is much less significant than the 10% level of significance, so there is no reason to suppose that the batches differ from each other in their internal variability.

The use of Bartlett's Test thus leads to the same conclusion as the control chart for ranges. It requires more calculation, but on the other hand has the advantages of being more sensitive and precise.

(d) Between Batch Variability: the Control Chart for Means

We wish to test whether the batches differ significantly in their means, having regard to the observed amount of variability of the individuals.

We obtain the mean for each batch (first row in lower part of Table 8.1) and plot this consecutively as in Figure 7. We calculate the grand mean $\bar{\bar{X}}$ as —0.67, and draw in inner control lines at $\bar{\bar{X}} \pm A'_{0\cdot025}\,\bar{w} = -0.67 \pm 0.668 \times 2.50$ or 1.60 and —1.74 and outer control lines at $\bar{\bar{X}} \pm A'_{0\cdot001}\,\bar{w} = -0.67 \pm 1.054 \times 2.5$ or 2.57 and —2.70. Thus, if the Between Batch variability is no greater than that due to the Within Batch variability, 1 point out of 20 will lie outside the inner control lines and 2 out of 1000 outside the outer control lines. Here 4 out of 10 lie outside the inner control lines and 2 out of 10 outside the outer control lines. It is thus evident that the hypothesis of no between batch variability is untenable.

CONTROL CHART FOR MEANS.

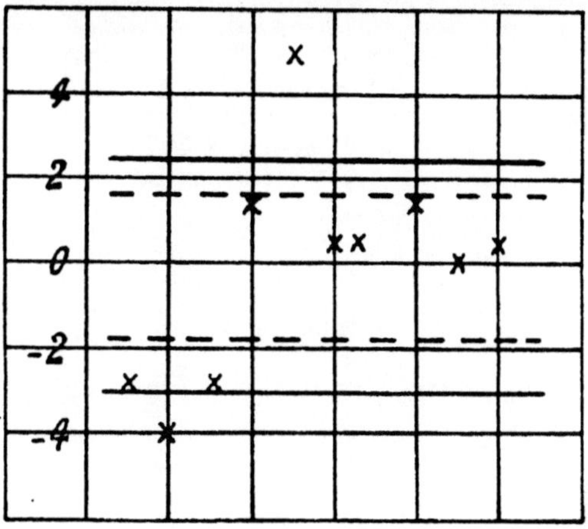

Figure 7.

This is in complete agreement with the conclusion reached using the analysis of variance in Chapter VII (b). With the control chart the arithmetical labour is much less, but the analysis of variance has the advantage of giving numerical estimates of the relative importance of the Between Batch and Within Batch variabilities, and of the exact significance of the existence of the Between Batch variability. For detailed and exact work, therefore, the analysis of variance is to be preferred, but for preliminary and exploratory investigations the control chart is very useful.

An important proviso in the use of control charts is that the control lines should be based upon at least 10 and, preferably, 20 batches: otherwise the estimate of the mean range $\bar{w}$ is not very accurate.

(e) The Conversion of Range to Standard Deviation

It frequently happens that we have a series of samples of n individuals drawn from a population and we wish to know their standard deviation. We can of course calculate the variance for each sample and take the average (since the samples are all of n individuals the simple average variance will be the same as that obtained by pooling the sums of squares and the degrees of freedom). The arithmetic required is much less, however, if we obtain the range for each sample, calculate the average range, and divide this average range by the factor d_n given in the last column of Table V in the Appendix, selecting that d_n corresponding to the actual size of sample. The resulting figure is the standard deviation. The standard deviation so calculated is an approximation and can only be used when the number of samples taken is reasonably large, say not less than 20. The estimate is then assumed to have nearly infinite degrees of freedom.

It will be seen that except when the sample size is 2 we are sacrificing some accuracy in our estimate of σ, the compensating gain being the ease of computation, of course. This loss of information is not very serious, however, being less than 20% for samples of size 10 and less for smaller samples. Under the conditions in which we use this method this does not really matter, as since we have such a large sample our estimate will be accurate enough for almost all purposes.

The reader will note that it is this factor d_n which is the basis of the factor $A'_{0.025}$ and $A'_{0.001}$ used for the formulation of the control lines for means. Thus it is clear, that for a sample of size n, control lines for 1 in 40 limits (1 in 40 about the upper limit and 1 in 40 below the lower limit, i.e. 1 in 20 outside the limits) should be at $1.96\sigma/\sqrt{n}$, where σ is the standard deviation, 1.96 is the value of t for infinite degrees of freedom (it is assumed that σ is known exactly as we have supposedly taken a large number, preferably greater than 20, of samples) and the 5% probability level, and n is the size of sample. If for example n is 4, and $\bar{w}$ is the mean range, then the limits should be at $1.96(\bar{w}/2.059)/\sqrt{4} = 0.476\,\bar{w}$, where 2.059 is the value of d_n for $n = 4$. It will be seen that this is the value for $A'_{0.025}$ given in Table V of the Appendix.

CHAPTER IX

THE RELATION BETWEEN TWO VARIABLES

(a) Introduction [1]

A problem that arises frequently is to determine whether an apparent relation between two variables is significant, and having shown it to be significant, to determine the best form of representation.

The statistical methods available for dealing with this problem are not very satisfactory. The treatment in general is to test whether the data can be represented by the equation for the simple straight line, $y = a + bx$, whether the deviations from this straight line are significant and if so can these deviations be represented by the equation $y = a + bx + cx^2$ or $y = a + bx + cx^2 + dx^3$, etc. In practice, the computational labour is excessively heavy for any of the steps but the first, namely, seeing whether the data can be approximately represented by a straight line of the form $y = a + bx$.[2]

It is clear where the unsatisfactory nature of this treatment lies: there is no *a priori* reason why a complex system should give a straight line relationship between two of its variables, or even the more complex relationship $y = a + bx + cx^2$, etc. The case where the treatment is most appropriate is where the data when plotted on a graph has the appearance of an elliptical cloud, and we are dubious whether this ellipticity is genuinely due to a real relationship or an accident of sampling. Alternatively there might be little doubt about the genuineness of

(1) A comprehensive survey of the field is given by W. E. Deming: "Statistical Adjustment of Data" (John Wiley: Chapman & Hall), 1943.

(2) An exception is where the independent variable is changing in equal stages: c.f. Fisher's "Statistical Methods for Research Workers," Sections 27 and 28. Also, G. Egloff and R. C. Kuder, Journal of Physical Chemistry: Vol. 46, page 926, 1942; and L. H. C. Tippett: "Methods of Statistics" (William & Norgate), Section 9. 3.

the existence of a relationship but we want to have the best estimate of the relationship.

If the data when plotted on a graph fall on a smooth curve of complex shape then the present techniques are not applicable. In practice, therefore, we should only use the present statistical treatment when the pairs of observations on the two variables plotted on a graph give something that looks approximately a straight line.

(b) Transformations

We may have *a priori* reasons, from the theory of the process, to suspect that the relationship should have the form

$$Y = AB^x$$

which is equivalent to the expotential form

$$Y = Ae^{Cx}$$

We can transform this to a linear function by taking logarithms,

$$\log Y = \log A + x \log B$$

or putting log Y = y, log A = a, log B = b, we now have the relation in the convenient linear form.

$$y = a + bx.$$

Also, if we suspect that relationship should have the form :—

$$Y = AX^B$$

where B can have any value, e.g. 2, when the relation would be

$$Y = AX^2$$

we can take logarithms

$$\text{Log } Y = \log A + B \log X$$

or putting log Y = y, log A = a, log X = x, we again have the relation in the convenient linear form

$$y = a + Bx$$

(c) The Correlation Coefficient

To test for the significance of an apparently linear relation we calculate the correlation coefficient r defined by (Σ denotes summation over all pairs of observations)

$$r = \frac{\Sigma(x - \bar{x})(y - \bar{y})}{\sqrt{(\Sigma(x - \bar{x})^2 \, \Sigma(y - \bar{y})^2)}}$$

It has the characteristics such that if the relationship between the data can be represented exactly by a straight line then $r = \pm 1$, positive if the straight line has a positive slope and negative if the line has a negative slope; if on the other hand there is no relation at all between the variables then $r = 0$. Even when the variables may have no relationship we will usually get a non-zero value for r, since the accidents of sampling will often lead to an apparent trend one way or the other. We can, however, test whether an observed value for r is larger than would have been obtained accidentally in the absence of a correlation. We enter the table for r with degrees of freedom two less than the number of observations (the reason for it being *two* less than the number of pairs of observations is that we have in effect fitted two constants, a and b, to the data). If our value for r exceeds that given in the table for say, the 5% level of significance, then we may regard it as being 19 to 1 that there really is a correlation.

We will illustrate the use of the statistical treatment of data suspected of being expressed in the form $y = a + bx$ with the data partially (there are actually 30 pairs of observations) given by

y	1.66	2.0	1.66	1.78	1.89	1.82	. . . . . . 2.07	2.29
x	6	8	17	16	19	16	13	12

In the table, y represents stick weight of cordite made from nitro-cellulose with acetone viscosities x. The variables have been transformed, however, to make the arithmetic lighter; y actually represents stick weight in ounces minus 13 lbs. 1 oz., and x actually viscosity in centipoises minus 50. On plotting y against x one obtains a graph with a wide scatter but, apparently, a decided tendency for higher viscosities to give lower stick weights.

We obtain the following terms (n = number of pairs of observations).

$$\Sigma(x - \bar{x})^2 = \Sigma(x^2) - \frac{(\Sigma x)^2}{n}$$

$$= (6^2 + 8^2 + \ldots + 12^2) - \frac{(6 + 8 + \ldots + 12)^2}{30}$$

$$= 3213$$

$$\Sigma(y - \bar{y})^2 = \Sigma(y^2) - \frac{(\Sigma y)^2}{n}$$

$$= (1.66^2 + 2.00^2 + \ldots + 2.29^2) - \frac{(1.66 + 2.00 + \ldots + 2.29)^2}{30}$$

$$= 9.060$$

$$\Sigma(x - \bar{x})(y - \bar{y}) = \Sigma(xy) - \frac{\Sigma(x)\ \Sigma(y)}{n}$$

$$= (1.66 \times 6 + 2.00 \times 8 + \ldots) - \frac{(1.66 + 2.0 + \ldots)(6 + 8 + \ldots)}{30}$$

$$= -47.84$$

We then calculate the correlation coefficient r, defined as

$$= \frac{\Sigma(x - \bar{x})(y - \bar{y})}{\sqrt{\Sigma(x - \bar{x})^2\ \Sigma(\bar{y} - y)^2}}$$

$$= \frac{-47.84}{\sqrt{9.060 \times 3213}} = -0.280$$

We see from the table for r (Table IV in the Appendix) that the probability of getting such a value for r in the absence of any correlation is about 0.10, that is to say 1 in 10 times we could get as large a value for r as we did here even in the absence of a correlation. The evidence for the correlation is thus inadequate.

(d) The Equation for the Regression Line

If r proved to be significantly greater than zero we would take the matter a little further: although in the example considered here r was not significantly greater than zero we will use its data to illustrate the point.

If we wished to use the data to predict values of y from known values of x we would calculate

$$a = \frac{\Sigma y}{n} = \bar{y} = 49.58/30 = 1.65$$

$$b = \frac{\Sigma(y - \bar{y})(x - \bar{x})}{\Sigma(x - \bar{x})^2} = \frac{-47.84}{3213} = -0.0149$$

$$\bar{x} = \frac{\Sigma x}{n} = \frac{670}{30} = 22.3$$

The formula for deducing the most probable value of y corresponding to a given value of x (technically known as the regression of y upon x) is then

$$y = a + b\,(x - \bar{x})$$
$$= 1.65 - 0.0149\,(x - 22.3)$$
$$= 1.98 - 0.0149\,x$$

This regression line of y upon x is the line which gives the squares of the deviation of every point, measured parallel to the y-axis in units of y, summed for all points, as a minimum. It gives the best estimate of y from a known value of x.

If we wished to predict the value of x from a known value of y we would use the similar but different equation derived by calculating

$$a' = \frac{\Sigma(x)}{n}$$

$$b' = \frac{\Sigma(y - \bar{y})(x - \bar{x})}{\Sigma(y - \bar{y})^2}$$

$$\bar{y} = \frac{\Sigma(y)}{n}$$

leading to the equation

$$x = a' + b'(y - \bar{y})$$

This line gives the deviations of every point, measured parallel to the x-axis in units of x, summed for all points, as a minimum. It gives the best estimate of x from a known value of y.

Non-statisticians frequently object to the concept of two "best" lines, two regression lines. They hold that there must be one line which represents the "true" relation. That may be so, but we are not concerned with "true" relations: we are concerned with making the best possible estimate of y from a known value of x, using a certain amount of experimental data to estimate the relationship. In one case we assume that we know x and wish to estimate y, in the other case we assume that we know y and wish to estimate x. These are two different operations, so it is not surprising that we use two different functions.

(e) The Residual Variance about the Regression Line

We assume that we now have our regression line of y upon x with the points scattered about on either side of it. The standard deviation σ_r of this scatter, measured in units of y parallel to the y-axis, is given by

$$\sigma_r = \sqrt{1 - r^2}\sqrt{\frac{\Sigma(y - \bar{y})^2}{N - 2}}$$

$$= \sqrt{1 - 0.280^2} \times \sqrt{\frac{9.06}{28}} = 0.546$$

This figure affords a good measure of the usefulness of the equation for the regression line for predicting values of y for given values of x.

Thus suppose we wish to draw 95% confidence limits on either side of the regression line, within which 95% of all points should lie, we look up the value of t for $N - 2 = 28$ degrees of freedom and the 5% level of significance, and calculate $t\,\sigma_r = 2.05 \times 0.546 = 1.12$. We then draw in two lines parallel to the regression line, but one displaced 1.12 units of y downwards and one displaced 1.12 units of y upwards. Thus if we use the regression line to predict the value of y from a known value of x, these confidence limits give us the limits between which we have a 95% chance of being correct in our prediction.(3)

(f) The Use of the Analysis of Variance for Examining Regression

An alternative method of testing the significance of a regression is by analysing the variance of the dependent variable y into its component factors.

The total sum of squares of y is $\Sigma(y - \bar{y})^2 = 9.060$. The sum of squares accountable for by the regression line is

$$\frac{[\Sigma(y - \bar{y})(x - \bar{x})]^2}{\Sigma(x - \bar{x})^2} = \frac{47.84^2}{3213} = 0.7123$$

(3) This statement is approximate: the exact treatment follows in Section (h)

We then enter these into a table of analysis of variance as below:

Source of Variance	Sums of Squares	Degrees of Freedom	Mean Squares
Regression ..	0.7123	1	0.7123
Residual	8.3477	28	0.2981
Total ..	9.060	29	

The degrees of freedom are 1 for the regression line, one less than the total number of pairs of observations for the Total, and the residual is the difference between these two. Similarly the residual sum of squares is obtained as the difference between the Total and the Regression.

The significance of the Regression Line is estimated by comparing its mean square with the residual in the usual way. Here it lies between the 20% and 5% levels.

The residual is the same as the residual variance about the regression line that we calculated earlier in the previous section; thus the square root of this residual variance is $\sqrt{0.2981} = 0.546$ as obtained earlier.

It will be noted that the results obtained by the present approach are identical with those found by calculating the correlation coefficient.

(g) Comparison of Regression Coefficients

We might wish to test whether two regression coefficients were significantly different. Thus we might be conducting experiments upon some system, (a) with clockwise stirring and (b) with anti-clockwise stirring. We might plot graphs for the two series and suspect that they were different.

We can make this test by using the fact that the variance of a regression coefficient is given by

$$\frac{\text{Residual Variance of y}}{\Sigma(x - \bar{x})^2}$$

i.e. in the present instance 0.2981/3213. The standard deviation is the square root of this, namely 0.0096, with two less than the total number of observations, namely 28, as its degrees of freedom.

If the two regression coefficients b_1 and b_2 have variances σ_1^2 and σ_2^2, then we calculate Student's t as

$$t = \frac{b_1 - b_2}{\sqrt{\sigma_1^2 + \sigma_2^2}}$$

and the degrees of freedom for this t are the sum of those of the two individual variances.

(h) Exact Formula for the Residual Variance about the Regression Line

As stated earlier, the formula given in Section (e) for the residual variance about the regression line is not quite exact. If σ_r^2 is the residual variance as already defined, and σ_b^2 is the variance of the regression coefficient itself, calculated as in Section (g), then the exact formula [4] for σ_{r1}^2 is

$$\sigma_{r1}^2 = (\sigma_r^2 + X^2\sigma_b^2)$$

where X is the distance in units of x from the midpoint of x, $\bar{x}$. For example,

[4] H. Schultz, Journal of the American Statistical Association, Vol. XXV, page 139, 1930, gives a full treatment of this and the more complicated cases of parabolas, etc.

in the case we have been considering, $\bar{x}$ is quoted in section (d) as 22.3. In section (e) $\Sigma(x - \bar{x})^2$ is quoted as 3213, whence $\sigma_x^2 = 110.79$. We have σ_x of the order of 10, and thus to select a point towards one end of the x scale we can take $\bar{x} + 2\sigma_x = 22.3 + 2 \times 10 = 42.3$: this corresponds to X = 20. Inserting the appropriate values for σ_r and σ_b we get

$$\sigma_{r^1}^2 = (0.2981 + 20^2 \times 0.00009278)$$

$$= 0.3352$$

whence $\sigma_{r^1} = 0.5790$

In the present instance, it is clear that the use of the approximate formula would have given results close to the truth, and of course the nearer we are to the midpoint of x the smaller is X and the less important the correction.

(i) The Use of the Analysis of Variance for Checking Linearity

A problem arising frequently is to determine whether a set of observations which to the first approximation can be represented by a straight line can be said to depart significantly from the straight line. This question can be readily settled if the data is in the symmetrical form suitable for the application of the analysis of variance.

Consider the data below :—

x	10	20	30	40
y	92.8 93.0	94.0 94.3	95.1 94.8	94.9 94.8
$\bar{y}$	92.9	94.15	94.95	94.85

We can regard x as representing the temperature in °C of a certain part of a process and the two values of y repeat determinations on the yield at that temperature. We are interested in the effect of temperature upon the yield. To the first approximation the yield y appears to increase linearly with the temperature x, but the value for x = 40 is less than that for x = 30. We shall test whether this apparent departure from linearity is significant.

We first transform the variables to give us smaller, and hence easier, numbers to work with. Thus we can use X = x/10, and Y = (y — 92) × 10. The data then becomes :

X	1	2	3	4
Y	8 10	20 23	31 28	29 28

We can in the first instance analyse the variance of the data into between columns (given values of X) and within columns.

Proceeding on these lines, we calculate the terms

(1) $= 8^2 + 10^2 + \ldots + 28^2 = 4463$
(2) $= [(8 + 10)^2 + (20 + 23)^2 + (31 + 28)^2 + (29 + 28)^2]/2 = 445/5$
(3) $= (8 + 10 + 20 + \ldots + 28)^2/8 = 3916.1$

We enter these terms into a table as below :—

Source of Variance	Sums of Squares	Degrees of Freedom	Mean Squares
Between Temperatures	(2) — (3) = 535.4	3	178.5
Within Temperatures	(1) — (2) = 11.5	4	2.87
Total	(1) — (3) = 546.9	7	

Testing the Between Temperature Mean Square against the Within Temperature Mean Square, we see that it is significant.

We now divide the Between Temperature Sum of Squares into that due to the linear regression line and that due to departure from it.

We calculate

$\Sigma(X) = 2\,(1 + 2 + 3 + 4) = 2 \times 10 = 20$

$\Sigma(X^2) = 2\,(1^2 + 2^2 + 3^2 + 4^2) = 2 \times 30 = 60$

$\Sigma(X - \bar{X})^2 = 60 - 20^2/(4 \times 2) = 10$

$\Sigma(XY) = 1\,(8 + 10) + 2\,(20 + 23) + 3\,(31 + 28) + 4\,(29 + 28) = 509$

$\Sigma(Y - \bar{Y})\,(X - \bar{X})) = \Sigma(XY) - \Sigma(X)\ \Sigma(Y)/N$

$= 509 - 20 \times 177/8 = 66.5$

The factor 2 in the expressions for $\Sigma(X)$ and $\Sigma(X^2)$ arises through there being 2 observations on Y for each level of X.

The sum of squares attributable to the regression line is then

$$\frac{[\Sigma(Y - \bar{Y})\,(X - \bar{X})]^2}{\Sigma(X - \bar{X})^2} = \frac{66.5^2}{10} = 442.22$$

Since the total sum of squares attributable to differences between temperatures is 535.4, the sum of squares due to deviations from the regression line is

$535.4 - 442.2 = 93.2$

The degrees of freedom for the regression line are 1 and for the deviations from it the remainder of those belonging to differences between temperatures.

We enter up these expressions in a table as below:

Source of Variance	Sums of Squares	Degrees of Freedom	Mean Squares
Between Temperatures :			
Regression	442.2	1	442.2
Deviation from Regression	93.2	2	46.6
Within Temperatures (Residual)	11.5	4	2.87
Total	546.9	7	

The general significance of the regression line can be tested by comparing the Regression Mean Square with the Residual. Here it is clearly highly significant. To test whether the departure from the straight line is significant, we calculate the variance ratio for the Deviation from Regression as $46.6/2.87 = 16.2$ for degrees of freedom $n_1 = 2$, $n_2 = 4$. This is nearly as significant as the 1% level, so we may take it with that degree of confidence that the data cannot be completely represented by a straight line.

The best estimate of the regression coefficient of Y upon X is given by

$$b = \frac{\Sigma[(Y-\bar{Y})(X-\bar{X})]}{\Sigma(X-\bar{X})^2} = \frac{66.5}{10} = 6.65$$

(j) The Calculation of Correlation Coefficient, etc., from Grouped Data

If the number of pairs of observations is large, say about 100, the labour in calculating the correlation coefficient as in Section X (c) becomes considerable, and can be lightened by grouping the data on the same general lines as in Chapter II (j).

We divide each axis into about 10 or 20 equal-sized groups, and count up the number of observations occurring in each cell.

The data in Table 9.1 refers to a manufacturing process involving the formation of an emulsion in water. The independent variable x is a function of the quality of the water (hardness) and the dependent variable y is a quality of the final product. Table 9.1 is a graph with Ax representing the x-axis and Ay the y-axis. For each set of values of Ax and Ay, i.e. for each point on the graph, the number gives the number of observations occurring with those values (when none occur then the space is left blank). The column headed B gives the frequency with which the corresponding values have occurred. Thus to take $Ax = 10$, it will be seen that there are points with $Ax = 10$ at $Ay = 23$, 17, and 16, so the corresponding entry for Bx is 3. C is the arbitrary scale with shifted origin used to lighten the arithmetic. D and E are the terms $B \times C$ and $B \times C^2$ respectively. The total number of observations is given by the sum of the frequencies in Column B, here 101.

Thus we have

$$\Sigma(x-\bar{x})^2 = \Sigma(x^2) - \frac{(\Sigma x)^2}{N}$$

$$= 915 - \frac{(25)^2}{101} = 908.8$$

$$\Sigma(y-\bar{y})^2 = \Sigma(y)^2 - \frac{(\Sigma y)^2}{N}$$

$$= 875 - \frac{(43)^2}{101} = 856.7$$

The calculation of the term $\Sigma(x-\bar{x})(y-\bar{y})$ is rather more difficult. For each level of Cy, we multiply the frequency for each cell by its value for Cx, and sum for all cells at this level of Cy. This is the column headed F. Thus for $Cy = -3$, we have three cells, the first with unit frequency at $Cx = -3$, the second with frequency 2 at $Cx = -2$, the third with unit frequency at $Cx = 1$. Thus $F = 1 \times (-3) + 2 \times (-2) + 1 \times 1 = -6$. As a check upon the accuracy of column F its sum should equal Σx. Column G is then obtained as the

Table 9.1

																			Ay	By	Cy	Dy	Ey	F	G
				1															25	1	—9	— 9	81	— 3	+27
																			24	0	—8	— 0	0	0	
	1				1														23	2	—7	—14	98	— 8	+56
																			22	0	—6	— 0	0	0	
			1		1														21	3	—5	—15	75	— 6	+30
					1	1													20	3	—4	—12	48	— 8	+32
				1	2			1											19	4	—3	—12	36	— 6	+18
		1	1	2	2	2	1	1											18	10	—2	—20	40	—20	+40
	1		1	1	1	2	3	2		1									17	12	—1	—12	12	—12	+12
	1		2		3	3	2	1	2	1		1							16	16	0	—94	0	—10	
					3		2	1	3			1	1						15	11	1	11	11	+12	+12
		1	1		2	4	3	1	1	1							1		14	15	2	30	60	— 1	— 2
				1	1	2	2	1	2	1	1								13	11	3	33	99	+ 5	+15
			1					2		1		1	1						12	6	4	24	96	+12	+48
						1				1				1					11	3	5	15	75	+ 9	+45
						1	1					1		1					10	4	6	24	144	+11	+66
Ax	10	11	12	13	14	15	16	17	18	19	20	21	22	23	24	25	26			N = 101		+137	875 = Σy^2		+401
Bx	3	3	7	6	17	16	15	10	8	6	1	4	2	2	0	0	1	101 = N				—94		—74	— 2
Cx	—6	—5	—4	—3	—2	—1	0	1	2	3	4	5	6	7	8	9	10							+49	
Dx	—18	—15	—28	—18	—34	—16	—129	10	16	18	4	20	12	14	0	0	10	104							
Ex	108	75	112	54	68	16	0	10	32	54	16	100	72	98	0	0	100	915 = Σx^2				+ 43 = Σy		Σx = —25	+399 = Σxy

Σx = +104 —129 = —25

product of Cy and F. Its sum is $\Sigma(xy)$. To correct this into terms of deviations from the means rather than the arbitrary zeros we subtract the correcting factor

$$\frac{\Sigma x \ \Sigma y}{N} = \frac{(-25) \times (+43)}{101} = -10.64$$

We thus obtain

$$\Sigma(x - \bar{x})(y - \bar{y}) = 399.0 - (-10.6)$$
$$= 409.6$$

The correlation coefficient is then

$$R = \frac{\Sigma(x - \bar{x})(y - \bar{y})}{\sqrt{\Sigma(x - \bar{x})^2 \ \Sigma(y - \bar{y})^2}}$$
$$= \frac{409.6}{\sqrt{(908.8 \times 856.7)}}$$
$$= 0.466$$

which for 99 degrees of freedom is much more significant than the 0.1% level of significance. The regression coefficient of y upon x can be calculated as before as

$$b = \frac{\Sigma(x - \bar{x})(y - \bar{y})}{\Sigma(x - \bar{x})^2}$$
$$= \frac{409.6}{908.8} = 0.451 .$$

and the regression equation then is

$$y = \frac{\Sigma y}{N} + b\left(x - \frac{\Sigma x}{N}\right) = 0.451\ x + 0.537$$

(k) Correlation and Causation

A significant correlation coefficient can be taken as an indication of association between two variables, but it is important to realize that this does not automatically imply causation.

Thus for example suppose we have plant data stretching over a period of some months, and we find that the temperature T_1 at a certain stage varies quite considerably. We may plot T_1 against the dependent variable y, obtain what seems a linear relation, calculate the correlation coefficient and find it significant. At this stage it would be dangerous to assume that y is necessarily a function of T_1, for it may be that the real operating variable is the temperature T_2 in some other part of the process, and that it happens that T_1 has been related to T_2 through some common operating factor such as weather.

This type of error is always liable to occur when our data is existing plant records which we observe. It is less likely to occur if the data is obtained by actual experiment. Thus in an experiment if we raise the temperature T_1 to a chosen value, and the running of the plant as measured by the dependent variable y (which may be yield, quality, etc.) improves, then for practical purposes it may be sufficient to say "run the plant with T_1 at this value." However, this still may not be real evidence of the causative effect of T_1 upon y, for the plant may be such that in raising T_1 to the new value we have at the same time affected the real causative variable T_2. Thus, for example, in a counter-current process, raising the temperature at one point will probably affect the temperature at other points.

The considerations outlined in the last three paragraphs do not in any way invalidate the desirability of the testing for significance of any apparent relation. They merely imply that having shown a correlation to be significant, caution is necessary in assuming that this association is evidence of a causative effect of one variable upon the other.

(l) Conclusions

Where it is suspected that the relation between two variables is approximately linear, there are three statistics which between them summarise the most important properties of the available data :—

(a) the correlation coefficient, with the associated number of degrees of freedom, which is a convenient measure of the degree of reliability of the association.

(b) the regression coefficient b that measures the slope of the regression line, i.e. the average increase in y per unit increase in x, and

(c) the residual variance σ_r that measures the scatter of values of y about the regression line, i.e. the reliability of estimates of y for given values of x when estimated from the regression line.

(d) If the experiment has been executed with appropriate replication, it is often desirable for the analysis of variance giving the significance of departure from linearity to be applied.

In using a regression equation it must be always remembered that it is only valid over the range of the independent variable which occurred in the data used in calculating it. Extrapolation is most unwise, except when there is a very sound theoretical basis. It is good practice to quote the range used of the independent variable in order to discourage extrapolation.[5]

CHAPTER X

MULTIPLE CORRELATION

(a) Introduction

We discussed in Chapter IX the determination of the relationship between a dependent and an independent variable In many of the cases which arise in practice, however, we find that there is more than one independent variable which may be of practical importance. In these circumstances it becomes necessary to isolate the effect of each independent variable from the effects of the other independent variables.

In the example we shall consider the stack loss from a Pressure Oxidation Plant for making nitric acid (about 55%—60%) by the oxidation of ammonia with air. The resulting nitric gases are absorbed by being passed upwards through a bubble cap absorption column, nitric acid being circulated down the column. The absorption is exothermic, i.e. gives rise to the liberation of heat, and the temperature tends to rise. The absorption of the nitric gases is less efficient at higher temperatures, so to keep the temperature down water is circulated through cooling coils in the column. The column also tends to cool itself by radiation, etc., to its surroundings. A small quantity of the nitric gases fails to be absorbed and escapes by the stack : this we will regard as the dependent variable. Its minimisation is, of course, of prime economic importance and we will first determine its dependence upon the two independent variables air temperature, x_a, and cooling water temperature, x_w. In a subsequent section we will consider a third independent variable, strength of the nitric acid being circulated in the absorption column.

(b) Two Independent Variables

We will determine the dependence of the P.O.P. stack loss (to be denoted by y) upon the cooling water temperature, x_w, and the air temperature, x_a.

[5] A full discussion of various aspects of correlation is to be found in Chapters 11 to 16 of Yule and Kendall's "An Introduction to the Theory of Statistics" (Charles Griffin).

Accordingly data was collected giving corresponding values for these three variables for 139 days.

It was assumed that the stack loss was to a first approximation related linearly to the two independent variables, so that it could be represented by an equation of the form

$$y = a_{y.wa} + b_{yw.a}(x_w - \bar{x}_w) + b_{ya.w}(x_a - \bar{x}_a)$$

The meaning of the symbols is as follows :—

$a_{y.wa}$ is the value y would have if x_a and x_w were held constant at their mean values.

$b_{yw.a}$ measures the rate of increase of y with increasing x_w, x_a being constant.

$b_{ya.w}$ measures the rate of increase of y with increasing x_a, x_w being constant.

If we had considered it more appropriate, we could, of course have used an equation of the type

$$y = a_{y.wa} + b_{yw.a}(x_w^2 - \overline{x_w^2}) + b_{ya.w}(x_a^2 - \overline{x_a^2})$$

which would be based on the assumption that the stack loss y increased as the square of the temperature, or in the first of the above equations we could have substituted for the temperature the reciprocal of the absolute temperatures, or whatever functions we considered most likely to represent the true behaviour of the system.

Taking the straightforward linear equation we will determine the values of these three coefficients which give the best general fit to the data. We proceed as follows.

It makes the computation lighter, particularly if we are not using a calculating machine, to use arbitrary zeros and to multiply by 10 or 100, etc., if necessary, to remove the decimal points. Thus in the present instance the variables used are actually :—

y = 10 (stack loss in gm/M³ — 3.0).
x_w = water temperature in °C — 20°C.
x_a = air temperature in °F — 50°F.

For each set of observations on the three variables, y, x_w, and x_a, we form the three pairs of products, yx_w, x_wx_a, and x_ay. Thus we have a table of 139 sets as below :—

Date	y	x_w	x_a	x_wx_a	x_ay	x_wy
30.12.43	—20	— 6	—11	66	220	120
29	— 9	1	— 3	— 3	27	— 9
28	—18	1	— 2	— 2	36	—18
27	— 6	— 1	— 1	1	9	6
25	— 3	2	— 3	— 6	6	— 6
22	— 5	— 5	—10	50	50	25
22	—20	2	—20	—40	400	—40
21	+19	5	+14	70	266	+95
18	— 4	— 1	—14	14	56	4
.	.	.	.	.	.	.
.	.	.	.	.	.	.
.	.	.	.	.	.	.
	1479	406	1	3533	17340	12797

We require the sums of the six columns as shown in the last row of the table. We will denote a summation by the letter Σ. Thus, e.g. $\Sigma(x_wx_a)$ is the sum of the 139 $x_w x_a$'s, here 3533. We also require the three sums of the squares of the individual observations on the three variables. We thus have :—

$$\begin{array}{llll} \Sigma y = 1{,}479 & \Sigma y^2 = 99{,}077 & & \\ \Sigma x_w = 406 & \Sigma x_w^2 = 3{,}456 & & \\ \Sigma x_a = 1 & \Sigma x_a^2 = 10{,}525 & & \\ \Sigma y x_w = 12{,}797 & \Sigma y x_a = 17{,}340 & \Sigma x_w x_a = 3{,}533 & \end{array}$$

So far these sums of squares and sums of products refer to deviations from the arbitrary zeros. We need to convert these into deviations from the means with the usual type of correcting factors. Thus, e.g. :—

$$\Sigma(y - \bar{y})^2 = \Sigma(y^2) - \frac{(\Sigma y)^2}{N}$$

$$= 99{,}077 - \frac{1479^2}{139}$$

$$= 83{,}340.0$$

and $$\Sigma(y - \bar{y})(x_w - \bar{x}_w) = \Sigma(y x_w) - \frac{(\Sigma y)(\Sigma x_w)}{N}$$

$$= 12{,}797 - \frac{1479 \times 406}{139}$$

$$= 8{,}477.0$$

In a similar manner we obtain the other terms as deviations from the means. In order to have our symbolism more compact we will denote a summation of deviations from the means by Σ'. Thus

$$\Sigma(y - \bar{y})(x_w - \bar{x}_w) = \Sigma' y x_w$$

and $\Sigma(y - \bar{y})^2 = \Sigma' y^2$.

We thus have

$$\Sigma' y^2 = 83{,}340.0 : \quad \Sigma' x_w^2 = 2270.1 : \quad \Sigma' x_a^2 = 10{,}525.0$$

$$\Sigma' y x_w = 8{,}477.0 : \quad \Sigma' y x_a = 17{,}329.4 : \quad \Sigma' x_w x_a = 3{,}530.1$$

To obtain the two regression coefficients $b_{yw.a}$ and $b_{ya.w}$ we have to solve the two simultaneous equations

$$\Sigma' y x_w = b_{yw.a} \,.\, \Sigma' x_w^2 + b_{ya.w} \,.\, \Sigma' x_w x_a$$

$$\Sigma' y x_a = b_{yw.a} \,.\, \Sigma' x_w x_a + b_{ya.w} \,.\, \Sigma' x_a^2$$

Substituting our values, we obtain

$$8{,}477 = b_{yw.a} \,.\, 2270 + b_{ya.w} \,.\, 3530 \qquad \text{(A)}$$

$$17{,}329 = b_{yw.a} \,.\, 3530 + b_{ya.w} \,.\, 10525 \qquad \text{(B)}$$

To solve these two simultaneous equations we can, e.g., multiply (A) by the ratio 10525/3530 = 2.9816 and obtain

$$25{,}275 = b_{yw.a} \,.\, 6768 + b_{ya.w} \,.\, 10525 \qquad \text{(C)}$$

and subtracting (B) we obtain

$$b_{yw.a} = 7946/3238 = 2.4540$$

To obtain the other regression coefficient we substitute this value for $b_{yw.a}$ in, say, (A) and find

$$8477 = 5570.6 + b_{ya.w} \,.\, 3530$$

whence

$$b_{ya.w} = 0.8234$$

Our equation for estimating y is thus

$$(y - \bar{y}) = 2.4540\,(x_w - \bar{x}_w) + 0.8234\,(x_a - \bar{x}_a)$$

$$y - 10.6403 = 2.4540\,(x_w - 2.9209) + 0.8234\,(x_a - 0.0072)$$

or $$y = 3.4665 + 2.4540\, x_w + 0.8234\, x_a.$$

Before proceeding, it is as well to test the significance of the two regression coefficients $b_{yw.a}$ and $b_{ya.w}$. This we can do with an application of the analysis of variance.

We first want the total Sum of Squares of the dependent variable y. This is obviously $\Sigma' y^2 = 83{,}340$.

We then calculate the Sums of Squares of y explained by the two independent variables independently of each other. These are

$$\frac{(\Sigma' yx_w)^2}{\Sigma' x_w^2} = \frac{8477^2}{2270} = 31,656.2$$

and $$\frac{(\Sigma' yx_a)^2}{\Sigma' x_a^2} = \frac{17,329^2}{10,525} = 28,531.5$$

for x_w and x_a respectively. We enter the larger of the two in the first line of the table below.

We next calculate the sums of squares of y explained by the two independent variables together. This sum of squares is

$$b_{yw.a}\ \Sigma' yx_w + b_{ya.w}\ \Sigma' yx_a$$
$$= 2.4540 \times 8477 + 0.8234 \times 17,329$$
$$= 35,071$$

Then the sum of squares explained by the addition of the second independent variable x_a is the difference between the sum of squares explained by x_w and x_a together and the sum of squares explained by x_w alone, i.e.

$$35,071.0 - 31,656.2 = 3414.8$$

We finally enter up these various sums of squares in a table of analysis of variance as below.

Table 10.1

Source of Variance	Sums of Squares	Degrees of Freedom	Mean Squares
Variation explained by x_w	31,656	1	31,656
Increment explained by the addition of x_a	3,415	1	3,415
Total explained by x_w and x_a together	35,071		
Residual	48,269	136	354.9
Total	83,340	138	

The degrees of freedom are such that each regression coefficient takes 1 and the residual takes what is left. Similarly the Residual sum of squares is what is left out of the Total after the total explained by the two regression coefficients has been subtracted.

To test for the significance of the second (smaller) regression term we compare its mean square with the residual. Here the variance ratio is 3415/354.9 = 9.6 with degrees of freedom $n_1 = 1$, $n_2 = 136$. This is more significant than the 1% level of significance, so there can be little doubt about the reality of the effect of x_a.

Accordingly, to estimate the value of y for any particular values of x_w and x_a we use the equation

$$y = 3.466 + 2.454\ x_w + 0.823\ x_a$$

and the variance of any estimate is given by the Residual variance in the above table of analysis of variance, namely 354.9. The standard deviation will be the square root of this, namely 18.8.

A modification, due to Fisher, of the above procedure is often useful. For generality we will use x_1 for x_w and x_2 for x_a. Thus we have

$\Sigma' y^2 = 83340.0.$ $\qquad \Sigma' yx_1 = 8477.0$

$\Sigma' x_1^2 = 2270.1.$ $\qquad \Sigma' yx_2 = 17329.4$

$\Sigma' x_2^2 = 10525.0.$ $\qquad \Sigma' x_1x_2 = 3530.1$

We first solve the simultaneous equations

$$b_1 \Sigma'(x_1^2) + b_2 \Sigma'(x_1x_2) = 1 \qquad (D)$$
$$b_1 \Sigma'(x_1x_2) + b_2 \Sigma'(x_2^2) = 0 \qquad (E)$$

and the solution of b_1 we denote by c_{a_1} and the solution of b_2 by c_{a_2}. The bs are, of course, the standard partial regression coefficients, and might be more completely defined as in the previous treatment by $b_{y1 \cdot 2}$ and $b_{y2 \cdot 1}$. In the present treatment we will understand the y and latter halves of the subscripts. Substituting our values in equations (D) and (E), we get

$$c_{a_1} \cdot 2270.1 + c_{a_2} \cdot 3530.1 = 1 \qquad (F)$$
$$c_{a_1} \cdot 3530.1 + c_{a_2} \cdot 10525.0 = 0 \qquad (G)$$

which can be solved by e.g. multiplying the first (F) by 10525.0/3530.1 = 2.9816, obtaining

$$c_{a_1} \cdot 6768.0 + c_{a_2} \cdot 10525.0 = 2.9816$$

From this we subtract the second equation, (G), to obtain

$$c_{a_1} \cdot 3238.0 = 2.9816$$

and

$$c_{a_1} = 0.9208 \times 10^{-3}$$

We can obtain c_{a_2} e.g. by substituting this value of c_{a_1} in the second equation as

$$c_{a_2} = -0.3088 \times 10^{-3}$$

We now require the solutions of

$$b_1 \Sigma'(x_1^2) + b_2 \Sigma'(x_1x_2) = 0 \qquad (H)$$
$$b_1 \Sigma'(x_1x_2) + b_2 \Sigma'(x_2^2) = 1 \qquad (I)$$

and we will denote the solutions b_1 and b_2 by c_{b_1} and c_{b_2} respectively.

It will be noted that equations (H) and (I) are identical with (D) and (E) except that the right hand sides have been interchanged. As before, we can multiply the first equation (H) by 2.9816, obtaining.

$$c_{b_1} \cdot 6768.0 + c_{b_2} \cdot 10525.0 = 0$$

from which we subtract (I).

We thus have

$$c_{b_1} = -0.3088 \times 10^{-3}$$

and substituting in either (H) or (I) we get

$$c_{b_2} = 0.1986 \times 10^{-3}$$

We now can calculate b_1 and b_2 as

$$\begin{aligned} b_1 &= c_{a_1} \cdot \Sigma'(yx_1) + c_{a_2} \Sigma'(yx_2) \qquad (J) \\ &= 0.9208 \times 10^{-3} \times 8477.0 - 0.3088 \times 10^{-3} \times 17329.4 \\ &= 2.454 \\ b_2 &= c_{b_1} \Sigma'(yx_1) + c_{b_2} \Sigma'(yx_2) \qquad (K) \\ &= -0.3088 \times 10^{-3} \times 8477.0 + 0.1986 \times 10^{-3} \times 17329.4 \\ &= 0.824 \end{aligned}$$

These solutions of b_1 and b_2 are of course the same as obtained previously for $b_{yw.a}$ and $b_{ya.w}$. It will be noted now where one of the principal advantages of this procedure lies. We can easily obtain the partial regression coefficients for a second dependent variable Y without the trouble of re-solving the simultaneous equations. Thus in the present instances we are only concerned with one dependent variable, the stack loss as combined nitrogen. We might in addition be interested in the ratio of nitrous to nitric gases and the variations of this ratio with the two independent variables. We merely need to obtain the sums of products of the new dependent vari ble Y with x_1, and x_2, $\Sigma'(Yx_1)$ and $\Sigma'(Yx_2)$ and substitute in equations (J) and (K). The additional labour is thus very slight, especially when compared with re-solving the simultaneous equations as with the earlier treatment.

The second advantage of the present procedure is that we can now readily obtain the standard error of each partial regression coefficient. We need the residual variance σ_r^2 which we already have in Table 10.1. To repeat, in the present symbolism, it is

$$\begin{aligned}\sigma_r^2 &= \frac{1}{(n-3)}\left[\Sigma'(y)^2 - b_1\,\Sigma'(yx_1) - b_2\,\Sigma'(yx_2)\right] \\ &= 354.9\end{aligned}$$

Then the standard error of b_1 is

$$\begin{aligned}\sigma_r\sqrt{c_{a_1}} &= \sqrt{354.9}\,\sqrt{0.9208 \times 10^{-3}} \\ &= 0.574\end{aligned}$$

and the standard error of b_2 is

$$\begin{aligned}\sigma_r\sqrt{c_{b_2}} &= \sqrt{354.9}\,\sqrt{0.1986 \times 10^{-3}} \\ &= 0.266\end{aligned}$$

These standard errors have degrees of freedom equal to $(n-3)$, and since n is generally large any regression coefficient twice its own standard error can be assumed significant at the 5% level. This procedure is thus a method of testing significance alternative to that set out previously in Table 10.1. We can also set the probable limits (95%) for b_1 as $2.454 \pm 2 \times 0.574 = 1.306$ and 3.602. Putting it this way makes it clear how many significant figures are worth retaining in the final statement of the regression equation.

(c) The Need for multiple Regression and Partial Correlation

In deriving the regression coefficients $b_{yw.a}$ and $b_{ya.w}$, we have kept the variable in the subscript after the full stop constant. For this reason these are known as "partial" regression coefficients. The simple regression coefficients would have been given by

$$b_{yw} = \frac{\Sigma' y x_w}{\Sigma' x_w^2} = \frac{8477}{2270} = 3.734$$

and

$$b_{ya} = \frac{\Sigma' y x_a}{\Sigma' x_a^2} = \frac{17329}{10525} = 1.646$$

It will be noted that these simple regression coefficients are appreciably larger than the corresponding partial regression coefficients. The explanation of this is easy to see. If we calculate the correlation coefficient of x_w and x_a we get

$$\begin{aligned}r_{wa} &= \frac{\Sigma'\, x_w\, x_a}{\sqrt{\Sigma' x_w^2\; \Sigma' x_a^2}} = \frac{3530}{\sqrt{2270 \times 10525}} \\ &= 0.7222\end{aligned}$$

There is thus a highly significant and very important correlation between x_w and x_a. This is a consequence of the nature of the process, of course. Weather conditions that lead to low air temperatures (x_a) will also tend to give low cooling water temperature (x_w).

Thus when we calculate the simple regression coefficient of y upon x_w, since the higher figures for x_w will tend to be associated with the higher figures for x_a, the values of y for the larger values of x_w will tend to be larger than they should be because they are also associated with the larger values of x_a. The partial regression coefficients, however, have the effect of the other variable eliminated, and measure only the effect of the variable specified.

In this connection the partial correlation coefficients are sometimes used. If the simple correlation coefficients are

$$r_{wa} = 0.7222$$

$$r_{yw} = \frac{\Sigma' y x_w}{\sqrt{\Sigma' y^2 \times \Sigma' x_w^2}} = \frac{8477}{\sqrt{83,340 \times 2270}} = 0.6165$$

$$r_{ya} = \frac{\Sigma' y x_a}{\sqrt{\Sigma' y^2 \times \Sigma' x_a^2}} = \frac{17,329}{\sqrt{83,340 \times 10,525}} = 0.5850$$

then the partial correlation coefficients are

$$r_{yw.a} = \frac{r_{yw} - r_{ya} \cdot r_{wa}}{\sqrt{(1 - r_{ya}^2)(1 - r_{wa}^2)}}$$

$$= \frac{0.6165 - 0.5850 \times 0.7222}{\sqrt{(1 - 0.5850^2)(1 - 0.7222^2)}}$$

$$= 0.3458$$

and

$$r_{ya.w} = \frac{r_{ya} - r_{yw} \cdot r_{aw}}{\sqrt{(1 - r_{yw}^2)(1 - r_{aw}^2)}}$$

$$= \frac{0.5850 - 0.6165 \times 0.7222}{\sqrt{(1 - 0.6165^2)(1 - 0.7222^2)}}$$

$$= 0.2567$$

For testing the significance of a simple correlation coefficient the degrees of freedom are $(n - 2)$, if n is the number of observations. For a partial correlation coefficient, another degree of freedom is lost, and the number is thus $(n - 3)$. In the present case, though both the correlation coefficients are markedly reduced in their transformation from simple to partial coefficients, they still remain significant with this large number of degrees of freedom $(139 - 3)$. In general, however, it is possible for a positive simple correlation coefficient to be transformed into a negative partial correlation coefficient, if, to quote the formula for $r_{ya.w}$, the product of r_{yw} and r_{aw} is greater than r_{ya}.

While the difference between the simple and partial coefficients was in this case of interest but not of immediate practical importance, it might well be otherwise in other cases. Thus suppose it had been decided that it would be economic to instal refrigeration equipment on the basis of the simple regression coefficient of 0.373. If the refrigeration would lower the mean cooling water temperature by 10°C., we could expect a reduction in the stack loss of 3.73 units on the simple correlation, and this might be sufficient to justify the installation. The reduction which would be actually achieved is 2.44 units (from the partial regression coefficient), and the difference between this and 3.73 might be the difference between an economic and an uneconomic installation.

(d) Multiple Correlation with Three Independent Variables

In the example we have been considering, the loss from a P.O.P. stack, there is a third variable of considerable interest, namely the strength of acid in the absorption tower, which we will denote by x_s.

We are setting out to determine the coefficients (a and the bs) in the equation

$$y = a_{y.was} + b_{yw.as}\, x_w + b_{ya.ws}\, x_a + b_{ys.aw}\, x_s$$

where the symbolism is as before: thus

$a_{y.was}$ is the value y would have if x_w, x_a, and x_s were held constant at their mean values.

$b_{yw.as}$ measures the rate of increase of y with increasing x_w, both x_a and x_s being constant at their mean values.

Similarly for $b_{ya.ws}$ and $b_{ys.aw}$.

We require the sums, the sums of squares, and the sums of products with the other three variables. As it is desirable to retain rather more decimal places, the complete set with the earlier ones recalculated are below :—

$\Sigma y = 1479$	$\Sigma y^2 = 99077$	$\Sigma' y^2 = 83340.014$
$\Sigma x_w = 406$	$\Sigma x_w^2 = 3456$	$\Sigma' x_w^2 = 2270.12950$
$\Sigma x_a = 1$	$\Sigma x_a^2 = 10525$	$\Sigma' x_a^2 = 10524.9928$
$\Sigma x_s = 70$	$\Sigma x_s^2 = 36364$	$\Sigma' x_s^2 = 36328.74820$
$\Sigma y x_w = 12797$	$\Sigma' y x_w = 8477.0431$	
$\Sigma y x_a = 17340$	$\Sigma' y x_a = 17329.3597$	
$\Sigma y x_s = 12931$	$\Sigma' y x_s = 12186.1799$	
$\Sigma x_w x_a = 3533$	$\Sigma' x_w x_a = 3530.07914$	
$\Sigma x_a x_s = 5365$	$\Sigma' x_a x_s = 5364.49640$	
$\Sigma x_s x_w = 1943$	$\Sigma' x_s x_w = 1738.5396$	

We now need to solve the three sets of three simultaneous equations (A), (B) and (C) below. The first set has as right hand side for (A), (B) and (C) 1, 0 and 0 respectively, and the solutions are c_{a_1}, c_{b_1}, and c_{c_1}. The second set has as right hand sides 0, 1 and 0 and solutions c_{a_2}, c_{b_2}, and c_{c_2}. Similarly the third set has right hand sides 0, 0, 1 and solutions c_{a_3}, c_{b_3}, and c_{c_3}.

$$c_a\, \Sigma' x_w^2 + c_b\, \Sigma' x_w x_s + c_c\, \Sigma' x_w x_a = 1,\ 0,\ 0 \qquad \text{(A)}$$
$$c_a\, \Sigma' x_s x_w + c_b\, \Sigma' x_s^2 + c_c\, \Sigma' x_s x_a = 0,\ 1,\ 0 \qquad \text{(B)}$$
$$c_a\, \Sigma' x_a x_w + c_b\, \Sigma' x_a x_s + c_c\, \Sigma' x_a^2 = 0,\ 0,\ 1 \qquad \text{(C)}$$

The solutions of these equations can be obtained empirically, but a systematic method is less liable to accidental errors.

Whittaker and Robinson(1) contain a general discussion, but the most satisfactory method is due to M. H. Doolittle. We set out the equations as (A′), (B′) and (C′) in a table as Table 10.2. Inserting the numerical values quoted above, we get (A″), (B″), (C″). It will be understood that all the figures occurring in the column headed c_a are effectively the coefficients of c_a in the successive equations, and similarly for c_b and c_c. The right hand sides have been multiplied by 10^4 temporarily to avoid the occurrence of excessively large numbers of 0's after the decimal points.

The next step is to write down again (A″) as (A‴), and then put underneath it the result of dividing it by the coefficient of c_a with the sign changed (here by —2270.12950). This gives us (D).

Now set down (B″) again as (B‴). Multiply (A‴) by the coefficient of c_b in (D) (here —0.76583279) ; this is (E). Add to (B‴) giving (F). Divide (F) by the coefficient of its first term with the sign changed (i.e. by —34997.3536) to give (G).

Now set down (C″) again as (C‴). Multiply (A‴) by the coefficient of c_c in (D) (i.e. by —1.55501223) to give (H). Also multiply (F) by the coefficient of c_c in (G) to give (I). Adding (C‴), (H) and (I) we get J, and dividing through by the coefficient of c_c (4833.3424) we get (K). The three figures on the right hand side are the solutions for c_{c_1}, c_{c_2}, and c_{c_3}, all multiplied by 10^4.

If we now take (G), and substitute these solutions for c_{c_1}, c_{c_2}, and c_{c_3} we get (L_1), (L_2) and (L_3) respectively. These lead immediately to (L'_1), (L'_2), and (L'_3), which give the solutions for c_{b_1}, c_{b_2}, and c_{b_3}, respectively.

We now substitute the solutions for c_b and c_c in $(D)_2$ getting (M_1), (M_2) and (M_3), leading to (M'_1), (M'_2) and (M'_3) as the solutions of c_{a_1}, c_{a_2}, and c_{a_3} respectively.

We can summarise these solutions in a matrix as in Table 10.3.

(1) E. T. Whittaker and G. Robinson, "The Calculus of Observations" (Blackie), 3rd edition, Chapter IX.

Table 10.2

	c_a	c_b	c_c
(A′)	$\Sigma' x_w^2$	$\Sigma' x_w x_s$	$\Sigma' x_w x_a$
(B′)	$\Sigma' x_s x_w$	$\Sigma' x_s^2$	$\Sigma' x_s x_a$
(C′)	$\Sigma' x_a x_w$	$\Sigma' x_a x_s$	$\Sigma' x_a^2$
A″	2270.12950	1738.5396	3530.07914
B″	1738.5396	36328.7482	5364.4960
C″	3530.07914	5364.4960	10524.9928
A‴	2270.12950	1738.5396	3530.07914
D	—1.00000	—0.76583279	—1.55501223
B‴	1738.5396	36328.7842	5364.4960
E	—1738.5396	—1331.4306	—2703.4503
F	0.0000	34997.3536	2661.0457
G		—1.0000	—0.076035630
C‴	3530.07914	5364.4960	10524.9928
(H)	—3530.07904	—2703.4502	—5489.3161
(I)		—2661.0458	—202.3343
J	0.0000	0.0000	4833.3424
K			1.00000
L_1		—1.0000	0.2354659
L_2		—1.0000	0.0119615
L_3		—1.0000	—0.1573148
L'_1		1.0000	
L'_2		1.0000	
L'_3		1.0000	
M_1	—1.0000	—0.0127435	4.8155366
M_2	—1.0000	—0.2279864	0.2446261
M_3	—1.000	0.1204768	—3.2172607
M'_1	1.0000		
M'_2	1.0000		
M'_3	1.0000		

Table 10.2—*contd.*

	First Set $\times 10^4$	Second Set $\times 10^4$	Third Set $\times 10^4$
(A′)	10,000	0	0
(B′)	0	10,000	0
(C′)	0	0	10,000
A″	10,000	0	0
B″	0	10,000	0
C″	0	0	10,000
A‴	10,000	0	0
D	—4.4050351	0	0
B‴	0	10,000	0
E	—7658.3279	0	0
F	—7658.3279	10,000	0
G	0.218825915	—0.28573589	0
C‴	0	0	10,000
(H)	—15550.1223	0	0
(I)	582.3058	—760.35630	0
J	—14967.8165	—760.35630	10,000
K	—3.0967838	—0.1573148	2.0689617
L_1	0.2188259		
L_2		—0.2857359	
L_3			0.0
L'_1	0.0166400		
L'_2		0.2976974	
L'_3			—0.1573148
M_1	—4.4050351		
M_2		0	
M_3			0
M'_1	9.2078282		
M'_2		0.0166397	
M'_3			—3.0967839

Table 10.3

All solutions multiplied by 10^4

	a	b	c
1	9.2078282	0.0166400	—3.0967838
2	0.0166397	0.2976974	—0.1573148
3	—3.0967839	—0.1573148	2.0689617

Like the original equations, this matrix is axi-symmetric ; $c_{b_1} = c_{a_2}$, $c_{c_1} = c_{a_3}$, and $c_{c_2} = c_{b_3}$.

A good check on the correctness of the solutions is to take the set for c_a and substitute them in (C″). There we get for the left hand side:

$$(3530.07914 \times 9.2078282 + 5364.4960 \times 0.01663970 - 10524.9928 \times 3.0967839) \times 10^{-4} = 0.00000025$$

which is close enough to the expected value of 0.

We now have as our values for the regression coefficients

$$\begin{aligned} b_{w.as} &= c_{a_1}\, \Sigma'(y\, x_w) + c_{a_2}\, \Sigma'(y\, x_s) + c_{a_3}\, \Sigma'(y\, x_a) \\ &= [9.2078282 \times 8477.0431 + 0.0166397 \times 12186.1799 \\ &\qquad - 3.0967839 \times 17329.3597] \times 10^{-4} \\ &= [78055.1564 + 202.7744 - 53665.2795] \times 10^{-4} \\ &= 2.4592651 \\ b_{s.aw} &= c_{b_1}\, \Sigma'(y\, x_w) + c_{b_2}\, \Sigma'(y\, x_s) + c_{b_3}\, \Sigma'(y\, x_a) \\ &= 0.1042687 \\ b_{a.sw} &= c_{c_1}\, \Sigma'(y\, x_w) + c_{c_2}\, \Sigma'(y\, x_s) + c_{c_3}\, \Sigma'(y\, x_a) \\ &= 0.7685143 \end{aligned}$$

A useful check on the accuracy of these last proceedings is to substitute these values in the equation

$$b_{w.as}\, \Sigma' x_a x_w + b_{s.aw}\, \Sigma' x_a x_s + b_{a.ws}\, \Sigma' x_a^2 = \Sigma' y\, x_a$$

Here we get 17329.3566 = 17329.3597, a discrepancy of 0.0031 which is small enough to be ignored.

The residual variance is given by

$$\begin{aligned} \sigma_r^2 &= \frac{1}{n-4}[\Sigma' y^2 - b_{w.as}\, \Sigma' y x_w - b_{s.aw}\, \Sigma' y x_s - b_{a.sw}\, \Sigma' y x_a] \\ &= \frac{1}{135}[83340.014 - 2.4592651 \times 8477.0431 - 0.1042687 \times \\ &\qquad 12186.1799 - 0.7685143 \times 17329.3597] \\ &= 47904.221/135 = 354.846 \end{aligned}$$

The standard errors of the three regression coefficients are then given by

$$\begin{aligned} \sigma_{w.as} &= \sigma_r \sqrt{c_{a_1}} = \sqrt{354.847 \times 9.2078 \times 10^{-4}} \\ &= 0.5716 \\ \sigma_{s.aw} &= \sigma_r \sqrt{c_{b_2}} = 0.1028 \\ \sigma_{a.sw} &= \sigma_r \sqrt{c_{b_3}} = 0.2709 \end{aligned}$$

To test the significance of each coefficient, we obtain the value of t as the ratio of the regression coefficient to its standard error, and look up this value of t with degrees of freedom equal to those of the residual variance. For $b_{a.sw}$, for example, t = 0.7685143/0.2709 = 2.837 with 135 degrees of freedom. Reference to Table I in the Appendix shows that this corresponds to a level of significance of between 1% and 0.1%.

Confidence limits for each estimate can be derived in the usual way. For $b_{a.sw}$ and 95% limits these are $0.768514 \pm 1.98 \times 0.2709$, or between 0.232132 and 1.304896.

Incidentally, it will be obvious that we have retained an excessive number of significant figures, and we could comfortably discard the last 4. It is much better, however, to carry out this discarding at the very end of the process rather than at the beginning.

The final regression equation is

$$y - \bar{y} = b_{w.as}(x_w - \bar{x}_w) + b_{s.aw}(x_s - \bar{x}_s) + b_{a.sw}(x_a - \bar{x}_a)$$

$$y - 1479/139 = 2.459265\,(x_w - 406/139) + 0.104269\,(x_s - 70/139) + 0.768514\,(x_a - 1/139)$$

$$\text{or } y = 2.459\,x_w + 0.104\,x_s + 0.768\,x_a + 3.399$$

(e) Conclusions

The use of this multiple regression technique involves rather heavy arithmetic, but when we have a mass of data with several independent variables it is the only sound way of assessing their several effects.

Thus in the present instance, we were particularly interested in the independent variable with the smallest regression coefficient, x_s. Completely eliminating the effects of the other two independent variables we obtained an estimate of the regression coefficient and were able to test its significance against a residual of 354.8, against which it was quite non-significant. If we had ignored the other two variables we would have obtained the sum of squares due to x_s as 4088, with a residual of 79252/137=578.5. Tested against this x_s would appear significant at the 1% level, an entirely erroneous conclusion.

The second reason for using the multiple regression technique was discussed at length earlier with reference to the misleading results obtained when using simple regression when the independent variables happen to be correlated. In this case the independent variables both had positive regression coefficients and were positively correlated, and so gave fictitiously large values for both the regression coefficients. If, however, they were negatively correlated, we would obtain fictitiously small values for the regression coefficients using the simple regression technique. Of course, if the independent variables are not correlated, then this phenomenon will not occur, and the only loss through using simple regression instead of partial (or multiple) regression is the loss of precision in our estimate through the residual being much larger.

As with simple regression equations, extrapolation of a multiple regression equation is unwise unless there is a very sound theoretical basis. It is good practice to quote the ranges of the independent variables that have occurred in the data used for calculating the regression equation, in order to discourage extrapolation.

CHAPTER XI

THE GENERAL ANALYSIS OF VARIANCE

(a) Introduction

It is important to realize that a situation suitable for the analysis of variance may arise in several ways:—

(i) By accident: the process may have a suitable structure as it stands. An example of this is discussed in Section (i) of this chapter, where there are three factories each handling three types of weak acid. The statistician had no part in seeing that there were three factories for each type of weak acid: this happened quite fortuitously.

(ii) By slight modification of existing manufacturing procedure. Thus it may be that in a process to each unit is added a variable amount of rework material of uncertain history, and for the purpose of examination this practice could be discontinued temporarily.

(iii) By deliberate experiment. Thus several factors may be varied at the levels appropriate to a factorial design.

(b) Types of Analysis

One of the difficulties frequently experienced in the use of the analysis of variance is to decide which is the appropriate form of analysis. A further difficulty is deciding the procedure for tests of significance. An attempt will be made here to give an outline of a general treatment.

In the succeeding examples, we shall deal with a hypothetical polymer being processed into fibres and the dependent variable is the fibre tensile strength. We shall make various modifications to this basic idea in an attempt to show how the various forms of analysis of variances are related to each other. After each form of this general example we shall deal in detail with another example of similar structure. A number of aspects of the use of the analysis of variance follow in Chapter XII.

All analyses can be divided into two broad types :—

(i) Those in which categories preserve their one-to-one correspondence : these we can define as pure factorial analyses.

(ii) Those in which certain of the categories do not preserve their one-to-one correspondence. These we can define as incomplete analyses.

The meaning of these two classifications will become clear with detailed discussion.

(c) The Two Factor Analysis

We can frequently categorise a set of individuals in two ways : thus we can have the raw material classified into a number of grades g according to the nominal degree of polymerisation. There are available a number of batches of each grade, and one batch of each grade can be processed at each of t different temperatures. We then have two factors : grade of polymer with g levels and temperature of processing with t levels. If we specify the values of g and t for any individual, we have completely identified that individual.

Such an example was discussed in Chapter VII (e). Table 11.1 below gives the degrees of freedom and components of variance.

Table 11.1

Source of Variance	Degrees of Freedom	Components of Variance
G	$g - 1$	$t\sigma_g^3 + \sigma_o^2$
T	$t - 1$	$g\sigma_t^2 + \sigma_o^2$
Residual	$(g - 1)(t - 1)$	σ_o^2
Total	$gt - 1$	

The tests of significance are obvious. If factor G is to exist, i.e. if σ_g^2 is to be greater than zero, then we must have :—

$$t\sigma_g^2 + \sigma_o^2 \text{ must be greater than } \sigma_o^2$$

and we can readily check the significance of this with the variance ratio test. Factor T can be tested similarly.

(d) The Three Factor Analysis

(i) In the previous section, we had g grades of polymer, one batch of each grade being processed at each of t different temperatures. Suppose now that each of s supplier supplies g grades of polymer and from each grade of each supplier t batches are processed at each of t temperatures.

It is important that the first grade from Supplier 1 has the same nominal degree of polymerisation as the first grade from Supplier 2, and as the first grade from Supplier 3, etc. Thus, the first grades for all the suppliers have a certain common property which distinguishes them in some way from the second grades of all the suppliers, etc.

There are now gts individuals, and each can be uniquely determined by specifying particular values of g, t, and s. We thus have three factors: suppliers, grades of polymer and temperature of processing. The technique of the analysis of variance for three factors is given later. The degrees of freedom and the components of variance are reproduced in Table 11.2.

Table 11.2

Source of Variance	Degrees of Freedom	Components of Variance
G	$g-1$	$\sigma_0^2 + s\sigma_{gt}^2 + t\sigma_{gs}^2 + ts\sigma_g^2$
T	$t-1$	$\sigma_0^2 + g\sigma_{ts}^2 + s\sigma_{gt}^2 + sg\sigma_t^2$
S	$s-1$	$\sigma_0^2 + t\sigma_{sg}^2 + g\sigma_{st}^2 + gt\sigma_s^2$
G × T	$(g-1)(t-1)$	$\sigma_0^2 + s\sigma_{gt}^2$
T × S	$(t-1)(s-1)$	$\sigma_0^2 + g\sigma_{st}^2$
S × G	$(s-1)(g-1)$	$\sigma_0^2 + t\sigma_{sg}^2$
Residual	$(g-1)(t-1)(s-1)$	σ_0^2
Total	$gts-1$	

For the tests of significance we must start with the smallest interaction and test it against the residual. Thus, if the smallest interaction is, say, S × G, we test with the variance ratio test $(\sigma_0^2 + t\sigma_{sg}^2)$ against σ_0^2. If it is not significant, we pool it with the residual and obtain a new estimate of σ_0^2; similarly, with the other interactions, taking them in ascending order of magnitude.

For the testing of the main effects, there are a number of possibilities:—

(i) All three interactions are non-significant. Striking them out in the table of components of variance in Table 11.2, and pooling their degrees of freedom with the residual, we obtain Table 11.3. :—

Table 11.3

Source of Variance	Degrees of Freedom	Components of Variance
G	$g-1$	$\sigma_0^2 + ts\sigma_g^2$
T	$t-1$	$\sigma_0^2 + sg\sigma_t^2$
S	$s-1$	$\sigma_0^2 + gt\sigma_s^2$
Residual	$gts-(g+t+s)+2$	σ_0^2
Total	$gts-1$	

For the three main effects the tests of significance are quite obviously to compare $(\sigma_0^2 + ts\sigma_g^2)$ with σ_0^2 for the factor G, and similarly for T and S.

(ii) One interaction, say, G × T, is significant, and the others are not. Striking the latter out in Table 11.2, we thereby obtain Table 11.4 :—

Table 11.4

Source of Variance	Degrees of Freedom	Components of Variance
G	$g - 1$	$\sigma_0^2 + s\sigma_{gt}^2 + ts\sigma_g^2$
T	$t - 1$	$\sigma_0^2 + s\sigma_{gt}^2 + sg\sigma_t^2$
S	$s - 1$	$\sigma_0^2 + gt\sigma_s^2$
G × T	$(g - 1 (t - 1)$	$\sigma_0^2 + s\sigma_{gt}^2$
Residual	$(gt - 1) (s - 1)$	σ_0^2
Total	$gts - 1$	

To test for the existence of the S main effect, we need to demonstrate the existence of σ_s^2, and this can be rigorously done by testing $(\sigma_0^2 + gt\sigma_s^2)$ against σ_0^2. For the G main effect, we need to demonstrate the existence of σ_g^2, and to do this, we must show that

$$\sigma_0^2 + s\sigma_{gt}^2 + ts\sigma_g^2 \text{ is greater than } \sigma_0^2 + s\sigma_{gt}^2,$$

i.e. we test the G main effect against the G × T interaction. The T main effect is tested similarly.

(iii) The third possibility is that two interactions are significant, e.g. G × T and T × S. Table 11.2 then becomes Table 11.5 :

Table 11.5

Source of Variance	Degrees of Freedom	Components of Variance
G	$g - 1$	$\sigma_0^2 + s\sigma_{gt}^2 + ts\sigma_g^2$
T	$t - 1$	$\sigma_0^2 + g\sigma_{ts}^2 + s\sigma_{gt}^2 + sg\sigma_t^2$
S	$s - 1$	$\sigma_0^2 + g\sigma_{st}^2 + gt\sigma_s^2$
G × T	$(g - 1) (t - 1)$	$\sigma_0^2 + s\sigma_{gt}^2$
T × S	$(t - 1 (s - 1)$	$\sigma_0^2 + t\sigma_{st}^2$
Residual	$t (g - 1) (s - 1)$	σ_0^2
Total	$gts - 1$	

Studying the Components of Variance, it will be apparent that the significance of the G and S main effects can be established by testing their mean squares against the G × T and the T × S interactions respectively. However, there is no rigorous test to demonstrate the existence of the T main effect, for while we might prove that it was greater than the G × T interaction, this might be due to the existence of σ_{ts}^2 as much as to the existence of σ_t^2.

In practice this impasse is not of any great practical importance, as we would break down the analysis into separate two factor G × S analyses for each level of T. This procedure is illustrated in Section (e) of this chapter.

Let us consider the data in the table below, referring to a purification process. The figures (the dependent variable $\mathbf{x}$) refer to the purity of a product measured in a certain way. The factor T at three levels represented time of boiling. The factor A represents solvent used, and W_1 represents a cold final wash of the product and W_2 a hot final wash.

		T_1	T_2	T_3
A_1	W_1	3.1	2.0	1.3
	W_2	2.1	1.6	1.9
A_2	W_1	4.3	2.8	4.1
	W_2	6.1	3.9	2.6

In analysing this data, an arbitrary zero of 3.0 was taken. This reduces the magnitude of all the numbers, and therefore their squares, and the arithmetic becomes less burdensome. Also, to avoid confusion with the decimal point, the numbers were then multiplied by 10. This results in the sums of squares in the analysis of variance being $10^2 = 100$ times too large, which does not affect the analysis, as in the tests of significance all the terms are compared with each other, the change in scale thus being of no importance. If we proceed to calculate any particular variance, however, we must correct for this change of scales by dividing by 100.

The result of the transformation is as below:

		T_1	T_2	T_3
A_1	W_1	1	—10	—17
	W_2	—9	—14	—11
A_2	W_1	13	—2	11
	W_2	31	9	—4

It should be remembered that the data is completely symmetrical with respect to the three variables, A, W, and T. This might be clearer if we were able, using three-dimensional paper, to set the lower half of the table (for A_2) on top of the upper half of the table (for A_1). Then the horizontal axis across the page represents difference between times of boiling (T), the vertical axis down the page represents type of wash (W), and the axis perpendicular to the page represents type of solvent (A). The table as it stands has the form of tables for W and T for each value of A: that is an arbitrary choice and it might equally well have been W and A tables for each value of T, or A and T tables for each value of W.

We first form the three two-way tables by summing over each of the three variables in turn. Thus we sum over W for each value of A and T, getting the table below:

	T_1	T_2	T_3	Totals
A_1	—8	—24	—28	—60
A_2	44	7	7	58
Totals	36	—17	—21	—2

Summing over A for each value of T and W we get the table below

	T_1	T_2	T_3	Totals
W_1	14	—12	—6	—4
W_2	22	—5	—15	+2
Totals	36	—17	—21	—2

The third table is obtained by summing over T for each value of A and W, as below:

	A_1	A_2	Totals
W_1	—26	22	—4
W_2	—34	36	2
Totals	—60	58	—2

We analyse the first of these two-way tables, for A and T, as follows:

Form the following terms—

(1) Square the individuals, sum the squares, and divide by the number of original individuals that have been summed to give the individuals in this two-way table. Here each individual is the sum of two original individuals. Thus we have

$$[(-8)^2 + (-24)^2 + (-28)^2 + 44^2 + 7^2 + 7^2]/2 = 1729$$

(2) Obtain the total for each row, square these totals, sum these squares, and divide this total by the number of original individuals that have been summed to give the row totals. Here each row total is the sum of 6 original individuals (the row totals are each the sum of 3 two-way table individuals, each of which is the sum of 2 original individuals). Thus we have

$$[(-60)^2 + (58)^2]/6 = 1160.67$$

(3) Perform the identical operation for the column totals. Here each column total is the sum of 4 original individuals, so the divisor is 4. Thus we have

$$[36^2 + (-17)^2 + (-21)^2]/4 = 506.5$$

(4) Obtain the grand total for all individuals, square this grand total, and divide by the grand total number of original individuals

$$(-2)^2/12 = 0.33$$

It will be noted that these operations are similar to the analysis of a row and column table, discussed earlier, differing only in that each sum of squares is divided, not by the number of individuals in the two-way table in each total which is being squared, but by the number of original individuals in each total that is being squared.

We can now form a table for the analysis of variance of this row and column table.

Source of Variance	Degrees of Freedom	Sums of Squares	Mean Squares
Between A	$a - 1 = 2 - 1 = 1$	$(2) - (4) = 1160.33$	1160.33
Between T	$t - 1 = 3 - 1 = 2$	$(3) - (4) = 506.17$	253.08
$A \times T$ interaction	$(a - 1)(t - 1) = 2$	62.17	31.08
Total	$at - 1 = 5$	$(1) - (4) = 1728.67$	

a = number of levels of A
t = number of levels of T

This table corresponds closely to that previously discussed for row and column analysis, except that what was formerly "Residual" is now termed "A × T interaction." The reason for this will be discussed later. The Sum of Squares corresponding to this term is best obtained as the difference between the sum of the A and T terms and the Total, i.e.

$$1728.67 - (1160.33 + 506.17) = 62.17$$

Precisely similar operations are performed on the other two-way tables.

Finally, the Total Variance is obtained by squaring all the original individuals, summing these squares, and subtracting from this sum of squares the total squared divided by the total number of original individuals, i.e.

$$1^2 + (-10)^2 + (-17)^2 + (-9)^2 + \ldots (-4)^2 - \frac{(-2)^2}{12} = 2139.67$$

All these results are now gathered together in Table 11.6.

Table 11.6

Source of Variance	Degrees of Freedom	Sums of Squares	Mean Squares	Components of Variance
Between A	$(a - 1) = 1$	1160.33	1160.33	$wt\sigma_a^2 + w\sigma_{at}^2 + t\sigma_{aw}^2 + \sigma_o^2$
Between W	$(w - 1) = 1$	3.00	3.00	$at\sigma_w^2 + a\sigma_{wt}^2 + t\sigma_{wa}^2 + \sigma_o^2$
Between T	$(t - 1) = 2$	506.17	253.08	$wa\sigma_t^2 + w\sigma_{at}^2 + a\sigma_{wt}^2 + \sigma_o^2$
A × W Interaction	$(a - 1)(w - 1) = 1$	40.33	40.33	$t\sigma_{wa}^2 + \sigma_o^2$
W × T Interaction	$(w - 1)(t - 1) = 2$	45.50	22.75	$a\sigma_{wt}^2 + \sigma_o^2$
T × A Interaction	$(t - 1)(a - 1) = 2$	62.17	31.08	$w\sigma_{ta}^2 + \sigma_o^2$
Residual	$(a - 1)(t - 1)(w - 1) = 2$	322.17	161.08	$+ \sigma_o^2$
Total	$awt - 1 = 11$	2139.67		

a, w, and t are respectively equal to the number of levels of A, W, and T.

σ_a^2, σ_w^2 and σ_t^2 are respectively equal to the variances due to general differences between levels of A, levels of W, and levels of T.

σ_{aw}^2, σ_{wt}^2, σ_{ta}^2 are respectively equal to the variances due to interactions between A and W, between W and T, and between T and A.

σ_o^2 is the residual variance, unattributable to any of the above terms.

The sum of squares corresponding to the residual is obtained as the difference between the total sum of squares and the sum of the six other terms.

The meaning of these terms is as follows:

σ_a^2 is the variability that would occur if the other two factors W and T were held constant, similarly σ_w^2 is the variability that would occur if A and T were held constant and σ_t^2 the variability that would occur if A and W were held constant.

The A × W Interaction σ_{aw}^2 is a measure of the extent to which the A effect depends on the value of W, and conversely, to which the W effect depends on the value of A. Similarly for the other interactions.

The Residual σ_0^2 is that portion of the variability that cannot be allocated to the other six terms. It can be regarded as a measure of error. In the present experimental design, the possible second order interaction A × W × T, if it exists, will contribute to the same term. The second order A × W × T measures the extent to which the A × W interaction depends upon the level of T, or similarly, to which the A × T interaction depends on the level of W, similarly, to which the T × W interaction depends on the level of A. If this effect does exist, it will give us an inflated estimate of error, and hence the effects will be likely to not attain significance. This situation is discussed later in Chapter XII (e). For the present we will assume that the A × W × T interaction does not exist, or at any rate is not large.

We now need to apply a test of significance for the existence of these terms. We can see that if, for example σ_{ta}^2 is to exist, then $(w\sigma_{ta}^2 + \sigma_0^2)$ must be significantly greater than σ_0^2, i.e. the T × A interaction mean square must be significantly greater than the residual mean square.

Here we see that the Mean Squares for the W, A × W, W × T, and T × A are all less than the Residual Mean Square, so that σ_w^2, σ_{aw}^2, σ_{wt}^2, and σ_{ta}^2 do not exist, i.e. are zero. We can therefore use these mean squares as estimates of σ_0^2 to get a more accurate estimate. We pool their sums of squares and the degrees of freedom, i.e.

$$(3.00 + 40.33 + 45.50 + 62.17 + 322.17)/(1 + 1 + 2 + 2 + 2) = 59.1$$

This new residual has 8 degrees of freedom.

Considering the T term, the T mean Square now estimates wa $\sigma_t^2 + \sigma_0^2$ for σ_{at}^2 and σ_{wt}^2 have been shown to be zero. To establish the existence of σ_t^2 we therefore test the T mean square against the (new) residual. The variance ratio is $253.08/59.1 = 4.3$ for degrees of freedom $n_1 = 2$, $n_2 = 8$. This lies close to the 5% level of significance, so we may assume that T does have an effect.

Similarly the A term gives a variance ratio of $1160.33/59.1 = 19.6$ for degrees of freedom $n_1 = 1$, $n_2 = 8$, this being considerably more significant than the 1% level, so we assume that A does have an effect.

We now can take the means for each level of A and T, and conclude that for A_1 we have, translating back into terms of the original variable, a mean value 2.00 and for A_2 a mean value of 3.97. For T_1 the mean is 3.90, for T_2 2.58, and for T_3 2.48. It is clear that the difference between T_2 and T_3 is so slight as to be not significant, but the difference between these two and T_1 is quite considerable. We can also conclude that the difference between the two levels of W is quite insignificant.

Each of the averages for the three levels of T is the average of 4 results. In the units in which the analysis of variance was carried out the residual variance was 59.15, corresponding to a standard deviation of 7.691, or converting to original units 0.7691. Accordingly the standard deviation of the average of four results will be $0.7691/\sqrt{4} = 0.3845$. This then is the standard deviation of each of the three averages quoted above for the three levels of T. The standard deviation of the difference between any two is $0.3845\sqrt{2} = 0.5429$.

Proceeding similarly for the two averages for the two levels of A, these each have standard deviation of $0.7691/\sqrt{6} = 0.3140$, and the standard error of the difference between these two averages, which is $3.97 - 2.00 = 1.97$, is $0.3140\sqrt{2} = 0.4440$. The residual on which this standard error is based has 8 degrees of freedom, for which for the 5% level of significance $t = 2.31$ (see Table I, Appendix). Accordingly the 95% confidence limits for the difference between A_1 and A_2 are $1.97 \pm 2.31 \times 0.444$, or 3.00 and 0.94.

In this example, having demonstrated the significance of certain effects, we have proceeded to calculate the means for each level of these effects in order to demonstrate their mode of action. In this example each factor and its levels had precise and obvious meanings, and when we compared A_1 with A_2 we knew what comparison we were making (we were comparing one solvent with another). In some types of analysis, however, the difference between different levels of a particular factor may not be obvious. Thus a factor may be shift, with 3 levels. Or it may be day, with any number of levels. Or it may be machine for a group of allegedly similar machines. With this type of factor, where the distinction between the levels is rather vague and elusive, it is often better to calculate the actual magnitude of the variance due to each term.

(e) The Four Factor Analysis

(i) In the previous section, we had g grades of polymer by each of s suppliers being processed at each of t temperatures. If we suppose that the suppliers were supplied with raw material from each of r sources, then R becomes a fourth main factor. There are thus gtsr individuals, and each can be uniquely determined by specifying particular of values of the categories. It is important that every supplier draws from each source of raw material.

The components of variance are reproduced in Table 11.8 below, along with the respective degrees of freedom.

Table 11.8

Source of Variance	Degrees of Freedom	Components of Variance
G	$g - 1$	$\sigma_o^2 + r\sigma_{gts}^2 + t\sigma_{srg}^2 + s\sigma_{rgt}^2 + sr\sigma_{gt}^2 + ts\sigma_{rg}^2 + rt\sigma_{gs}^2 + tsr\sigma_g^2$
T	$t - 1$	$\sigma_o^2 + r\sigma_{gts}^2 + g\sigma_{tsr}^2 + s\sigma_{rgt}^2 + sr\sigma_{gt}^2 + rg\sigma_{st}^2 + gs\sigma_{rt}^2 + gsr\sigma_t^2$
S	$s - 1$	$\sigma_o^2 + r\sigma_{gts}^2 + g\sigma_{tsr}^2 + t\sigma^2_{srg} + rg\sigma_{ts}^2 + gt\sigma_{sr}^2 + rt\sigma_{gs}^2 + gtr\sigma_s^2$
R	$r - 1$	$\sigma_o^2 + g\sigma_{tsr}^2 + s\sigma^2_{rgt} + t\sigma^2_{srg} + gt\sigma^2_{sr} + ts\sigma^2_{rg} + gs\sigma^2_{rt} + sgt\sigma_r^2$
G × T	$(g - 1)(t - 1)$	$\sigma_o^2 + s\sigma_{rgt}^2 + r\sigma^2_{gts} + sr\sigma^2_{gt}$
T × S	$(t - 1)(s - 1)$	$\sigma_o^2 + r\sigma^2_{gts} + g\sigma^2_{tsr} + rg\sigma^2_{ts}$
S × R	$(s - 1)(r - 1)$	$\sigma_o^2 + g\sigma^2_{tsr} + t\sigma^2_{srg} + gt\sigma^2_{sr}$
R × G	$(r - 1 (g - 1)$	$\sigma_o^2 + t\sigma^2_{srg} + s\sigma^2_{rgt} + ts\sigma^2_{rg}$
G × S	$(g - 1)(s - 1)$	$\sigma_o^2 + r\sigma^2_{gts} + t\sigma^2_{srg} + rt\sigma^2_{gs}$
T × R	$(t - 1)(r - 1)$	$\sigma_o^2 + g\sigma^2_{tsr} + s\sigma^2_{rgt} + gs\sigma^2_{rt}$
G × T × S	$(g - 1)(t - 1)(s - 1)$	$\sigma_o^2 + r\sigma^2_{gts}$
T × S × R	$(t - 1)(s - 1)(r - 1)$	$\sigma_o^2 + g\sigma^2_{tsr}$
S × R × G	$(s - 1)(r - 1)(g - 1)$	$\sigma_o^2 + t\sigma^2_{srg}$
R × G × T	$(r - 1)(g - 1)(t - 1)$	$\sigma_o^2 + s\sigma^2_{rgt}$
Residual	$(g - 1)(t - 1)(s - 1)(r - 1)$	σ_o^2
Total	$gtsr - 1$	

The appropriate tests of significance can be worked out from the components of variance.

(ii) The data below is from a four factor experiment, each factor at two levels. The experiment is on a purification process, and high figures for the dependent variable correspond to an inferior product. The treatments were such that the crude material could be given a hot or cold wash (H_1 or H_2), then given a period of boiling or not given a period of boiling (B_2 or B_1), then dissolved, filtered, and precipitated from either of two solvents (S_1 or S_2), and finally given a cold or hot wash (W_1 or W_2).

S_1								S_2							
W_1				W_2				W_1				W_2			
B_1		B_2		B_1		B_2		B_1		B_2		B_1		B_2	
H_1	H_2	H_1	H_2	H_1	H_2	H_1	H_2	H_1	H_2	H_1	H_2	H_1	H_2	H_1	H_2
4.2	2.7	1.4	1.3	3.3	3.5	1.3	1.9	2.2	3.1	4.0	4.1	5.0	3.0	2.2	2.6
17	2	—11	—12	8	10	—12	—6	—3	6	15	16	25	5	—3	1

In carrying out the analysis of variance, for convenience 2.5 was subtracted from each figure, and the results multiplied by 10 to remove the decimal point, this giving the figures in the last row. The effect of this transformation is that all the sums of squares in the analysis of variance are $10^2 = 100$ times too large.

We proceed[1] as follows :—

(1) We form the four tables obtained by summing over each of the four variables in turn. Thus the table obtained by summing over S is as below:

W_1				W_2			
B_1		B_2		B_1		B_2	
H_1	H_2	H_1	H_2	H_1	H_2	H_1	H_2
14	8	4	4	33	15	—15	—5

The table obtained by summing over W is as below:

S_1				S_2			
B_1		B_2		B_1		B_2	
H_1	H_2	H_1	H_2	H_1	H_2	H_1	H_2
25	12	—23	—18	22	11	12	17

The other two three-way tables, obtained by summing over B and over H, are similar.

[1] For an alternative method of calculating the analysis of variance of a 2^n experiment see page 138.

(2) We form the six tables obtained by summing over the variables two at a time. Thus the tables obtained by summing over S and H, and over S and B, are as below:

Summed over H and S

	B_1	B_2	Totals
W_1	22	8	30
W_2	48	—20	28
Totals	70	—12	58

Summed over S and B

	H_1	H_2	Totals
W_1	18	12	30
W_2	18	10	28
Totals	36	22	58

The other two-way tables are as below:

Summed over H and W

	B_1	B_2	Totals
S_1	37	—41	—4
S_2	33	29	62
Totals	70	—12	58

Summed over B and W

	H_1	H_2	Totals
S_1	2	—6	—4
S_2	34	28	62
Totals	36	22	58

Summed over B and H

	W_1	W_2	Totals
S_1	—4	0	—4
S_2	34	28	62
Totals	30	28	58

Summed over S and W

	H_1	H_2	Totals
B_1	47	23	70
B_2	—11	—1	—12
Totals	36	22	58

(3) We take the square of the grand total and divide it by the grand total number of observations:—

$$58^2/16 = 210.25$$

We shall use this quantity a great deal, and refer to it as "the correcting factor," as it corrects all our sums of squares for the fact that they are deviations from the zero, not the mean.

(4) To form the Sum of Squares for the main effect of the factor S, we square the S totals, sum these squares, and divide by the number of original individuals forming each S total, and subtract from this the correcting factor, i.e.

$$[(-4)^2 + 62^2]/8 - 210.25 = 272.25$$

The other main effects are obtained similarly. Thus—

For W: $(30^2 + 28^2)/8 - 210.25 = 0.25$

For B: $(70^2 + (-12)^2)/8 - 210.25 = 420.25$

For H: $(36^2 + 22^2)/8 - 210.25 = 12.25$

(5) The first order interactions measure the extent to which the effect of one factor depends upon the value of the other factor. Thus there are three first order interactions involving S, namely S × W, S × B, and S × H.

The Sum of Squares corresponding to the first mentioned, S × W, is obtained by squaring the individuals in the two way table for S and W, summing these squares, and dividing by the number of original individuals making up the individuals in this table, and from this subtracting the correcting factor, the S Sum of Squares, and the W Sum of Squares, i.e.

$$[(-4)^2 + 0^2 + 34^2 + 28^2)]/4 - 210.25 - 272.25 - 0.25 = 6.25$$

Similarly, the B × H interaction sum of squares is given by

$$(47^2 + 23^2 + (-11)^2 + (-1)^2)/4 - 210.25 - 420.25 - 12.25 = 72.25$$

The other first order interactions are derived likewise.

(6) It will be apparent that there is a possibility that the effect of, say, the B × H interaction may depend upon the value of W or of S. The former is termed the S × B × H interaction and the latter the W × B × H interaction. Interactions of this type are known as second order interactions.

The sums of squares for these terms are derived from the three way tables. Thus to derive the Sum of Squares for the S × B × H interaction we first square the individuals in the S × B × H table, sum these squares, and divide by the number of original individuals making up each individual in the table, and subtracting the correcting factor, i.e.

$$(25^2 + 12^2 + (-23)^2 + (-18)^2 + 22^2 + 11^2 + 12^2 + 17^2)/2 - 210.25$$
$$= 1119.75$$

From this figure we subtract the sums of squares for all the main effects and all the first order interactions which do not involve the odd variable. Thus with the S × B × H sum of squares the odd variable is W, so we subtract from 1119.75 the sums of squares for the S, B, H, S × B, B × H, and H × S terms, i.e.

$$1119.75 - 272.25 - 420.25 - 12.25 - 342.25 - 72.25 - 0.25 = 0.25$$

The other second order interactions are obtained similarly.

(7) The Total Sum of Squares is the difference between the sum of the squares of the original individuals and the correcting factor, i.e.

$$17^2 + 2^2 + (-11)^2 + \ldots + (-3)^2 + 1^2 - 210.25 = 1877.75$$

(8) The Sum of Squares corresponding to the Residual is obtained by subtracting the four main effects, the six first order interactions, and the four second order interactions from the Total Sum of Squares.

We thus have a complete analysis as in Table 11.9 below. The degrees of freedom are of the following form (small letters represent the number of levels at which the factor denoted by the capital letter occurs).

Table 11.9

Source of Variance	Sums of Squares
B	420.25
H	12.25
S	272.25
W	0.25
B × H	72.25
H × S	0.25
S × W	6.25
W × B	182.25
W × H	0.25
B × S	342.25
B × H × S	0.25
H × S × W	156.25
S × W × B	272.25
W × B × H	30.25
Residual	110.25
Total	1877.75

(a) for the main effects, e.g. for B, (b — 1)
(b) for the first order interactions, e.g. for H × B, (h — 1) (b — 1)
(c) for the second order interactions, e.g. for H × B × W, (h — 1) (b — 1) (w — 1)
(d) for the residual, (h — 1) (b — 1) (w — 1) s — 1)
(e) for the total, (h b w s — 1).

In the present case, the degrees of freedom are in every case 1 except for the total.[2] Accordingly, the column for Degrees of Freedom is omitted. Also, since the Sums of Squares thus equal their respective Mean Squares the latter column is omitted.

Analysing the various terms it is clear that the W × B × H and B × H × S interactions do not exist, so we can pool them with the residual giving a new residual of 140.75/3 = 46.92 with 3 degrees of freedom. The H × S × W interaction is not significant, and we get a new residual of 297.00/4 = 74.25 with 4 degrees of freedom. Tested against this the S × W × B interaction does not reach the 5% level of significance, but it is suspiciously large, and it is desirable to split the experiment up into two three factor experiments to check that the factors are not interacting.

With one second order interaction significant, say the S × W × B interaction, there is a choice of three methods of splitting, viz. H × W × B for each level of S, H × S × W for each level of B, or H × S × B for each level of W.

Which method of breakdown we employ is largely a matter of choice ; sometimes it may be informative to employ more than one. Here one particular method of breakdown is strongly indicated, namely according to the solvent used (factor S).

Accordingly, we carry out two three factor analyses, one for S_1 and the other for S_2. The results of such analyses are below in Table 11.10.

Table 11.10

Source of Variance	Mean Squares	
	Experiment with S at S_1	Experiment with S at S_2
B	760.5	2.0
H	8.0	4.5
W	2.0	4.5
B × H	40.5	32.0
H × W	72.0	84.5
W × B	4.5	450.0
Residual	12.5	128.0
Total	900.0	705.5

(2) In this respect the present example constitutes a special case. The adaptation of these methods of computation to the more general case is quite straightforward. The formulae for the degrees of freedom have just been given. With regard to the sums of squares, if we have a four factor experiment with factors A, B, C, and D at 2, 3, 4, and 5 levels respectively, there are two A totals each the total of 3 x 4 x 5 = 60 observations, so the sum of the squares of the A totals is divided by 60 before having the correcting factor subtracted from it to give the A sum of squares. There are five D totals, each the total of 2 x 3 x 4 = 24 observations, so the division of the sum of the squares of the D total is 24. For the interaction, for example, the B x C table has 3 x 4 = 12 entries, each the total of 2 x 5 = 10 observations ; accordingly the sum of the squares of these 12 entries is divided by 10 before having subtracted from it the correcting factor and the B and C Sums of Squares to give the B x C Sum of Squares.

The Degrees of Freedom for each of the terms except the Total are 1 in every case, so the Mean Squares equal their respective Sums of Squares, and therefore columns for Degrees of Freedom and Sums of Squares are omitted from the above table.

Let us consider the S_1 experiment first. The W × B interaction is not significant, and neither is the B × H interaction. The H × W interaction is also found to be non-significant. Clearly the H and W main effects are non-significant. Pooling all these non-significant terms we get a residual of 23.2 with 6 degrees of freedom. The only term left is the B main effect, giving a variance ratio of $760.5/23.2 = 32.8$ with degrees of freedom $n_1 = 1$, $n_2 = 6$. This lies near the 0.1% level of significance.

We can thus conclude that the B factor has an effect upon the quality of the product, B_1 giving a mean of 3.47 and B_2 a mean of 1.47. The significance of the other factors W and H has not been established, the means for H_1 and H_2 being 2.55 and 2.35 respectively and for W_1 and W_2 being 2.4 and 2.5 respectively.

It thus seems a matter of indifference which level of H and of W we use, but it is very important to select the right level of B.

Now let us consider the S_2 experiment. We have a large residual. The B × H and H × W interactions cannot be significant, and pooled give a new residual for 81.5 with 3 degrees of freedom. The H main effect does not contain amongst its components of variance σ_{wb}^2, which is contained amongst the components of variance of the outstanding interaction W × B : the H term is non-significant and can therefore be pooled to give a new residual of 62.25 with 4 degrees of freedom. Tested against this the W × B interaction gives a variance ration of $450.00/62.25 = 7.2$ with degrees of freedom $n_1 = 1$, $n_2 = 4$, this being close to the 5% level of significance.

The fact that the W × B interaction is marked for S_2 but non-existent for S_1 implies the existence of a W × B × S interaction, which we had suspected from the four factor analysis. The non-existence of a B main effect for S_2 as compared with its great significance for S_1 indicates the existence of a S × B interaction : the four factor analysis had showed that this exists but actually in the more complicated guise of an S × B × W interaction.

Here we have a three factor analysis with a significant first order interaction, W × B. Accordingly we need to break the three factor experiment down, either into W × H experiments for B_1 and for B_2 or into B × H experiments for W_1 and for W_2.

The results of the former are below in Table 11.11. Here again the Degrees of Freedom for each term except the total are 1, so that column and the Mean Square column are omitted.

Table 11.11

Source of Variance	Sums of Squares	
	B at	
	B_1	B_2
H	30.25	6.25
W	182.25	272.25
Residual	210.25	2.25
Total	422.75	280.75

Considering the B_2 experiment, the H term is not significant, and can be pooled to give a new residual of $8.50/2 = 4.25$ with two degrees of freedom. The W term then gives a variance ratio of $272.25/4.25 = 64.0$ for $n_1 = 1$, $n_2 = 2$, this being more significant than 5%.

We can thus conclude that using the solvent S_2 and treatment B_2 (boiling) it is a matter of indifference which level of H we use, but that it is important to select the correct level of W, the averages for W_1 and W_2 being 4.05 and 2.40 respectively.

Turning now to the B_1 experiment, we have a large residual, which suggests that the $H \times W$ interaction exists. From the fact that it clearly does not exist for $B = B_2$, this suggests that it takes the guise of a $B \times H \times W$ interaction. This was not shown up on the full four factor analysis, but the evidence here is suggestive. With such a large residual, the H and W terms will not be significant, but we may get an idea of the behaviour of the system by forming an $H \times W$ table, Table 11.12.

Table 11.12

$S = S_2$, $B = B_1$

	W_1	W_2
H_1	2.2	5.0
H_2	3.1	3.0

This table suggests that with S_2 B_1, we should use W_1, and possibly that H_1 is better. However, these suggestions cannot be made as definite assertions.

That is as much as can be done with that method of breakdown. Turning to the other, the results of the analysis are below in Table 11.13. The degrees of freedom are 1 for each term (except the total) so that column and the Mean Square column are omitted.

Table 11.13

Source of Variance	Sum of Squares W at W_1	Sum of Squares W at W_2
H	25	64
B	196	256
Residual	16	144
Total	237	464

Considering the experiment for W_1, clearly the H term is not significant. Pooling it we get a new residual of $41/2 = 20.5$ with 2 degrees of freedom. The B term then has a variance ratio of $196/20.5 = 9.55$ for $n_1 = 1$, $n_2 = 2$. This is considerably more significant than the 20% level but less significant than the 5%. However, we may regard it provisionally as real.

We can thus conclude that using solvent S_2 and treatment W_1 it is a matter of indifference which level of H we use but it is important to use the correct level of B, the means for B_1 and B_2 being 2.65 and 4.05 respectively.

Considering the experiment for W_2, we have a large residual, and therefore we cannot expect significance for the H and B terms. However we may get an idea of the behaviour of the system by inspecting a B × H table, as below.

$S = S_2$, $W = W_2$

	B_1	B_2
H_1	5.0	2.2
H_2	3.0	2.6

This table suggests that with S_2 W_2, we should use B_2, and possibly H_1 is better.

Let us now see whether the two methods of breakdown give consistent conclusions. The B_1 and B_2 method gave that with B_2 we should use W_2 to get a low figure for the impurity, but that with B_1 we should use W_1. The W_1 and W_2 method gave that with W_1 we should use B_1, and with W_2 we should use B_2. As regards H, the B_1 and B_2 method did not give significant results, but the W_1 and W_2 method suggested (qualitatively, not with an exact test of significance) that H_1 should be used to give low figures for the impurity. The two methods of breakdown thus lead to similar conclusions.

The effect of the W × B interaction for S_2 is shown in Table 11.14 below.

Table 11.14

$S = S_2$ (*H averaged*)

	B_1	B_2
W_1	2.65	4.05
W_2	4.0	2.4

This table shows clearly that to obtain a low figure for the impurity, if we use treatment B_1, then we must use W_1, and if we use B_2 then we must use W_2. There is no "best" level for either B or for W: the "best" levels depend upon the levels of the other factor. Also solvent S_2 behaves differently in this respect to Solvent S_1, for which treatment B_2 was always best irrespective of the values of H or W. The interaction shown above is the B × W interaction, and since it operates for S_2 but not for S_1 we can say that the S × W × B interaction exists.

It is of interest to note the type of error into which we might have fallen if we had carried out this experiment classically rather than factorially. Classically we would have investigated each factor at one level. If we were unlucky we would have investigated B at W_2 and W at B_1. From the first experiment we would have decided that in order to get a low figure for the impurity we should use B_2 and from the second experiment that we should use W_1. We thus would have decided to use W_1 B_2, an entirely faulty conclusion.

This has been a lengthy analysis, and we might recapitulate the conclusions reached :—

(1) Using the solvent S_1
  (a) it is a matter of indifference whether we use H_1 or H_2
  (b) it is a matter of indifference whether we use W_1 or W_2
  (c) it is desirable to use B_2 giving a mean figure for the impurity of 1.47 as compared with 3.42 for B_1.

(2) Using the solvent S_2

(a) it is a matter of indifference whether we use H_1 or H_2.

(b) using B_1 we should use W_1, when we get a figure of 2.65 for the impurity.

(c) using B_2 we should use W_2, when we get a figure of 2.4 for the impurity.

These conclusions have all been reached rigorously, with no guess work, and give a complete picture of the behaviour of the system.

It will be noted that this experiment has been complicated in the sense that there have been second order interactions significant. It would have been simpler if only the main effects, or first order interactions, had been significant. With second order interactions existing, however, the operation of the system is complicated, so it is inevitable that its analysis should be also.

It will also be noted that with significant interactions the factorial experiment loses its superiority in the sense of efficiency over the classical, and in effect reduces to a series of classical experiments. The point is that if a factorial design is not used, then these interactions cannot be detected.,

These questions are discussed further in Chapter XII (d), but meantime it must be noted that Tables 11.11 and 11.13 must be considered not satisfactory owing to the inadequate number of degrees of freedom. When thesee high order interactions are significant we require more experiments than were made in this instance.

(f) The Five Factor Analysis

(i) In the previous section, we had four factors, source of raw material (R), supplier of polymer (S), grade of polymer (G), and temperature of Processing (T). Let us now assume there is a fifth factor, namely, pressure of processing (P).

The procedure for five factor analysis of variance can be readily generalised from the two, three, and four factor analyses discussed earlier :—

(1) Sum over each of the variables in turn. This will give us five tables, each containing four variables.

(2) Sum over the variables taken two at a time. This will give us ten tables, each containing three variables.

(3) Sum over the variables taken three at a time. This will give us ten tables, each containing two variables.

(4) Derive the marginal totals of the tables (3). This is equivalent to summing over the variables taken four at a time.

(5) Sum over the variables taken five at a time, i.e. take the grand total.

(6) Sum the squares of all the figures in the tables described in (1) to (5) and divide each sum of squares by the number of original individuals forming the individuals in each table. Thus, in the table of class (3) formed by summing over G, T, and S, i.e. the table for R and P, the divisor is gts.

(7) The main effects are given by subtracting (5) from each of the sums of squares in (4) (both having been divided by their appropriate divisors).

(8) To get say the GTS interaction, we take the table for G, T, and S (i.e. the table of class (2) summed over R and P), take its sum of squares divided by the appropriate divisor (here rp) and subtract from this the correcting factor (5) divided by its divisor (gtsrp) and also subtract the sums of squares already derived for G, T, S, S $\times$ G, G $\times$ T and T $\times$S.

Studying the components of variance for a four factor analysis in Table 11.8, and comparing them with Table 11.2 for three factors and Table 11.1 for two factors, we can readily see how for a five factor experiment the components of variance would be built up :—

(a) The highest order interaction, used as a residual, σ_0^2 has no coefficient.

(b) The interactions of the next highest order have σ_0^2 and the component corresponding to the interaction, the latter having as its coefficient the letters *not* included in the subscripts of the interaction. Thus the G × T × S × R components are

$$p\sigma_{gtsr}^2 + \sigma_0^2$$

(c) The interactions of the next highest order have σ_0^2, the component corresponding to the interaction, and all the intermediate interactions whose suffices include the interaction suffices. The general rule for coefficients applies throughout: the coefficients are those letters which are not included in the subscripts.

Thus the G × T × S components are :—

$$rp\sigma_{gts}^2 + r\sigma^2_{gtsp} + p\sigma^2_{gtsr} + \sigma_0^2$$

(d) The first order interactions are built up according to the same general rules. Thus the S × R components are :—

$$gtp\sigma^2_{sr} + gt\sigma^2_{psr} + tp\sigma^2_{gsr} + pg\sigma^2_{srt} + g\sigma^2_{psrt} + t\sigma^2_{gsrp} + p\sigma^2_{gsrt} + \sigma_0^2$$

(e) The main effects are built up similarly. Thus, the S main effect includes σ_s^2, the first order interactions of S, namely, σ^2_{sg}, σ^2_{sr}, σ^2_{sp} and σ^2_{st}, the second order interactions of S, namely σ^2_{sgr}, σ^2_{sgp}, σ^2_{srp}, σ^{2s}_{tp} σ^2_{str} and σ^2_{stg}, the third order interaction of S, namely σ^2_{rgst}, σ^2_{strp}, σ^2_{srpg} and σ^2_{spgt}, and the residual σ_0^2. All these components have their coefficients determined by the general rule mentioned earlier: thus σ_s^2 has as its coefficient prgt.

(ii) A five factor experiment was carried out on a process for purifying a crystalline product, all factors being at two levels. The quantity of the substance per cycle (T) was tested, one level actually corresponding to double the concentration of the other. The time to dissolve (D) the crystalline substance in the solvent was tested, one level being four times the time of the other level. Time was relevant because the dissolving was done in hot solution and as the formation of impurities is auto-catalytic a long period at a high temperature might have deleterious effects. The third factor W represented two slightly different liquids used in the next stage of the process, in which there were two speeds of stirring (S) and two times (G) to precipitate the pure crystal by steam distillation.

The original data is given in Table 11.15. The decimal point has been removed and large figures represent an inferir products.

Table 11.15

Original Data on Five Factor Crystal Purification Experiment.

		W_1				W_2			
		G_1		G_2		G_1		G_2	
		D_1	D_2	D_1	D_2	D_1	D_2	D_1	D_2
T_1	S_1	138	108	113	95	103	137	106	116
	S_2	116	119	106	114	122	122	128	148
T_2	S_1	155	170	131	172	146	152	135	144
	S_2	133	172	138	181	150	156	124	146

In the analysis of variance, all factors being at two levels, the degrees of freedom for all terms are unity, and hence the Mean Squares are equal to the Sums of Squares. In Table 11.16 giving the Analysis of Variance below the fourth-order interactions have not been calculated but have been pooled with the Residual whose degrees of freedom are thus $(1 + 5) = 6$. Strictly speaking, these interactions should be calculated, but in practice it is difficult to attach any great importance to them, and it is the effects earlier in the table which are of practical interest. In Table 11.16 the figures 31 and 6 in brackets after the Total and the Residual are the numbers of degrees of freedom for the Total and Residual respectively.

Table 11.16

Analysis of Variance for Five Factor Experiment on Crystal Purification.

Source of Variance	Sums of Squares
S	91.1
G	325.1
W	21.1
T	8256.1
D	1352.0
S × G	264.5
G × W	12.6
W × T	924.5
T × D	741.2
D × S	171.1
G × T	18.0
W × D	1.2
T × S	128.1
D × G	120.1
W × S	112.5
S × G × W	21.1
G × W × T	406.1
W × T × D	1200.4
T × D × S	0.4
D × S × G	24.6
S × W × T	91.1
S × G × T	91.1
T × D × G	40.5
G × W × D	31.9
D × W × S	288.0
Residual (6)	661.6
Total (31)	15396.0

It is apparent that all the second order interactions except W × T × D are non-significant, but the latter is large. To test W × T × D, we must note that its components of variance are included amongst the components of variance of W × T, T × D, D × W, W, T, and D, and therefore the latter terms cannot be less than W × T × D. Of these latter terms, only the T and W main effects are greater than W × T × D. Accordingly we pool the others with W × T × D and obtain a new estimate of the latter of $2888.4/5 = 577.7$ with 5 degrees of freedom. Testing this against the residual of $1656.4/15 = 110.4$ with 15 degrees of freedom, we get a variance ratio of 5.2 for $n_1 = 5$, $n_2 = 15$, corresponding to a probability of 1%. Since T is the more prominent main effect, it would seem most profitable to break down the five factor analysis into two four factor analyses for each level of T, as in Table 11.17.

Examining the terms for T_1, starting from the Residual and working towards the top of the table, we find none of them significant. T_1 actually corresponds to the use of the dilute solution. Under these conditions, therefore, we are at liberty to choose the four factors at whatever levels may be convenient on practical grounds secure in the knowledge that this will not have a deleterious effect upon the purity of the product.

Table 11.17

Analysis of Variance for two four factor experiments in Crystal Purification.

Source of Variance	Sums of Squares	
	T_1	T_2
W	333.06	612.56
S	217.56	1.56
G	95.06	248.06
D	45.56	2047.56
W × S	203.07	0.57
S × G	333.07	22.57
G × D	10.57	150.07
D × S	76.57	95.07
W × D	637.57	564.07
G × W	280.57	138.07
W × S × G	45.55	175.55
G × S × D	85.55	5.08
S × D × W	430.55	10.55
W × G × D	27.55	7.55
Residual	162.58	76.55
Total	2984.44	4155.44

Reverting to Table 11.16, it will be noted that the T main effect, when tested against W × T × D (all the first order interactions involving T are non-significant) is significant at the 5% level, nearly at the 1% level. The mean for T_1 is lower than T_2, and thus for purity we should choose T_1. However, since the charge is only half of that for T_2, the throughput of material through the plant will be only half, and it may be necessary therefore to use T_2 if at all possible.

Reverting to Table 11.17, and examining the analysis for T_2, we find W × D is at the 5% level of significance, and accordingly separate analyses were made for each level of D, as in Table 11.18.

Table 11.18

Source of Variance	Sums of Squares	
	D_1	D_2
G	392.0	6.15
W	0.5	1176.15
S	60.5	36.15
G × W	40.5	105.10
W × S	8.0	3.10
S × G	24.5	3.10
Residual	242.0	10.15
Total	768.0	1339.90

For the D_1 Series, all terms are non-significant with the possible exception of G, the means for G_1 and G_2 being 146 and 132 respectively. For the D_2 series, on the other hand, the only prominent term is W, the means for W_1 and W_2 being 173.8 and 149.5 respectively.

We may recall that using T_1, with any value of D, W, S and G, the mean obtained was 118.2, so as far as purity goes we prefer T_1. If we use T_2, however, we should prefer D_1, when we will use any value of G, W, and S and get an average purity of 139. Should we need to use D_2, then we can use either G and S but it is important to use W_2, giving an average of 149.5.

It is clear that the complicated behaviour of this system could not possibly have been followed without the use of a factorial design. Also, the analysis of variance was absolutely necessary in order to identify those effects and interactions which were significant. It would have been quite impossible to do this by qualitative inspection of the results in Table 11.15.[3]

(g) Incomplete Two-Factor analysis : One Factor with Replication

In our two factor analysis (Section (c)), we have g grades of material being processed at t different temperatures. Suppose, now, that we make t batches all at the same temperature from each of the g grades. Under these circumstances, the first unit of Grade 1 has no more correspondence with the first unit of Grade 2 than it has with the second unit of Grade 2, etc.

The two-factor analysis has thus become one factor (Grades) with t replications. This amounts to pooling the degrees of freedom and the sums of squares of the T main effect in Table 11.1 with the Residual. This gives us Table 11.19 :

Table 11.19

Source of Variance	Degrees of Freedom	Components of Variance
G	$g-1$	$t\sigma^2_g + \sigma_0^2$
Residual (within G's)	$(t-1)+(t-1)(g-1)$ $= g(t-1)$	σ_0^2
Total	$gt-1$	

It is this type of analysis which was discussed in detail in Chapter VII Section (c).

(h) Incomplete Three-Factor Analysis : Two Factors with Replication

(i) In our complete three factor analysis we had s suppliers each supplying g grades of polymer which were processed at each of the t temperatures. Let us now assume that t batches were processed at the same temperature, i.e. we have two factors G and S, with t replications. Considering Table 11.2, we have that the G × T and T × S interactions and the T main effect all do not exist. The reason for the interactions mentioned disappearing is that, for example, the G main effect is by definition the same for all the replications, and any irregularity in it is synonymous with error, for which we use the residual. We then obtain Table 11.20.

Consider the problem in which we wish to investigate a factor in a process, in which, say, we wish to determine its effect at three levels, F_1, F_2, and F_3.

[3] An example of a seven factor experiment on a factory process will be found in R. L. Cunningham and J. Ansel Anderson : "Cereal Chemistry," Vol. XX, page, 482, 1943.

Table 11.20

Source of Variance	Degrees of Freedom	Components of Variance
G	$(g-1)$	$\sigma^2_o + t\sigma^2_{gs} + ts\sigma^2_g$
S	$(s-1)$	$\sigma^2_o + t\sigma^2_{gs} + tg\sigma^2_s$
G × S	$(g-1)(s-1)$	$\sigma^2_o + t\sigma^2_{gs}$
Residual	$(g-1)(s-1)(t-1)+(t-1)+$ $(g-1)(t-1)+(s-1)(t-1)$ $= gs(t-1)$	σ^2_o
Total	$gst-1$	

Suppose that the material at one stage passes through a particular process which we know or suspect may give rise to variability. Then it will be necessary to eliminate the errors due to this other factor.

The experimental design below would satisfy the requirements. A comparison of the means of the Fs is valid since the disturbing effect of the machines M_1, M_2 and M_3 is eliminated. The same experiment also gives us a valid comparison of the three machines, M_1, M_2 and M_3. The data from such an experiment would be analysed by the analysis of variance by rows and columns, previously discussed in Chapter VII (e) and Section (c) of the present chapter.

	Machine		
	M_1	M_2	M_3
F_1 F_2 F_3			

This experimental design has been presented as a means of eliminating errors due to a particular factor, but of course it is exactly the same as for a two factor experiment, i.e. we might be equally interested in both the factors.

As the design stands we cannot determine whether there is any interaction between the terms, for though we can compare, say $(M_1 - M_2)$ for $F = F_1$ with $(M_1 - M_2)$ for $F = F_3$, our comparison is pointless because we have no estimate of the error of either term and hence of theii difference. Without the estimate of the error we cannot estimate the significance of any apparent difference.

We would get an estimate of error if we had repeated each experiment, when the design would be called a row and column or two factor analysis with replication.

Consider the data in the table below.

	N_1		N_2		Totals
D_1	—12	—5	27	27	37
D_2	—29	—22	34	24	7
Totals	—68		112		44

It refers to a two factor experiment N × D, each factor at two levels, and there are two observations for each point. We proceed as follows:—

(1) Form the total of each cell, square these totals, sum these squares, and divide by the number of original individuals per cell, i.e.

$$[(-12-5)^2 + (-29-22)^2 + (27+27)^2 + (34+24)^2]/2 = 4585$$

(2) Form the total for each level of D, square these totals, sum these squares, and divide by the number of individuals per total being squared, i.e.

$$(37^2 + 7^2)/4 = 354.5$$

(3) Similarly for each level of N, i.e.

$$[(-68)^2 + 112^2]/4 = 4292$$

(4) Form the grand total, square it and divide by the grand number of individuals, i.e.

$$44^2/8 = 242.$$

(5) Square every individual and sum these squares, i.e.

$$(-12)^2 + (-5)^2 + (27)^2 + \ldots + 24^2 = 4684$$

The table of the analysis of variance is as below:

Source of Variance	Sums of Squares	Degrees of Freedom	Mean Squares	Components of Variance
Between Rows (D)	(2) — (4) = 112.5	$n_1 - 1 = 1$	112.5	$n_2n_3\sigma_1^2 + n_3\sigma_{12}^2 + \sigma_0^2$
Between Columns (N)	(3) — (4) = 4050.0	$n_2 - 1 = 1$	4050.0	$n_1n_3\sigma_2^2 + n_3\sigma_{12}^2 + \sigma_0^2$
Row × Column interaction (D × N)	180.5	$(n_1-1)(n_2-1) = 1$	180.5	$n_3\sigma_{12}^2 + \sigma_0^2$
Residual	(5) — (1) = 99.0	$n_1n_2(n_3-1) = 4$	24.75	σ_0^2
Total	(5) — (4) = 4442.0	$n_1n_2n_3 - 1 = 7$		

n_1 rows, n_2 columns, n_3 replications.

σ_1^2 = variance due to differences between rows.

σ_2^2 = variance due to differences between columns.

σ_{12}^2 = row × column interaction.

σ_0^2 = residual error.

The Sum of Squares for the Row × Column Interaction is obtained by subtracting the total of the Sums of Squares for the other three components from the Total Sum of Squares, (5) — (4).

In general, in testing the mean squares for significance, the row mean square and the column mean square are tested against the row × column interaction, for if they are significantly greater than the interaction, this can only be so if σ_1^2 and σ_2^2 respectively are greater than zero. Similarly the existence of the interaction can be checked by comparing the interaction mean square with the residual.

Here we test the Interaction against the Residual, getting a variance ratio of 180.5/24.75 = 7.3 for degrees of freedom $n_1 = 1$, $n_2 = 4$, this lying close to the 5% level of significance.

Accordingly we should conclude that D and N interact, and we should inspect the data broken down into one factor experiments. We can compare D_1 with D_2 at each level of N, using the Student t test to compare the two means for D. We find that the difference between D_1 and D_2 is not significant for N_2 but is quite considerable for N_1. Similarly we can compare the difference between N_1 and N_2 for each level of D, when we find that the difference between the two levels of N is greater for D_2 than for D_1.

It will be noted that this two factor analysis with replication is really a three factor analysis with all the terms involving the third factor R, i.e. the R main effect and the R × N and R × D interactions, pooled with the residual.

(i) Doubly Incomplete Three Factor Analysis: One Factor with Double Order Replication

(i) In the previous example, we had s suppliers each supplying g different grades of polymer, and from these t batches were processed, all at the same temperature. Now suppose that the s suppliers, instead of each supplying g different grades of polymer, supplied g nominally identical consignments of polymer, all of the same grade. The system then has the structure given by the sketch below:

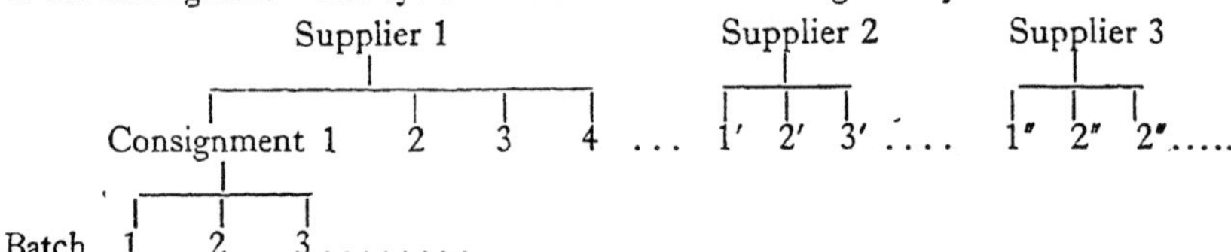

Each consignment is made up of a number of batches; these are only indicated for consignment 1 of supplier 1, but should be understood for all the consignments. Since the consignments are nominally of similar grade, there is no point in comparing the mean of all the 1s, 1, 1′, 1″ etc. with the mean of all the 2s, 2, 2′, 2″ etc. The different consignments 1, 2, 3, etc. from Supplier 1 may differ among themselves, however, and similarly for the other suppliers. We can use the consistency of the batches processed from each consignment as a measure of error against which the difference between consignments can be compared. It may be noted that should the first batch in all instances be processed at temperature t_1, the second batch in all instances at another temperature t_2, etc., then we have an incomplete two factor analysis as in the previous section, the factors being supplier (S) and temperature (R).

The variance can then be analysed into the components given in Table 11.21. Table 11.20 is derived from Table 11.21 by pooling the sums of squares and degrees of freedom of the G and G × S terms. The component of variance corresponding to the G effect in Table 11.21 is more of the nature of an interaction than a main effect, but we will symbolically use G (rather than g) as a suffix to the component of variance to denote its rather different character.

Table 11.21

Source of Variance	Degrees of Freedom	Components of Variance
Suppliers (S)	$(s-1)$	$\sigma_0^2 + t\sigma_G^2 + tg\sigma_s^2$
Between Consignments (G)	$(g-1)+(g-1)(s-1) = s(g-1)$	$\sigma_0 + t\sigma_G^2$
Within consignments (Residual)	$gs(t-1)$	σ_0^2
Total	$gst-1$	

(ii) A certain type of plant for concentrating dilute acid was subject to failure through corrosion. The figures below in Table 11.22 represent the quantity of acid obtained from a number of units before failure. From the mass of data 7 units were selected from each of 9 factories, and the 9 factories fell naturally into three groups according to the type of weak acid they were concentrating.

To analyse this data we form the following terms:—

(1) Square every individual and sum all the squares, i.e. $40^2 + 49^2 + 25^2 + \ldots + \ldots + \ldots + \ldots + \ldots + 122^2 + 113^2 = 339{,}900$

Table 11.22

Type of Weak Acid	Factory	Throughputs							Totals
A	1	40	49	25	30	32	25	22	223
	2	40	46	41	30	50	39	31	277
	3	38	38	32	33	42	45	44	272
B	4	16	50	40	54	80	64	59	363
	5	49	35	70	64	23	70	88	399
	6	68	20	66	36	34	45	40	309
C	7	90	90	104	62	78	88	93	605
	8	84	93	73	80	210	137	89	766
	9	152	70	122	143	72	122	113	794

(2) Obtain the total for each block (factory), square these totals, sum these squares, and divide by the number of individuals in each block, i.e. $(223^2 + 277^2 + \ldots + 794^2)/7 = 310{,}016$

(3) Obtain the total for each super-block (type of weak acid), square these totals, sum these squares and divide by the number of individuals in each super-block, i.e. $[(223 + 277 + 272)^2 + (363 + 399 + 309)^2 + (605 + 766 + 794)^2]/21 = 306{,}202$

(4) Obtain the grand total for all individuals, square it, and divide by the grand number of individuals, i.e. $(223 + 277 + 272 + 363 + \ldots + \ldots + \ldots + 794)^2/63 = 254{,}985$

From these terms we form the analysis of variance below in Table 11.23.

Table 11.23

Source of Variance	Degrees of Freedom	Sums of Squares	Mean Squares	Components of Variance
Between super-blocks (type of weak acid)	$n_1 - 1 = 2$	(3) — (4) = 51,217	25,609	$n_2 n_3 \sigma_1^2 + n_3 \sigma_2^2 + \sigma_3^2$
Between blocks (Factories) within super-blocks	$n_1 (n_2 - 1) = 6$	(2) — (3) = 3,814	636	$n_3 \sigma_2^2 + \sigma_3^2$
Residual : Within blocks (within factories)	$n_1 n_2 (n_3 - 1) = 54$	(1) — (2) = 29,884	553	σ_3^2
Total	$n_1 n_2 n_3 - 1 = 62$	(1) — (4) = 84,915		

n_1 = number of super-blocks

n_2 = number of blocks within a super-block.

n_3 = number of individuals within a block.

σ_1^2 = variance due to differences between super-blocks.

σ_2^2 = variance due to differences between blocks within super-blocks.

σ_3^2 = variance due to differences between individuals within blocks.

From the last column, "Components of Variance," we see that σ_2^2 can be greater than zero only if $n_3\sigma_2^2 + \sigma_3^2$ is significantly greater than σ_3^2. Thus we compare the Between Blocks Mean Square with the Within Blocks Mean Square. Similarly, in general we test the Super-blocks Mean Square against the Between Blocks (within Super-blocks) Mean Square, for if it is significantly greater than the latter this can only be so because σ_1^2 is greater than zero.

Here we see that the Between Blocks Mean Square is not significantly greater than the Residual, so we can assume that $\sigma_2^2 = 0$ and pool the two sets of Sums of Squares and Degrees of Freedom to get a new Residual of $33{,}698/60 = 561.6$ with 60 degrees of freedom.

Testing the Between Super-blocks Mean Square against this residual we have a variance ratio of $25{,}609/561.6 = 45.6$ for degrees of freedom $n_1 = 2$, $n_2 = 60$. For these degrees of freedom and the 0.1% level of significance the variance ratio needs to be not less than 7.8. It follows that the Between Super-blocks Mean Square is very much more significant than the 0.1% level. Solving the equations $3 \times 7\ \sigma_1^2 + \sigma_3^2 = 25{,}609$, $\sigma_3^2 = 562$, (we have shown $\sigma_2^2 = 0$) we obtain the value 1192 for σ_1^2. We thus get

$$\sigma_1^2 = 1192$$
$$\sigma_2^2 = 0$$
$$\sigma_3^2 = 562$$

The value of this analysis is that it shows that differences between factories within an acid group are not detectable, and that the larger part of the variability in throughput achieved is due to differences between acid groups.

The use of the first point is that it enables us to pool data for all factories within an acid group for any detailed comparison: e.g., for comparisons between foundries, in some instances there are 10 pots of foundry A and 1 pot of foundry B at one factory, 1 pot of foundry A and 10 pots from foundry C at a second factory, and so on. So long as we are confined to comparisons within a factory, our estimates of foundry differences will be very inaccurate. Having proved that we can pool the data for all factories within an acid group, our comparisons will be much more useful.

The use of the second point is that it throws great emphasis upon the importance of the type of acid being concentrated. It can only be followed up using orthodox chemical considerations, of course.

(j) Incomplete Four-Factor Analysis: Three Factors with Replication

(i) In our complete four-factor analysis we had s suppliers working from each of r sources of raw material and providing g grades of polymer which were worked at each of t temperatures. If, instead, we work t batches all at the same temperature, we then have a three factor analysis with replication, the three factors being grade of polymer (G), supplier (S) and source of raw material (R).

We derive the analysis of variance for this situation from the complete four factor analysis given in Table 11,8. We have the T main effect, the first order interactions involving T and the second order interactions involving T, all non-existent. We can therefore pool their degrees of freedom and sums of squares with the residual, and we obtain Table 11.24 :—

Table 11.24

Source of Variance	Degrees of Freedom	Components of Variance
G	$(g-1)$	$\sigma_o^2 + t\sigma^2_{srg} + ts\sigma^2_{rg} + rt\sigma^2_{gs} + tsr\sigma^2_g$
S	$(s-1)$	$\sigma_o^2 + t\sigma^2_{srg} + gt\sigma^2_{sr} + rt\sigma^2_{gs} + gtr\sigma^2_s$
R	$(r-1)$	$\sigma^2_o + t\sigma^2_{srg} + gt\sigma^2_{sr} + ts\sigma^2_{rg} + gts\sigma^2_r$
G × S	$(g-1)(s-1)$	$\sigma^2_o + t\sigma^2_{srg} + rt\sigma^2_{gs}$
S × R	$(s-1)(r-1)$	$\sigma_o^2 + t\sigma^2_{srg} + gt\sigma^2_{sr}$
R × G	$(r-1)(g-1)$	$\sigma_o^2 + t\sigma^2_{srg} + ts\sigma^2_{rg}$
G × S × R	$(g-1)(s-1)(r-1)$	$\sigma^2_o + t\sigma^2_{srg}$
Residual	$(g-1)(t-1)(r-1)(s-1)$ $+ (r-1)(g-1)(t-1)$ $+ (t-1)(s-1)(r-1)$ $+ (g-1)(t-1)(s-1)$ $+ (t-1)(r-1) + (t-1)(s-1)$ $+ (g-1)(t-1) + (t-1)$ $= gsr(t-1)$	σ_o^2
Total	$gsrt - 1$	

(ii) Suppose we carry out a three factor experiment, and replicate each point. This could be regarded as a four factor experiment, the fourth factor being the order of replication and when the complete analysis of variance is obtained pooling with the residual all factors involving A, viz., if N, D, and R are the three main factors, pooling A, A × N, A × D, A × R, A × N × D, A × D × R, and A × R × N.

The arithmetic is lighter, however, if we total over all levels of A, i.e. sum over all replications, for each value of N, D, and R, thus getting a three factor table in which each figure is the sum of the replications.

Consider the data in the table below :—

	N_1				N_2			
	D_1		D_2		D_1		D_2	
	R_1	R_2	R_1	R_2	R_1	R_2	R_1	R_2
A_1	—3	—1	—8	—6	8	8	10	7
A_2	—7	—6	—3	—5	—6	1	0	—3
S(A)	—10	—7	—11	—11	2	9	10	4

The row S(A) is the sum of A_1 and A_2 for each value of N, D, and R. The data in this row is subjected to the same three factor analysis previously described, except for the following difference :

(1) Whenever we sum a set of squares, we divide by the number of replications, here 2, in addition to the other divisors.

Thus one of our three two-way tables is

	D_1	D_2	Totals
N_1	—17	—22	—39
N_2	11	14	25
Totals	—6	—8	—14

The correcting factor is $(-14)^2/8 \times 2 = 12.25$

The sum of squares for N is

$[(-39)^2 + (25)^2]/4 \times 2 - 12.25 = 256.00$

The sum of squares for D is

$[(-6)^2 + (-8^2]/4 \times 2 - 12.25 = 0.25$

The N × D interaction is given by

$[(-17)^2 + (-22)^2 + (11)^2 + (14^2)]/2 \times 2 - 12.25 - 256.00 - 0.25$
$= 4.00$

The Sums of Squares of the R, R × D, and R × N effects are obtained similarly.

(2) An independent estimate of the Residual is obtained as the difference between the sum of the squares of all the original individuals and (the sum of the squares of the values for S(A) divided by the number of replications, here 2), i.e.

$(-3)^2 + (-1)^2 + \ldots (-3)^2 - ((-10)^2 + (-7)^2 + \ldots 4^2)/2 = 256$

(3) The Total Sum of Squares is given by the difference between the sum of the squares of the original individuals and correcting factor, i.e.

$(-3)^2 + (-1)^2 + \ldots + (-3)^2 - 12.25 = 539.75$

(4) The N × D × R Interaction Sum of Squares is obtained as the difference between the Total Sum of Squares and the sum of all the other terms.

The results of this analysis are as below:

Source of Variance	Sums of Squares	Degrees of Freedom	Mean Squares
N	256.00	$n - 1 = 1$	256.00
D	0.25	$d - 1 = 1$	0.25
R	1.00	$r - 1 = 1$	1.00
N × D	4.00	$(n - 1)(d - 1) = 1$	4.00
D × R	16.00	$(d - 1)(r - 1) = 1$	16.00
R × N	0.25	$(r - 1)(n - 1) = 1$	0.25
N × D × R	6.25	$(n - 1)(d - 1)(r - 1) = 1$	6.25
Residual	256.00	$n\,d\,r\,(a - 1) = 8$	32.00
Total	539.75	$r\,n\,d\,a - 1 = 15$	

The N × D× R interaction is tested against the Residual, and is obviously not significant. In fact, all the terms except the N main effect are not significant and can be pooled to give a new residual of $283.75/14 = 20.2$: the N main effect then gives a variance ratio of $256.00/20.2 = 12.7$ with degrees of freedom $n_1 = 1$, $n_2 = 14$, this being more significant than the 1% level of significance. We can then calculate the means for N_1 and N_2 as — 4.875 and 3.125 respectively.

It may have been in this example that the second replication (series R_2) may be at a different general level from the first (series R_1), due to an adjustment of the plant between the two series, a new batch of raw material, etc. The variance due to such an effect will be included in the Residual, and if large will give us an inflated estimate of the Residual, thus lowering the accuracy of our experiment.

Accordingly we may take out from the Residual the Sum of Squares corresponding to the replication by forming the total for series $R_1 = 15$ and for series $R_2 = (-29)$ and then calculating

$$[15^2 + (-29)^2]/8 - 12.25 = 121.00$$

Thus the Sum of Squares for the Residual is now $256.00 - 121.00 = 135.00$ and its Degrees of Freedom are $8 - 1 = 7$ giving a Mean Square of 19.29.

In this case, therefore, we have gained considerably by taking out the series Sum of Squares, and we have increased the likelihood of detecting significance in the Terms very considerably.

(k) Doubly Incomplete Four Factor Analysis: Two Factors with Double Order Replication

(i) Let us now suppose that in the previous example the suppliers, instead of working to product g different grades, actually produced g nominally identical grades. We still process t batches from each of these also at the same temperature as before.

The variance can be analysed now into between source of raw material (R), between suppliers (S), and the R × S interaction, and the two further components shown below in Table 11.25. The degrees of freedom and sums of squares for the new G term are obtained by pooling them together with the G × S, S × R and G × S × R terms. The Residual is the same as in Table 11.24.

Table 11.25

Source of Variance	Degrees of Freedom	Components of Variance
R	$(r - 1)$	$\sigma^2_0 + t\sigma^2_G + gt\sigma^2_{rs} + gts\sigma^2_r$
S	$(s - 1$	$\sigma^2_0 + t\sigma^2_G + gt\sigma^2_{rs} + gtr\sigma^2_s$
R × S	$(r - 1)(s - 1)$	$\sigma^2_0 + t\sigma^2_G + gt\sigma^2_{rs}$
Between G Within R and S	$(g - 1) + (g - 1)(r - 1) + (g - 1)(s - 1) + (g - 1)(r - 1)(s - 1) = rs(g - 1)$	$\sigma^2_0 + t\sigma^2_G$
Within G (Residual)	$gsr(t - 1)$	σ^2_0
Total	$gsrt - 1$	

(ii) The purpose of this experiment was to determine whether the position of a scroll of nitrated paper in a stabilising vat had any effect upon its nitrogen content. Two scrolls (S) were stabilised in each of two positions (P) and samples were taken from the top and bottom of each scroll (F). Duplicate determinations of the nitrogen content were performed on each of these eight samples.

At first sight this would appear to fall in the class of three factors ($P \times S \times F$) with replication, the class which we discussed in the previous section.

Position of Scroll	Scroll Number	Fraction of Scroll	% Nitrogen
P_1	S_1	F_1	12.20, 12.20
		F_2	12.26, 12.26
	S_2	F_1	12.10, 12.10
		F_2	12.39, 12.38
P_2	S'_1	F_1	12.31, 12.30
		F_2	12.44, 12.44
	S'_2	F_1	12.23, 12.21
		F_2	12.37, 12.35

However, a moment's reflection will show that there is no true one-to-one correspondence between S_1 and S'_1, or between S_2 and S'_2. S_1 has no more association with S'_1 than with S'_2. It is thus evident that the factor S is really a form of replication.

The second point is that the duplication of analysis does not constitute a genuine replication, i.e. a genuine repeat of the whole experiment (to perform the latter we should have to use different scrolls in a different vat).

To carry out the analysis of variance we might carry out the full analysis, and then pool together the degrees of freedom and sums of squares on the lines indicated previously. However, it is less trouble to evaluate the relevant terms directly. In the calculation below the zero used is 12.20 and the scale has been multiplied by 100.

(1) We need the square of the grand total divided by the number of individuals in that total (the usual correcting factor):

$$134^2/16 = 1122.25$$

(2) We need the two-way table for P and F.

	F_1	F_2	
P_1	—20	49	29
P_2	25	80	105
	5	129	134

From this table the P, F, and $P \times F$ sums of squares are obtained in the usual manner:—

$$P = (29^2 + 105^2)/8 - 1122.25 = 361.00$$
$$F = (5^2 + 129^2)/8 - 1122.25 = 961.00$$
$$P \times F = (20^2 + 49^2 + 25^2 + 80^2)/4 - 1122.25 - 361.00 - 961.00 = 12.25$$

(3) The sum of squares between analyses is

$$(0^2 + 0^2 + 6^2 + \ldots + 15^2) - [(0 + 0)^2 + (6 + 6)^2 + \ldots]/2 = 5.00$$

(4) The total sum of squares is

$$(0^2 + 0^2 + 6^2 - \ldots . + 15^2) - 1122.25 = 1731.75$$

(5) The sum of squares for Error is obtained by difference.
The resulting table is below :

Sources of Variance	Sums of Squares	Degrees of Freedom	Mean Square
Between position in vat (P)	361.00	1	361.00
Between fraction of scroll (F)	961.00	1	961.00
F × P	12.25	1	12.25
Error	392.50	4	98.12
Between analyses	5.00	8	0.62
Total	1731.75	15	

The F × P interaction, tested against the Error is clearly non-significant; we can pool it with the Error. The P main effect, the principal object of the experiment, can then be tested against this Error. The F main effect is not of direct interest, but can also be tested against the Error. It was advisable to have included F in the experiment, however, as it was quite possible that P would interact with it.

(l) Trebly Incomplete Four Factor Analysis : One Factor with Triple Order Replication

(i) In the previous example, the Factor R represented source of raw material. Suppose, on the contrary, that it represented operator in the factory. Then obviously, there is no point in comparing the first operator in all the factories with the second operator in all the factories, and we are only interested in this respect in the variation between the operators within a factory.

The sums of squares and degrees of freedom for the new R term are given by pooling them for R and R × S in Table 11.25, thus giving us Table 11.26.

Table 11.26

Source of Variance	Degrees of Freedom	Components of Variance
S	$(s-1)$	$\sigma_0^2 + t\sigma^2_G + gt\sigma^2_R + gtr\sigma^2_S$
Between R within S	$(r-1)+(r-1)(s-1)$ $= s(r-1)$	$\sigma_0^2 + t\sigma^2_G + gt\sigma^2_R$
Between G within R	$rs\,(g-1)$	$\sigma_0^2 + t\sigma^2_G$
Within G (Residual)	$gsr\,(t-1)$	σ^2_0
Total	$gsr\,(t-1)$	

The system has the structure indicated below, where there are similar assemblies for subsequent super-blocks.

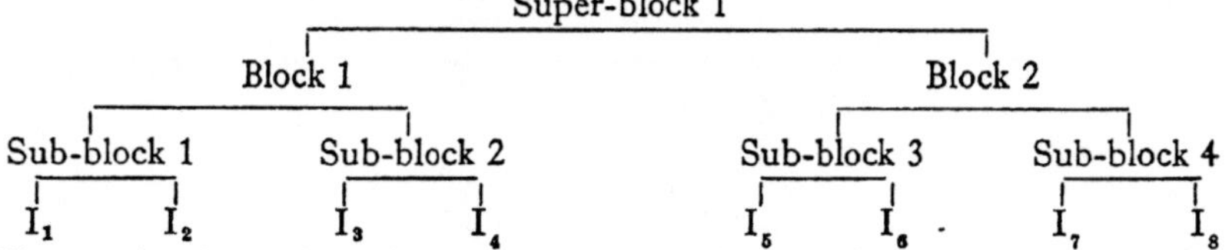

The number into which the larger units are split can of course be anything from 2 upwards.

(ii) Consider the data in the table below. We have an allegedly homogeneous batch of material contained in vats V_1 to V_6. The contents of each vat are wrung in a centrifuge and bagged. We select two bags B_1 and B_2 from each vatload and take two samples S_1 and S_2 from each bag. On each sample we perform an analysis for percentage of an ingredient, in duplicate, A_1 and A_2.

	V_1				V_2				V_3			
	B_1		B_2		B_1		B_2		B_1		B_2	
	S_1	S_2	S_1	S_2	S_1	S_2	S_1	S_2	S_1	S_2	S_1	S_2
A_1 ..	29	28	29	27	29	27	26	24	32	29	25	30
A_2 ..	29	27	29	28	29	28	27	25	30	30	27	31

	V_4				V_5				V_6			
	B_1		B_2		B_1		B_2		B_1		B_2	
	S_1	S_2	S_1	S_2	S_1	S_2	S_1	S_2	S_1	S_2	S_1	S_2
A_1 ..	29	30	28	30	30	27	25	26	29	31	29	29
A_2 ..	29	31	28	28	29	27	28	26	31	32	30	31

In carrying out the analysis of variance it lightens the arithmetic to take an arbitrary zero, e.g. by subtracting 20 from every observation. We form terms

(1) Square every individual and sum the squares, i.e.
$9^2 + 8^2 + 9^2 + 7^2 + \ldots + 10^2 + 11^2 = 3636$

(2) Obtain the total for each sub-block, square the sub-block totals, sum these squares, and divide by the number of individuals per sub-block, i.e.
$[(9 + 9)^2 + (8 + 7)^2 + (9 + 9)^2 + \ldots + (9 + 10)^2 + (9 + 11)^2]/2 = 3616,$

(3) Obtain the totals for each block, square the block totals, sum these squares, and divide by the number of individuals per block, i.e.
$[(9 + 9 + 8 + 7)^2 + (9 + 7 + 9 + 8)^2 + \ldots + (9 + 10 + 9 + 11)^2]/4 = 3570.5$

(4) Obtain the totals for each super-block, square the super-block totals, sum these squares, and divide by the number of individuals in each super-block, i.e.
$(66^2 + 55^2 + 74^2 \ldots\ldots + 82^2)/8 = 3534.25$

(5) Obtain the grand total for all individuals, square it, and divide by the grand number of individuals, i.e.
$408^2/48 = 3468$

From these terms we form the analysis of variance in Table 11.27 below.

Table 11.27

Source of Variance	Degrees of Freedom	Sum of Squares	Mean Squares	Components of Variance
Between Super-blocks (vats)	$n_1 - 1 = 5$	(4) — (5) = 66.25	13.25	$n_2n_3n_4\sigma_1^2 + n_3n_4\sigma_2^2 + n_4\sigma_3^2 + \sigma_4^2$
Between Blocks within Super-Blocks (Bags within vats)	$n_1(n_2 - 1) = 6$	(3) — (4) = 36.25	6.04	$n_3n_4\sigma_2^2 + n_4\sigma_3^2 + \sigma_4^2$
Between Sub-blocks within Blocks (Samples within Bags)	$n_1n_2(n_3 - 1) = 12$	(2) — (3) = 45.50	3.79	$n_4\sigma_3^2 + \sigma_4^2$
Between Individuals within Sub-blocks (Analyses within Samples)	$n_1n_2n_3(n_4 - 1) = 24$	(1) — (2) = 20.00	0.833	σ_4^2
Total	$n_1n_2n_3n_4 - 1 = 47$	(1) — (5) = 168.00		

n_1 = number of super-blocks = 6
n_2 = number of blocks within a super-block = 2
n_3 = number of sub-blocks within a block = 2
n_4 = number of individuals within a sub-block = 2

σ_1^2, σ_2^2, σ_3^2, σ_4^2 are respectively the variances due to the four terms listed under the heading "Source of Variance."

Proceeding to the analysis of Table 11.27, the Between Samples with Bags Mean Square, tested against the Between Analyses within Sample Mean Square (to test for the existence of σ_3^2—see the Components of Variance), gives a variance ratio of $3.79/0.833 = 4.6$ for degrees of freedom $n_1 = 12$, $n_2 = 24$: this is more significant than the 0.1% level of significance.

To test for the existence of σ_2^2, we test the Between Bags within Vats Mean Square against the Between Samples within Bags Mean Square. The variance ratio is $6.04/3.79 = 1.6$ for degrees of freedom $n_1 = 6$, $n_2 = 12$. This is less significant than the 20% level, so we can take it that σ_2^2 does not exist. We pool the two terms to get a new estimate of $(n_4\sigma_3^2 + \sigma_4^2)$ of $81.75/18 = 4.53$ with 18 degrees of freedom.

To test for the existence of σ_1^2, we test the Between Vats Mean Square against the Between Samples within Bags Mean Square. We have shown that σ_2^2 does not exist, so we are testing $(n_2n_3n_4\sigma_1^2 + n_4\sigma_3^2 + \sigma_4^2)$ against $(n_4\sigma_3^2 + \sigma_4^2)$. The variance ratio is $13.25/4.53 = 2.93$ with degrees of freedom $n_1 = 5$, $n_2 = 18$. This is more significant than the 5% level of significance.

We can now calculate σ_1^2 as $(13.25 - 4.53)/8 = 1.09$ and σ_3^2 as $(4.53 - 0.83)/2 = 1.85$.

Our final conclusion thus is that the variability can be accounted for by the terms

$$\sigma_1^2 = 1.09$$
$$\sigma_2^2 = 0.00$$
$$\sigma_3^2 = 1.85$$
$$\sigma_4^2 = 0.83$$

We see that there is an appreciable variability between vats, the variability between bags from a given vat is not large enough to be detected, the variability between samples within a given bag is quite large, in fact the most important component, and the variability between duplicate analyses on a given sample is quite appreciable. The total variance of a single analysis is thus $(1.09 + 0.00 + 1.85 + 0.83) = 3.77$.

It is further clear from this analysis of variance that the allegedly homogeneous batch is significantly inhomogeneous, and that the larger part of this inhomogenity arises in bagging the material ($\sigma_3^2 = 1.85$). Each vat is apparently homogeneous ($\sigma_2^2 = 0.00$), but there is an appreciable difference between vats ($\sigma_1^2 = 1.09$).

(m) An Incomplete Five Factor Analysis

When we come to five factor analyses the number of different types of incomplete analysis is considerable. We will discuss only one type[4], but from such a viewpoint that it is hoped that the general method of treatment will be clear.

The table below gives the data of an experiment on a process using a cellulose derivative. The final product was subject to fluctuations in a certain property, and it was required to find out at what stages the variability was arising. The cellulose derivative reaches the process in large homogeneous blends, and from these a number of batches are mixed. Normally the whole of each mix is put into a single truck and then dried, after which it is possible to observe the quality of the product. Under this procedure it is impossible to disentangle the effects of mixing from those of drying: to do this requires that a truck should contain parts of more than one mix (in order to compare mixes independently of their drying) and that a mix should be dried in more than one truck (in order to compare

[4] A complicated example dealing with glass manufacture is described by C. E. Gould and W. M. Hampton: Supplement to Journal of the Royal Statistical Society, Vol. III, page 137, 1936. See particularly E. S. Pearson's contribution to the discussion, page 156. This example is also discussed by Tippett, "Methods of Statistics," Section 10, 31, and by Kendall, "The Advanced Theory of Statistics," Vol. II, page 202, where he treats it as a complete analysis.

dryings independently of the material of the mix). For practical reasons it was impossible to split a mix into more than two portions. Accordingly a mix was made and split into two portions, one portion going into one truck and the other into another truck. The next mix was also split and the two portions filled up the previous two trucks. A second pair of mixes taken from the same blend of the cellulose derivative were similarly tested. The whole was repeated on three subsequent blends. On every individual (that is, material from a particular truck and mix from a particular pair from a particular blend) a duplicate determination of quality was made.

Blend Numbers	Pair Numbers	Mix Numbers					Mix Totals	Pair Totals	Blend Totals
1	1	1	11 16	27	17 16	33	60		
		2	0 0	0	14 13	27	27		
				27		60		87	
	2	3	12 12	24	10 8	18	42		
		4	6 6	12	1 3	4	16		
				36		22		58	145
2	3	5	9 9	18	19 18	37	55		
		6	3 1	4	6 6	12	16		
				22		49		71	
	4	7	8 9	17	14 13	27	44		
		8	6 8	14	6 7	13	27		
				31		40		71	142
3	5	9	15 17	32	22 21	43	75		
		10	21 20	41	13 13	26	67		
				73		69		142	
	6	11	18 18	36	19 21	40	76		
		12	6 6	12	6 4	10	22		
				48		50		98	240
4	7	13	11 10	21	3 2	5	26		
		14	5 6	11	1 0	1	12		
				32		6		38	
	8	15	8 8	16	6 6	12	28		
		16	4 4	8	7 8	15	23		
				24		27		51	89

In the table the first two figures 11 and 16 are the duplicate determinations of quality on Mix 1 Pair 1 Blend 1, first truck. The 27 is the total of 11 and 16. The next pair of figures 17 and 16 are the determinations on the second truck of mix 1, and the 33 following is their total. The last figure in the row is the mix total. The second row is for the second mix and is precisely identical. The third row has 27 as the total for the first truck, 60 as the total for the second truck, and 87 as the pair total. The same follows for the second pair for blend 1, with the addition of 145 as the blend total.

Prima facie this is a five factor analysis, the factors being Blends (B), Pairs (P), Mixes (M), Trucks (T) and Determination of Quality (A). It is immediately apparent that it is not a complete five factor analysis, however, as A is obviously a simple replication: there is no distinction between all the first determinations as compared with the second. Further, there is nothing special to distinguish the first pairs from the second pairs, so the pair main effect P will not exist and we will have a Between Pairs within Blends effect formed by pooling the sums of squares and degrees of freedom of the P and B $\times$ P terms.

We will proceed to calculate this term and the B main effect. The correcting factor, the grand total over the grand number of individuals, is

$$616^2/64 = 5929$$

The Blend main effect is of course given by the blend totals

$$(145^2 + 142^2 + 240^2 + 89^2)/16 - 5929 = 740.37$$

The Between Pairs within Blends term is given directly by squaring the pair totals and dividing by the number of individuals therein, and subtracting the correcting factor and the Blend sum of squares, i.e.

$$(87^2 + 58^2 + \ldots + 51^2)/8 - 5929 - 740.37 = 184.13$$

We would of course get the same result if we formed a B × P table, calculated the B, P, and B × P (residual) and then pooled P with B × P.

We now come to consider the M effect. There can be no M main effect, as the first mix in all pairs are not systematically distinguished from the second mixes: we therefore have that $\sigma_m^2 = 0$. Further the M effect is only of interest within a given pair, which is within a given blend: this term is σ_{mbp}^2, and σ_{mb}^2 and σ_{mp}^2 are both zero. If we strike out σ_m^2, σ_{mb}^2 and σ_{mp}^2 from the components of variance of the M, M × B, and M × P mean squares, we find we have in each case left as the components of variance

$$\sigma_a^2 + a\sigma^2_{mtbp} + at\sigma^2_{mbp}$$

which is the same as for the M × B × P mean square. We therefore pool these four terms, M, M × B, M × P, and M × P × B, and call the resulting term "Between Mixes within Pairs and Blends." The pooled degrees of freedom are

$$(m-1) + (m-1)(b-1) + (m-1)(p-1) + (m-1)(p-1)(n-1) = bp(m-1).$$

It is clear that this is a reasonable answer: looking at it in a rather different way, each pair of mixes contribute (m — 1) degrees of freedom, and there are bp pairs, so the total is bp(m — 1).

To calculate this pooled M × B × P term we need a M × B × P table, i.e. a table formed by totalling over A and T. Such a table is already formed in the column headed "Mix Totals," 60, 27, 4, 16, 55, etc. The total sum of squares for this table is

$$(60^2 + 27^2 + 4^2 + \ldots + 23^2)/4 - 5929 = 1771.5$$

To obtain our pooled M × B × P term we could calculate in full M, M × B, B × P, M × B × P and then pool them. We may note, however, that the Total of an M × B × P table is made up of these terms plus B, P, and B × P. These latter we already have, so the pooled M × B × P term is very easily obtained as

$$1771.5 - 740.37 - 184.13 = 847.00$$

Its degrees of freedom are

$$bp(m-1) = 4 \times 2(2-1) = 8$$

The T term is obtained in exactly the same way as the M term. We require the term formed by pooling T, T × B, T × P, and T × B × P, so we work from the T × B × P table formed by totalling over A and M. The total sum of squares for this table is

$$(27^2 + 60^2 + 36^2 + 22^2 + 22^2 + \ldots + 27^2)/4 - 5929.0 = 1274.5$$

From this we subtract the sums of squares of B, P, and B × P as before, and we obtain as the sum of squares for the B × P × T term

$$1274.5 - 740.37 - 184.13 = 350.00$$

The degrees of freedom are

$$bp(t-1) = 4 \times 2(2-1) = 8.$$

We now want the M × T interaction. As for M and T, this only exists within Pairs and Blends, so we pool M × T with M × T × B, M × T × P and M × T × B × P. We therefore work from the M × T × B × P table, i.e. the table formed by totalling over A. The total sum of squares for this table is

$$(27^2 + 60^2 + 0^2 + 27^2 + 24^2 + \ldots + 15^2)/2 - 5929.0 = 2316.00$$

To obtain the sum of squares for our pooled M × T × B × P term we can subtract from this total all the other terms arising in an M × T × B × P table.

These are

(a) B and B × P : these we have as 740.37 + 184.13.
(b) M, M × B, M × P and M × B × P : this we have calculated as 847.00
(c) T, T × B, T × P, and T × B × P : this we have calculated as 350.00.

The sum of squares is thus

$$2316.00 - 740.37 - 184.13 - 847.00 - 350.00 = 194.50$$

Its degrees of freedom are

$$\begin{aligned}&(m-1)(t-1)+(m-1)(t-1)(b-1)+(m-1)(t-1)(p-1)\\&\quad+(m-1)(t-1)(p-1)(b-1)\\&\quad=bp(m-1)(t-1)\\&\quad=4\times 2(2-1)(2-1)\\&\quad=8.\end{aligned}$$

The final term is the Between Analyses which is

$$(11^2+16^2+17^2+16^2+0^2+\ldots 8^2)-(27^2+33^2+0^2+\ldots+15^2)/2$$
$$=8278-8245=33.00$$

The total sum of squares is the usual

$$(11^2+16^2+\ldots+8^2)-5929=2349.00$$

We can now enter all these terms into a table of analysis of variances.

Source of Variance	Mean Squares of Complete Analysis being Pooled	Sums of Squares	Degrees of Freedom	Mean Squares	Components of Variance
Between Blends	B	740.37	3	246.79	$\sigma_a^2+a\sigma^2_{mtbp}+am\sigma^2_{tbp}+at\sigma^2_{mbp}+amt\sigma^2_{bp}+amtp\sigma^2_b$
Between Pairs within Blends	P P × B	184.13	4	46.03	$\sigma_a^2+a\sigma^2_{mtbp}+am\sigma^2_{tbp}+at\sigma^2_{mbp}+amt\sigma^2_{bp}$
Between Trucks within Pairs and Blends	T T × B T × P T × B × P	350.00	8	43.75	$\sigma_a^2+a\sigma^2_{mtbp}+am\sigma^2_{tbp}$
Between Mixes within Pairs and Blends	M M × B M × P M × B × P	847.00	8	105.87	$\sigma_a^2+a\sigma^2_{mtbp}+at\sigma^2_{mbp}$
Mix × Truck Interaction within Pairs and Blends	M × T M × T × B M × T × P M × T × B × P	194.50	8	24.31	$\sigma_a^2+a\sigma^2_{mtbp}$
Between Analyses		33.00	32	1.03	σ_a^2
Total		2349.00	63		

The appropriate tests of significance can be worked out from the components of variance. It may be noted, however, that if both the Between Mixes and Between Trucks terms are significant when tested against the Mix × Truck interaction, i.e. if both σ^2_{mbp} and σ^2_{tbp} are greater than zero, then there is no valid test for the Between Pairs Mean Square This circumstance is similar to that arising in Table 21 (Chapter XI (d)).

The Between Trucks Mean Square is not significant, but it is probably worth while calculating its component of variance. We obtain

$$\begin{aligned}\sigma_a^2&=1.03\\\sigma^2_{mt}&=11.64\\\sigma_m^2&=15.40\\\sigma_t^2&=4.86\\\sigma_p^2&=0.00\\\sigma_b^2&=10.05\end{aligned}$$

It is clear that the origins of variability are rather widespread, Mixing and its interaction with Trucks (drying) and Blends being responsible for the greater part of the variability.

CHAPTER XII

MISCELLANEOUS ASPECTS OF THE ANALYSIS OF VARIANCE

(a) Introduction

In this Chapter a number of miscellaneous aspects of the use of the analysis of variance will be discussed. The next five sections contain matter which might be borne in mind in planning and analysing the results of factorial experiments, Section (g) is an account of a useful experimental device (the Latin Square), and the subsequent sections describe various applications of the analysis of variance.

(b) The Use of Components of Variance[1]

In the systematic discussion of the Analysis of Variance in Chapter XI for each type of analysis the components of variance corresponding to each mean square were given.

It should be realized that the mean square only estimates these terms, and one must not regard them as precise algebraic identities. Thus in the complete three factor analysis (Table 22) we had

31.08 estimates $w\sigma^2_{ta} + \sigma_0^2$
161.08 estimates σ_0^2

It is evident that σ_{ta}^2 does not exist, i.e. is zero, and so we have two estimates of σ_0^2 which we can pool in the usual way, taking into account the degrees of freedom (i.e. the simplest way is to pool the sums of squares and the degrees of freedom and calculate the new mean squares, estimating σ_0^2 as the former divided by the latter).

This pooling is of course only valid when the estimates being pooled are consistent as tested with the variance ratio test. If $(w\sigma^2_{ta} + \sigma_0^2)$ was significantly greater than σ_0^2 then of course we would not pool. It is possible that $(w\sigma_{ta}^2 + \sigma_0^2)$ may be significantly smaller than σ_0^2. This is very unlikely to happen and if it does then the meaning is rather obscure. Either it is an accident (the 1 in 20 chance which will occur 1 in 20 times) and we can ignore it, or some human agency is entering in a certain way to bias the results.

The Components of Variance are useful for indicating the sequence of tests in the testing of the various terms of significance. They are also useful for estimating the actual amount of variability each part of the process is giving rise to, in order to decide on which part of the process the control must be improved to increase the uniformity of the product. This application was discussed in Chapter VII (Section (c)) and Chapter XI (Section (m)).

The coefficients of the components of variance given in the various tables in Chapter XI are strictly only valid when the supposed populations are infinite. If the population is made up of batches of raw material, we can comfortably suppose that there is an infinite population of batches even if we are only concerned with a few dozen or a few hundred. If the populations are factories, then there may be only two or three factories and unlikely to be any others built in the future. Under these circumstances it becomes a little difficult to regard the population as infinite, and strictly the coefficients of the components of variance become modified.[2]

For practical purposes the modifications can be generally ignored, because

(a) the sequence of tests of significance is unaltered, and therefore no mistakes will be made by using the unmodified coefficients.

(b) the actual estimates of the component of variance using the simple coefficients should be multiplied by the factor (k − 1)/(k where k is the size of the population). It is only for k = 2 or 3 that the factor is appreciable, being

(1) On this point see S. L. Crump : Biometrics Bulletin, Vol. 2, No. 1, page 7, 1946.
(2) cf. H. E. Daniels, Supp. Journ. Roy. Stat. Soc. VI No. 2, 1939, p. 188).

0.5 and 0.66 respectively. For larger values of k the difference of the factor from unity is rarely important compared with the fairly large standard error that is of course attached to these components of variance.

In the case where a factor is made up of arbitrarily chosen different levels of a continuous variable, the population can of course be reasonably regarded as infinite, but we are probably more interested in the actual mean values and it will probably be of no interest to calculate the component of variance.

(c) Partitioning a Sum of Squares into Linear, Quadratic, etc. Components

Frequently we have a factor at 3, 4, 5 or more levels, where the factor has a numerical nature, the levels being chosen at intervals on the range of the continuous variable, e.g. temperature. We may wish to know whether the relation between the independent variable and the dependent variable can be regarded as linear, or whether there is appreciable curvature. If the steps between successive levels have been made equal, e.g. if the temperatures are 20, 25, 30, 35°C., then the question can be answered with the greatest of ease.

Consider the data in Table 12.1. The four values of T represent four temperatures, increasing in equal steps, of nitration of cellulose in mixed acid of four different water contents, represented by W, this also varying in equal steps. The dependent variable whose values are given in the table is the viscosity of the resulting nitro-cellulose.

Table 12.1

	T_1	T_2	T_3	T_4	Totals
W_1	6	32	45	63	146
W_2	24	27	45	62	158
W_3	6	24	44	45	119
W_4	1	22	23	39	85
Totals	37	105	157	209	508

A straightforward two factor analysis of variance gives the results in Table 12.2.

Table 12.2

Source of Variance	Degrees of Freedom	Sums of Squares	Mean Squares
Temperature	3	4052.0	1350.67
Water Content	3	787.5	262.50
Residual	9	367.5	40.83
Total	15	5207.0	

Both the effects are obviously highly significant. We can proceed to partition each of the two sums of squares into three components, one degree of freedom for the linear term, one for the quadratic term, and one for the cubic term.

For the linear term, the sum of squares is

$$(3\ T_4 + T_3 - T_2 - 3\ T_1)^2/N\Sigma\ k^2$$

The T's represent the totals of N observations, and Σk^2 in the sum of the squares of the co-efficients of the numerator. Here

$$\Sigma k^2 = 3^2 + 1^2 + (-1)^2 + (-3)^2 = 20$$

Accordingly the linear component of the sum of squares is

$$(3 \times 37 + 105 - 157 - 3 \times 209)^2/4 \times 20 = 4032.80$$

The quadratic component of the sum of squares is

$$(T_4 - T_3 - T_2 + T_1)^2/N\Sigma k^2$$
$$= (37 - 105 - 157 + 209)^2/4 \times 4 = 16.00$$

The cubic component is

$$(T_4 - 3\ T_3 + 3\ T_2 - T_1)/N\Sigma k^2$$
$$= (37 - 3 \times 105 + 3 \times 157 - 209)^2/4 \times 20 = 3.20$$

A ready check on the correctness of the arithmetic is obtained by noticing that the sum of the three components equals the total given in Table 12.2.

The Sum of Squares for Water Content can be partitioned exactly similarly and we get the results in Table 12.3.

Table 12.3

Source of Variance		Degrees of Freedom	Sums of Squares	Mean Squares
Temperature :	Linear	1	4032.80	4032.80
	Quadratic	1	16.00	16.00
	Cubic	1	3.20	3.20
Water Content :	Linear	1	616.06	616.06
	Quadratic	1	132.25	132.25
	Cubic	1	39.20	39.20
Residual		9	367.50	40.83
Total		15	5207.00	

The linear components in each case are obviously significant, and the significance of the quadratic and cubic terms can be tested in the usual manner against the Residual. It is interesting to note that the apparent bend over from W_2 to W_1 for decreasing W is not significant.

In the case where there are only three levels, there are 2 degrees of freedom, one for the linear component and one for the quadratic component. These sums of squares are respectively

$$(T_1 - T_3{}^2/N\Sigma k^2, \quad \Sigma k^2 = 2$$
$$(2\ T_2 - T_1 - T_3)^2/N\Sigma k^2, \Sigma k = 6$$

For more than four levels, Fisher and Yates. "Statistical Tables for Biological, Agricultural and Medical Research" (Oliver and Boyd) give the appropriate factors up to 52 levels.

In the case where two factors are numerical variables changing in equal steps, their interaction can be split up in an analogous manner. Consider the 3 × 3 table below (Table 12.4).

Table 12.4

	X_1	X_2	X_3	Totals
Y_1	17	20	24	61
Y_2	14	19	25	53
Y_3	10	18	30	58
Totals	41	57	79	177

We can use the coefficients

$$(T_1 - T_3)^2/N\Sigma k^2$$

$$\text{and } (-T_1 + 2T_2 - T_3)/N\Sigma k^2$$

to partition the two main effects into their linear and quadratic components, which we can represent as X_L, X_Q, Y_L and Y_Q respectively. We can also partition the 4 degrees of freedom for the interaction into that attributable to $X_L Y_L$, $X_Q Y_L$, $X_L Y_Q$, and $X_Q Y_Q$. To do this we set up a table of the type shown in Table 12.5.

Table 12.5

X_L	1	0	—1		
X_Q	—1	2	—1	Y_L	Y_Q
				1	—1
				0	2
				—1	—1

To form a table of coefficients for obtaining $X_L Y_L$, we take the coefficients for X_L and multiply them by the first coefficients for Y_L to give the first row, by the second coefficient for Y_L to give the second row, and similarly for the third row. For Y_L we multiply the coefficients for X_Q by those for Y_L in a similar manner.

Proceeding thus, we obtain the table of coefficients in Table 12.6.

Table 12.6

X_LY_L			X_QY_L			X_LY_Q			X_QY_Q		
1	0	—1	—1	2	—1	—1	0	1	1	—2	1
0	0	0	0	0	0	2	0	—2	—2	4	—2
—1	0	1	1	—2	1	—1	0	1	1	—2	1

$\Sigma k^2 = 4$ $\Sigma k^2 = 12$ $\Sigma k^2 = 12$ $\Sigma k^2 = 36$

The Σk^2 quoted below each table is the sum of the squares of the coefficients. To obtain the sum of squares due to e.g. $X_Q Y_L$, we operate on the figures in Table 12.4 by the coefficients for $X_Q Y_L$ in Table 12.6, square this result, and divide by Σk^2 times the number of observations in each figure that has been multiplied by the coefficients. In the present instance the latter figure is of course 1, but if the figures in Table 12.4 were the totals of N observations then it would be N. Accordingly we have as the Sum of Squares for $X_Q Y_L$

$$(-1 \times 17 + 2 \times 20 - 1 \times 24 + 1 \times 10 - 2 \times 18 + 1 \times 30)^2/12$$
$$= 0.750$$

We can now assemble the complete analysis of variance as in Table 12.7. The column "Sums of Squares" is obtained by squaring the figures in column two and dividing by column three. A good check on the arithmetic is given by the agreement of the sum of all the components with the sum calculated directly from the original observations.

Table 12.7

Source of Variance	Products of Coefficients and Data	$N\Sigma k^2$	Sums of Squares
X_L	—38	3 × 2	240.667
X_Q	— 6	3 × 6	2.000
Y_L	— 3	3 × 2	1.500
Y_Q	— 3	3 × 6	0.500
X_L Y_L	13	1 × 4	42.250
X_Q Y_L	3	1 × 12	0.750
X_L Y_Q	5	1 × 12	2.083
X_Q Y_Q	3	1 × 30	0.250
Total			290.000

If we had not made this detailed analysis, but merely an analysis by rows and columns, we would have obtained Table 12.8.

Table 12.8

Source of Variance	Degrees of Freedom	Sums of Squares	Mean Squares
X	2	242.667	121.333
Y	2	2.000	1.000
Residual	4	45.333	11.333
Total	8	290.000	

This analysis, though better than nothing, is not nearly so informative as that of Table 12.7. Table 12.8 is completely unable to give any information on the possible X Y interaction. With Table 12.7 we of course have to pool the smaller terms X_Q, Y_Q, X_L Y_Q, X_Q Y_L, and against this X_L Y_L is found to be significant.

This device is applicable generally for any number of levels. From a table of the type of Table 12.5 we can form tables of the type of Table 12.6, and this procedure will work for mixed levels, e.g. a 3 × 4 or a 3 × 5 or a 4 × 5. Further, there can be other factors present, and this is taken account of by adjusting N in the divisor $N\Sigma k^2$ to correspond to the number of original observations that have been summed to give us the table, as Table 12.4, on which we operate with the coefficients.

In the case of four or more levels for each factor, the number of components rises rapidly, e.g. for a 4 × 4 experiment the residual has 9 degrees of freedom and hence 9 components, for a 5 × 5 experiment the corresponding number is 16. The calculation of all of them is time-consuming and also really unnecessary. Normally the only components that are likely to be of interest are X_L Y_L, X_Q X_L and X_L, Y_Q. Even the latter two are unlikely to be of interest if X_Q and Y_Q respectively have proved to be small. Accordingly it normally suffices to calculate the total interaction in the usual manner and obtain a residual as the difference between it and the sum of the three components mentioned. In this case, of course, there is no explicit check on the arithmetic, so the steps taken need careful checking.

It might be emphasised again that this whole procedure rests on the assumption that each factor is increasing in equal steps, for example, 10°C, 15°C, 20°C, 25°C. However, if we prefer, we can make the steps equal on a logarithmic scale, for example 1%, 2%, 4%, 8%. In this case, X_L will measure the fit to linearity on this scale, and similarly X_Q and the higher terms deviations from linearity on this scale.

(d) The Assumption Underlying Factorial Design

A factorial experiment is much more useful, in that its interpretation is simplest and that its efficiency in the sense of giving more information for a given number of experiments than the corresponding classical design is greatest, when the interactions are not significant.

It may be interesting to note that the non-existence of interactions presupposes that the dependent variable y can be expressed as the sum of a series of functions of the independent variables x_1, x_2, etc., each of the latter involving one and only one independent variable, i.e.

$$y = f(x_1) + f(x_2) + \ldots \qquad (1)$$

The functions can be anything, of course, with no limit to the degree of complexity.

To take a simple example, let

$$y = x_1 + 2x_2 \qquad (2)$$

If the two independent variables were at two levels both equal to 1 and 2, we would obtain the results in the table below for y:

	$x_2 = 1$	$x_2 = 2$
$x_1 = 1$	2	5
$x_1 = 2$	3	6

It will be readily seen that there is no $x_1 \times x_2$ interaction. Thus the effect in y of changing x_2 for $x_1 = 1$ is $5 - 2 = 3$ which is identical with that for $x_1 = 2$, $6 - 3 = 3$, i.e. the effect on y of changing x_2 is independent of the level of x_1.

Now consider a relationship of the type

$$y = f(x_1)\, f(x_2) \qquad (3)$$

where the functions $f(x_1)$ and $f(x_2)$ can be of any form.

To take an example of the simplest form, let

$$y = x_1 x_2^2 \qquad (4)$$

With the two independent variables at two levels 1 and 2, we could obtain the results as in the table below for y.

	$x_2 = 1$	$x_2 = 2$
$x_1 = 1$	1	4
$x_1 = 2$	2	8

It will be readily seen that there is an $x_1 \times x_2$ interaction. Thus the effect in y of changing x_2 from 1 to 2 for $x_1 = 1$ is equal to $4 - 1 = 3$ but for $x_1 = 2$ is equal to $8 - 2 = 6$, i.e. the effect on y of changing x_2 is dependent on the level of x_1.

It will be apparent that if we take logarithms throughout, equation (3) becomes

$$\log y = \log f(x_1) + \log f(x_2) \qquad (5)$$

and we now have an equation of the same form as (1), and the analysis will be non-interacting.

(e) The Use of Interactions as Estimates of Error

In our original two factor (row and column) analysis what was termed the Residual included not only variance due to error but also to any possible interaction between the factors. If the latter exists and is large, then we have a large Mean Square for the Residual, and hence neither of the main effects is likely to be significant, i.e. we conclude the experiment knowing little more about the behaviour of the system than when we began.

There are two possible courses of action open under these circumstances.

We can replicate, and carry out an analysis as described in the section on Two Factor Analysis with Replication, which would give us an estimate of error independent of the Interaction.

Alternatively, we could repeat the series of observations, but with a third factor, held constant at a certain level in the first series, held constant at another level in the second series. The experiment would now be a three factor one, and we would be relying upon the second order interaction (P × Q × R) to be small or non-existent so as not to inflate the Residual.

It may happen, however, that this second order interaction is large. A good example of this was in the Section on a Four Factor Experiment, when the four factor experiment was broken down into two three factor experiments, and the S_2 had a large Residual almost certainly because it contained a large second order interaction.

Under these circumstances there are two possible alternatives. We can either replicate, in which case we would analyse the data as in the Section on Three Factor Analysis with Replication.

Alternatively, we could add a fourth factor, and use the third order interaction as an estimate of error. It may happen that this third order interaction is large, and so we will have an inflated estimate of error, and still not be much better off. However, if this interaction is large, it is valuable to know this, so it will have been as well to include this additional factor.

A further example is in the Five Factor experiment discussed in Chapter XI (f), where the W × T × D interaction was very large. If the experiment had been carried out as a three factor one on W, T, and D, this large W × T × D interaction would have been used as the residual, and no conclusions could have been drawn. Actually, of course, the experiment included two further factors, S and G, and fortunately neither of these interacted, so a reasonably small residual was obtained.

We can thus formulate some general ideas about the planning of factorial experiments. We have first to decide what are the main factors in which we are interested, and the number of levels at which we will test them. We then need to decide which are the factors which normally vary in the process and are likely to interact with our main factors, and include these, possibly only at two levels. We now need to decide whether the combination of factors so far introduced will give us a satisfactory residual as given by some non-existent high order interaction. To make this decision is of course frequently difficult. With a certain amount of prior information as to the general behaviour of the system we can frequently have some confidence in our conclusion, but often it is quite impossible to guess. We can only go on the general rule that it is not very frequent for high order interactions to exist, or if they do exist, to be very large, and be prepared to replicate the whole experiment if we end up with a large residual. Alternatively, if it is absolutely essential to be certain of getting results on the first experiment, then we must include a replication in the first experiment, perhaps at the cost of omitting a factor.

It is probably generally desirable to include batch of raw material as one of the factors, for it may be that all batches do not react identically to particular treatments. In an example in the author's experience, a crude chemical was subjected to a purifying process, and a factorial experiment established with a greater significance than 1% that level 1 of a particular factor gave a much better product than level 2. This experiment was only carried out on a single batch of crude material, however, and subsequent experience showed that in general this conclusion was erroneous. If the experiment had been replicated on one or more batches this mistake would have been avoided. If we can afford to carry out replications, we should therefore replicate on different batches rather than within a single batch, this really being to introduce an additional factor, batch of raw material.

(f) The Amount of Detail Required in Reports

In presenting in a paper or report the results of an investigation using a factorial design with an analysis of variance upon the results, it is desirable to give

(a) the factors and the levels at which they were used,

(b) the analysis of variance. It is a useful practice to mark with asterisks the significant terms, one (*) for the 5% level, two (**) for the 1% level, and three (***) for the 0.1% level.

(c) If we are interested in components of variance then we should calculate those which are significant. If we are interested in means then these should be given. In the case where two factors interact, a two-way table is necessary, e.g. Table 29.

(d) In general it is not necessary to give the original data, particularly when it is extensive: the statistics specified above contain the essential facts. However, when the original data is not very extensive, there is no harm in giving it.

(g) The Latin Square

A statistical device that was originally introduced by Fisher to overcome difficulties arising out of differences in soil fertility in agricultural experiments is the Latin Square.

Suppose we wished to investigate the effects of two factors, P and Q, each at four levels, upon a process. P might be the pressure at which cordite was pressed and Q might be the angle of the choke plate in the press. Then we would carry out the experiment below: i.e. 16 experiments are carried out, one for each value of Q for each value of P, thus P_1Q_1, P_1Q_2, P_1Q_3, P_1Q_4, P_2Q_1, P_2Q_2 and so on.

	Q_1	Q_2	Q_3	Q_4
P_1				
P_2				
P_3				
P_4				

To the first order, our comparison of the Qs is independent of our comparison of the Ps (ignoring interactions), and the results of such an experiment could be tested for significance by carrying out the analysis of variance for rows and columns.

However, suppose that the material for pressing comes from the previous (incorporation) stage in homogeneous batches of such a size that only (say) ten pressings could be made from one batch. Then we could not carry out the above design, because it involves 16 pressings, and thus part of the series would be carried out on one batch and part on another batch and possible differences between batches would be hopelessly mixed up with the P and Q comparisons.

This difficulty can be avoided by the use of a Latin Square design. Consider the arrangement below, where A, B, C and D represent four different batches. Thus with batch A, four readings are taken in which for the first P is at P_1 and Q at Q_1, the second P at P_2 and Q at Q_4, etc. Similarly for the other batches.

	Q_1	Q_2	Q_3	Q_4
P_1	A	B	C	D
P_2	B	C	D	A
P_3	C	D	A	B
P_4	D	A	B	C

It will be noticed that each row contains A, B, C and D each once and only once. Thus whatever disturbing effects possible differences between the batches may introduce occur equally for each row, and hence are completely eliminated when we take the average of the rows for our comparison of the Ps.

Exactly similarly each column contains A, B, C and D each once and only once and all disturbing effects due to differences between the batches are eliminated from the comparison of the Qs.

The results of such an experiment would be tested for significance with an analysis of variance on the following lines :—

(1) Square every observation and sum these squares.

(2) Obtain the total for each row, square these totals, sum these squares, and divide this total by the number of individuals in each row.

(3) Similarly for columns.

(4) Similarly for batches.

(5) Square the grand total and divide by the grand number of individuals.

We then form a table of this analysis of variance (Table 12.9).

Table 12.9

Source of Variance	Sums of Squares	Degrees of Freedom	Mean Squares
Rows	(2) — (5)	$n - 1$	
Columns	(3) — (5)	$n - 1$	
Batches	(4) — (5)	$n - 1$	
Residual		$(n - 1)(n - 2)$	
Total	(1) — (5)	$n^2 - 1$	

n = size of square.

The Residual Sum of Squares is as usual the difference between the Total Sum of Squares and all the other components.

The various mean squares are tested for significance with Fisher's variance ratio test. Here we are principally interested in the Row and Column effects, corresponding to our factors P and Q. If the effects prove not significant we can regard it as there being no significant difference between the P (or the Qs). If the effect proves significant, we can calculate the means for each level of P (or Q). For making a detailed comparison of any two levels of P (or Q) each mean has the standard error given by the square root of the Residual Mean Square divided by the square root of n.

We have discussed the 4 × 4 Latin Square, but there is in general no restriction upon square size. Designs are available for sizes up to 12 × 12.

One of the assumptions underlying the use of a Latin Square is that there should be no interaction between the factors. Since the existence of interaction in industrial chemical systems appears to be common, the Latin Square may not be of wide applicability in this field.

An alternative method for dealing with the situation of restricted batch size, where we need to carry out a given number of experiments for a factorial experiment and the batch size of raw material is not large enough, is known as confounding (see Chapter XIV).

(h) Graeco-Latin and Higher Order Squares

Consider the Latin Square in Table 12.10. It is possible to construct another Latin Square, using Greek Letters (Table 12.11) such that when they are superimposed (Table 12.12) to each Latin letter corresponds all Greek letters and vice-versa. Such a square is called "Graeco-Latin."

Table 12.10

A	B	C	D	E
B	C	D	E	A
C	D	E	A	B
D	E	A	B	C
E	A	B	C	D

Table 12.11

α	β	γ	δ	ε
δ	ε	α	β	γ
β	γ	δ	ε	α
ε	α	β	γ	δ
γ	δ	ε	α	β

Table 12.12

Aα	Bβ	Cγ	Dδ	Eε
Bδ	Cε	Dα	Eβ	Aγ
Cβ	Dγ	Eδ	Aε	Bα
Dε	Eα	Aβ	Bγ	Cδ
Eγ	Aδ	Bε	Cα	Dβ

The applications of this to experimental design are obvious. If as in the previous example different columns were different angles, the rows different pressures, and Latin letters different batches, then the Greek letters could be any further factor such as rate of pressing.

The analysis of variance proceeds exactly as in the previous section, except that now there is a further item derived exactly in the same way as the first three in Table 12.9, again with (n — 1) degrees of freedom. The Sum of Squares for the Residual, obtained by difference as before, now has (n — 1) (n — 3) degrees of freedom.

It is possible to superimpose on Table 12.12 a fifth factor which still satisfies the appropriate conditions, when the degrees of freedom for the Residual will be (n — 1) (n — 4), or in this case 4.

Generally speaking, except for n = 6, on a square of side n we can superimpose n factors still leaving (n — 1) degrees of freedom for the residual. These designs can thus be extremely useful for rough surveys, as for example in a total of 25 runs we can get good estimates of 5 factors each at 5 levels. The disadvantages, of course, is that they do not estimate interactions: nevertheless, for a quick survey of a new field, in which we are principally interested in the main effects and propose to examine those which turn out to be of practical importance in more detail later, these designs are valuable.

Fisher and Yates' Tables (Table XVI) give the structure of such squares from n = 3 to 9. It is remarkable that for n = 6 nothing higher than a Latin Square is possible.

(i) The Theory of Chemical Sampling[*]

(i) The techniques outlined above can be made the basis of a scientific study of sampling, a field that has been not adequately dealt with in chemical industry.

Thus consider the variances derived for the problem in Chapter XI (f).

Between Vats	$= \sigma_1^2 = 1.09$
Between Bags within Vats	$= \sigma_2^2 = 0.00$
Between Samples within Bags	$= \sigma_3^2 = 1.85$
Between Analyses within Samples	$= \sigma_4^2 = 0.83$

Suppose we have one analysis on one sample from one bag from one vat. This will have a variance of (1.09 + 0.00 + 1.85 + 0.83) = 3.77 or a standard deviation of 1.94. It will then have a 95% chance of being less than 1.96 × 1.94 = 3.80 out from the true mean (1.96 is the value of t for infinite degrees of freedom for the 5% level of significance).

If this is too inaccurate an estimate of the quality of the batch, we might reduce the error in our estimate by doing duplicate analyses. It would then have a variance of (1.09 + 0.00 + 1.85 + 0.83/2) = 3.35 or a standard deviation of 1.83. It is clear that this is very little improvement upon our original estimate of 1.94 based on a single analysis.

We might take a pair of samples from a bag, and perform single analyses upon them. Our estimate would thus have a variance of (1.09 + (1.85 + 0.83)/2) = 2.43, or a standard deviation of 1.56. This is a definite improvement upon our earlier estimates.

Alternatively we might take a pair of samples, one from one bag from one vat and the other from another bag from another vat. Our estimate of the mean batch quality would now have a variance of (1.09 + 0.00 + 1.85 + 0.83)/2 = 1.88 or a standard deviation of 1.37.

It is thus clear that it is much less profitable, if we are going to have the laboratory doing two analyses, to have them doing duplicate analyses upon the same sample or separate analyses from two samples from the same bag than have them doing separate analyses upon samples drawn from separate bags from separate vats.

If we are dealing with a chemical substance, samples of which can be blended, such as liquids, powders, etc., then a further possibility is open to us. We can take a pair of samples, one from one bag from one vat and one from one bag from another vat, blend them, and carry out one analysis upon the blended sample.

[*] Interesting papers on sampling problems are: D. J. Finney: Biometrics Bulletin, Vol. 2, No. 1, 1946, page 1. C. S. Pearce: Journal of the Royal Statistical Society, Vol. CVII, page 117, 1944. F. Yates: Journal of the Royal Statistical Society, Vol. CIX, page 12, 1946. Chapter 17 of G. W. Snedecor's "Statistical Methods" 4th Edition (Iowa State College Press) is also stimulating.

Our estimate would now have an error variance of $((1.09 + 0.00 + 1.85)/2 + 0.83) = 2.30$ or a standard deviation of 1.52. Or if we took four samples from four vats and blended them and carried out one analysis upon the blended sample our estimate would have an error variance of $((1.09 + 0.00 + 1.85)/4 + 0.83) = 1.56$ or a standard deviation of 1.25. Thus with a little extra trouble in sampling, and no more work on the part of the laboratory, we have got an estimate of the batch mean quality with an error standard deviation of 1.25, to be compared with the simple estimate from one sample of 1.94.

It is on the basis of such an exploratory analysis of variance that we can deduce what is the error of our present sampling scheme and if the latter proves to have too high an error the analysis of variance will show the most economical method of improving its accuracy.

(ii) Further examples of the application of the analysis of variance to the study of chemical sampling are given below. An allegedly homogeneous blend had been bagged. To test its homogeneity three analyses were performed on three samples taken from three bags from the blend. The material was nitrocellulose, and it was analysed for nitrogen content and viscosity.

Nitrogen (%)

Sample \ Bag	1	2	3
I	12.20 12.22 12.21	12.23 12.24 12.23	12.19 12.21 12.22
II	12.21 12.20 12.19	12.22 12.23 12.25	12.24 12.21 12.23
III	12.21 12.22 12.20	12.22 12.21 12.24	12.22 12.22 12.22

Viscosity (poises)

Sample \ Bag	1	2	3
I	116 112 114	124 130 126	109 128 119
II	128 127 132	134 114 127	114 127 119
III	116 118 117	126 129 132	119 119 130

The data was analysed as in Chapter XI (i), with results as below:

Source of Variance	Degrees of Freedom	Nitrogen		Viscosity	
		Sums of Squares	Mean Squares	Sums of Squares	Mean Squares
Between Bags	2	24.51	12.25	267.56	133.78
Between Samples within Bags	6	10.23	1.70	427.11	71.19
Between Analyses within Samples	18	25.33	1.40	614.00	34.11
Total	26	60.07		1308.67	

Units for nitrogen: hundredths of a per cent.

In the case of Nitrogens, the Between Sample Mean Square is not significant but the Between Bags is, at the 1% level. In the case of Viscosity, the Between Samples Mean Square is not significant but the Between Bags Mean Square is nearly significant at the 5% level.

It is thus apparent that there is appreciable inhomogeneity in the blend from bag to bag but not within bags. We can calculate the components of variance as below:

Source of Variance	Nitrogen	Viscosity
Between Bags ..	1.20	10.0
Between Samples ..	0.00	0.0
Residual	1.48	43.4
Total	2.68	53.4

The figure under "Total" is the variance of a single analysis upon a sample from one bag.

To effect improvement in the nitrogen figure, we need to concentrate attention upon both operating sources of error. It is not sufficient to take n samples and bulk them and perform one analysis on the blended sample: thus if n was 4, the variance of the estimate thus obtained would be $(1.48 + 1.20/4) = 1.78$. This is an improvement, but no matter how many samples we bulk, so long as we perform only one analysis the variance will never be less than 1.48. If we performed two analyses upon a blended sample derived from four bags, the variance of the mean would be $(1.20/4 + 1.48/2) = 1.04$.

With the viscosity determination, it is clear that our main efforts must be directed at obtaining more analyses. If we had four analyses upon one sample the variance of our estimate of the mean would be $(10 + 43.4/4) = 20.8$, or four analyses upon separate samples gives a variance of $(10/4 + 43.4/4) = 13.3$. The gain by taking separate samples is appreciable, therefore.

(j) The Homogeneity of Data

At the end of Chapter III on the comparison of means it was mentioned that complications arise in the calculation of standard deviations if the observations are not independent of each other.

In general, with an analysis of variance between and within batches (One Factor with Replication) if we have m batches of n individuals then let us define the simple variance given by the Total Mean Square (i.e. the variance we would calculate if we ignored the inhomogeneity of the data and regarded it as referring to nm independent individuals) as σ_t^2. Then

$$\sigma_t^2 = \frac{m(n-1)}{mn-1} \sigma_A^2 + \sigma_B^2$$

where σ_A^2 and σ_B^2 are the components of variances corresponding to differences between batches and differences within batches.

Rearranging, this can be expressed as

$$\sigma_t^2 = [1 - \frac{(m-1)}{mn-1}] \sigma_A^2 + \sigma_B^2$$

It is evident that σ_t^2 is always smaller than $\sigma_T^2 = \sigma_A^2 + \sigma_B^2$, and the error will be greatest when σ_B^2/σ_A^2 tends to 0 and when m is large and n = 2. Under these circumstances σ_t^2 is only half σ_T^2, the correct value for the total variance.

Consider the block of 30 observations discussed in Chapter VII (b), Analysis Between and Within Columns. Suppose we wished to calculate the standard deviation of the mean of these observations.

If we ignored the fact that these 30 observations are not independent of each other, but are actually 10 groups, each group being 3 observations, we should calculate the variance from its ordinary definition which corresponds to terms (1) — (3) in that section divided by the total degrees of freedom, i.e. 203.87/29 = 7.030, and the standard deviation of the individual observations would be 2.65, and the standard deviation of the mean would be $2.65/\sqrt{30} = 0.484$.

However, this is a false result, for our mean is not the mean of 30 independent individuals, but actually the mean of 10 column means.

The variance of each column mean is $(\sigma_B^2/3 + \sigma_A^2)$ and since there are 10 column means the variance of the grand mean is $(\sigma_B^2/3 + \sigma_A^2)/10$, i.e. $(2.17/3 + 5.22)/10 = 0.594$. The standard deviation of the grand mean is thus $\sqrt{0.594} = 0.771$.

This true standard error of the grand mean of 0.771 is very much larger than the false one of 0.484 we obtained by ignoring the inhomogeneity of the data. If we had been using the standard error to compare the mean with some other value using the Student t test we would have fallen into serious errors, for not only is the true value of the standard error of the grand mean much larger than the incorrect one, but also the true degrees of freedom are only 9, not 29. This is why it is in general very desirable to plan experiments of this type in a form suitable for the application of the analysis of variance.

Thus, if the thirty units (ten batches) referred to had been made of one consignment of raw material, and we wished to compare the grand mean of another consignment, it would be most convenient to make ten batches (thirty units) with the second consignment. This would then be suitable for an analysis of variance as below:

Source of Variance	Degrees of Freedom	Sums of Squares	Mean Squares
Between Consignments	(2 — 1) = 1		
Between Batches within Consignments	2 (10 — 1) = 18		
Between Units within Batches	2 × 10 (3 —1) = 40		
Total	2 × 10 × 3 — 1 = 59		

It will be noted that it would not be possible to apply this technique if the experiment had been done haphazardly, unplanned, so that units were missing from some of the batches and the numbers of batches made from each consignment were unequal.

(k) The Use of Logarithms in the Analysis of Variance

We discussed earlier the possibility of using the logarithm of the dependent variable rather than the dependent variable itself in cases where deviations were likely to be proportional to the mean, i.e. constant if we use logarithms.

An example of this is occurring in the case of acid plant throughputs discussed in Chapter XI (i) (Table 11.22). The Between Factories Within Acid Group term is not significant, so we can form a pooled residual variance with $3 \times 6 = 18$ degrees of freedom for each type of weak acid. These become 57.19, 405.21, and 1197.84 respectively. These are severely inconsistent when tested with the variance ratio test. However, the standard deviations are 7.56, 20.13, and 34.61, and when expressed as fractions of the means 26.7, 51.0, and 103.3, we get 0.294, 0.396 and 0.334 respectively. It seems that these fractions are roughly constant, and we are encouraged to try an analysis of the logarithms of the data.

The natural logarithms of one-tenth of the throughput was selected as being the most convenient function to handle. Residual variances of 0.04489, 0.22450, and 0.08891 were obtained, each with 18 degrees of freedom, for each of the three acid types as before. While not strictly consistent, these are much more so than the simple variable. The Analysis of Variance on the logarithm of the data is in Table 12.13.

Table 12.13

Analysis of Variance of Logarithm of Acid Plant Throughputs.

Source of Variance	Degrees of Freedom	Sums of Squares	Mean Squares
Type of weak acid	2	11.4670	5.7335
Factories	6	0.6769	0.1128
Within Factories	54	6.4494	0.1194
Total	62	18.5933	

The conclusions to be reached from the above analysis are identical with those obtained from Table 11.23, the analysis of the simple data.

This is a reassuring aspect of the analysis of variance: we can disregard the underlying assumptions with comparative impunity.

(l) Other Transformations in the Analysis of Variance[4]

Sometimes in an analysis of variance the dependent variable is not a continuous variable but discontinuous.

For example, in discussing blemishes in objects, the number of blemishes of course has the lower limit zero but can go to very large numbers. Technically, the distribution is probably Poissonian. Under these circumstances it is more appropriate to use the square root of the number of blemishes as the dependent variable[5]. Where the number of blemishes are in many cases less than 10, it is slightly preferable to use, where x is the number of blemishes, $\sqrt{x + 1/2}$

[4] A very interesting paper on the effects of various transformations in a 3 x 3 x 2 x 2 experiment is by Thorp *et al*: Phytopathology XXXI, page 26, 1941.

[5] M. S. Bartlett: Supplement to the Journal of the Royal Statistical Society, 3 : 68 (1936).

In the case where the number of incidents x being counted has a finite upper limit, being able to range from O to X, it is best to take the angle θ.

$$\theta = \sin^{-1}\sqrt{x/X}$$

For example, if $x = 40$, $X = 120$, then $\sqrt{x/X} = \sqrt{1/3} = 0.5774$, and $\sin^{-1} 0.5774 = 35.2°$.

In practice convenient tables of the transformation are available.[6]

(m) **Missing Values**[7]

Occasionally runs fail to produce results: the sample may get lost or any similar accident may happen. In the case of a two factor experiment, of r rows and c columns, one missing value may be efficiently estimated by the formula[8]

$$X = \frac{rR + cC - T}{(r-1)(c-1)}$$

where r = number of rows
c = number of columns
R = total for the row with the missing item
C = total for the column with the missing item
T = grand total

Thus, in Table 12.1, if the value of T_2W_2 (actually the observed value was 27) had been missing, we would have estimated it as

$$X = \frac{4 \times 131 + 4 \times 78 - 481}{(4-1)(4-1)} = 39.4$$

In carrying out the analysis of variance, this value is inserted as though it had actually been observed, and the analysis then proceeds normally. However, the degrees of freedom for the Residual and for the Total are both decreased by unity.

It is wiser to regard conclusions from an experiment with a missing observation with rather more caution than if it had been complete. That is to say, we had better only attach something of the order of a 5% significance to what apparently is a 1% significance.

When two observations are missing, they can be inserted by an iterative method. We insert for X_1 an assumed value, say the grand mean, and then calculate the expected value of X_2. Using this value of X_2, we delete the assumed value for X_1, and then calculate its expected value, say X'_1. Using this value of X'_1 we delete the previous value X_2 and recalculate its new value X'_2. Using this new value X'_2 we delete X'_1 and recalculate a new value for X_1, X_1''. After a very few cycles of this process the new values will be the same as the old. The analysis of variance then proceeds with two degrees of freedom subtracted from both the Residual and the Total.

It is obvious that an inserted value can never be as good as an observed one, and so every effort should be made to avoid having to handle incomplete data. Where the lack of balance is on a large scale, the simplest case can be handled rigorously with little increase in trouble as in Chapter VII (d). Snedecor[9] (page 281-301) discusses some more complicated instances. However, in practice we can frequently obtain a moderately satisfactory result by discarding sufficient data randomly from the larger classes so that we have only one or two missing values which can be inserted by the methods above.

(6) Fisher and Yates "Statistical Tables for Biological Agriculture, and Medical Research" (Oliver and Boyd), Table XII in Second Edition.
G. W. Snedecor: "Statistical Methods," Iowa State College Press: Fouth Edition page 449.

(7) A full discussion with bibliography of missing plot techniques is by R. L. Anderson: Biometrics Bulletin, Vol. 2, No. 3, page 41, 1946.

(8) F. Yates: Empire Journal of Experimental Agriculture, 1, 129, 1933.

(9) G. W. Snedecor: "Statistical Methods applied to Experiments in Agriculture and Biology," (Iowa State College Press), 4th Edition, 1946.

CHAPTER XIII

BALANCED INCOMPLETE BLOCKS

(a) Introduction

A general description of the experimental design known as balanced incomplete blocks have been given in Chapter I Section (f), and will not be repeated here. This chapter will give the methods of computation for such experiments, the method and notation being based on Yates[1].

Yates has developed a rather more sensitive method of analysing the results[2] but generally, particularly when the number of blocks in the experiment is not very large, the increase in accuracy is not very great, and the earlier method of analysis reproduced here will normally suffice.

(b) Computation

Table 13.1 gives the results of an experiment for comparing 7 treatments in 7 blocks of 3 units, there thus being 3 replications of each treatment. Block A, for example, contained treatments T_1, T_3, and T_5, and the figures in the table in the columns A to G are the yields obtained.

Table 13.1

Blocks / Treatments	A	B	C	D	E	F	G	Totals	Q	v	Corrected Treatment Means
T_1	50	42	91					183	—84	—12.000	57.238
T_2			118	94	94			306	163	23.285	92.523
T_3	76			64		80		220	69	9.857	79.095
T_4			72			53	31	156	—160	—22.857	46.381
T_5	44				65		54	163	—81	—11.571	57.667
T_6		102			119	92		313	254	36.286	105.524
T_7		38		38			37	113	—161	—23.000	46.238
Totals	170	182	281	196	278	225	122	1454	0	0.000	

In Yates' notation—

Number of treatments	=	$t = 7$
Number of units per block	=	$k = 3$
Number of replications of each treatment	=	$r = 3$
Number of blocks	=	$b = 7$
Total number of units	=	$N = tr = bk = 21$
Sum of all N observations	=	$G = 1454$
Sum of all r observations for treatment 1	=	T_1
Sum of all k observations for block 1	=	B_1
Error variance of a single observation within blocks of k units	=	σ_k^2

For each of the t treatments we calculate the quantities Q given by

$$Q_1 = kT_1 - B_1 - B_2 - \dots - B_r$$

where the Bs for Q_1 are the totals for the r blocks containing treatment 1. For example,

$$Q_1 = 3 \times 183 - 170 - 182 - 281 = -84$$

The Sum of Squares for treatments is then

$$\frac{t-1}{Nk(k-1)} \Sigma Q^2 = \frac{7-1}{21 \times 3(3-1)} (84^2 + 163^2 + \dots + 161^2)$$

$$= 7665.905$$

(1) F. Yates : Annals of Eugenics, Vol. 7, page 121, 1936.
(2) F. Yates : Annals of Eugenics, Vol. 10, p. 317, 1940.

The Sum of Squares for Blocks is obtained from the Block totals in the usual manner:—

$$\frac{1}{k}\Sigma B^2 - G^2/N$$

$$= \frac{1}{3}(170^2 + 182^2 + \ldots + 122^2) - 1454^2/21 = 6725.810$$

The Total Sum of Squares is also as usual

$$50^2 + 42^2 + 91^2 + 116^2 + \ldots 37^2 - 1454^2/21 = 15057.810$$

We enter up these items in a table of analysis of variance and obtain the Error Sum of Squares and Degrees of Freedom by difference.

Table 13.2

Source of Variance	Degrees of Freedom	Sums of Squares	Mean Squares
Blocks	6	6725.810	1120.968
Treatments	6	7665.905	1277.651
Error	8	666.095	83.261
Total	20	15057.810	

The Error Mean Square is σ_k^2 and the standard error of the difference between any two treatment means is

$$\sqrt{2}\sqrt{\frac{k(t-1)}{N(k-1)}\sigma_k^2} = \sqrt{2}\sqrt{\frac{3(7-1)}{21(3-1)} \times 83.261}$$

$$= 8.448$$

To form these treatment means, corrected for block differences, we obtain the t quantities.

$$v_1 = \frac{(t-1)}{N(k-1)}Q_1 = \frac{(7-1)}{21(3-1)}(-84) = -12.000$$

These vs represent the deviation of each of the t treatments from the grand mean, which is $G/N = 1454/21 = 69.238$. The corrected treatment mean for treatment 1 is thus

$$v_1 + G/N = -12.000 + 69.238 = 57.238$$

Should we also be interested in the Block means, in the case of designs such as the present example, in which every pair of blocks has the same number of treatments in common, we can estimate the corrected block means by calculating Q′s similar to the Qs, e.g.

$$Q^1_A = 3 \times 170 - 183 - 220 - 163 = -56$$

and $v'_A = Q_A \dfrac{(t-1)}{N(k-1)} = 56 \dfrac{(7-1)}{21(3-1)} = -8.000$

whence the corrected mean for block A is $(69.238 + (-8.000)) = 61.238$.

More generally, we obtain the corrected block mean as, here,

$$\frac{1}{3}(170.000 - 57.238 - 79.095 - 57.667) + 69.238 = 61.238$$

In the particular case discussed, where each pair of blocks has the same number of treatments in common, the standard error of the difference between corrected block means is the same as that quoted above for corrected treatment means. In the more general case, the variance is, on the average.

$$\overline{V_b} = \frac{2\sigma_k^2}{k}\left(1 + \frac{(t-1)(t-k)}{t(k-1)(b-1)}\right)$$

which of course gives identical results in the present instance.

(c) **Possible Designs**

A list of possible designs is given in Fisher and Yates' Tables (Table XVII). Broadly speaking, if the number of treatments and the size of block are both determined, then the minimum number of replications of each treatment is fixed. If we are anxious to have only a small number of replications we can often avoid the straightforward solution. For example, working with blocks of 4, to compare 6 treatments then for balance we require 10 replications. If we are of the opinion that 10 replications is more than sufficient for our purpose, we can instead use the design for 7 treatments which requires only 4 replications : the seventh treatment can be a replication of one of the 6 or an additional one as we choose.

The most useful designs are that already given ($k = 3$, $b = 7$, $t = 7$, $r = 3$, that is to say, 3 units per block, 7 blocks, 7 treatments, 3 replications) and those in Table 13.3.

Table 13.3

$k = 3, b = 4, t = 4, r = 3$

A	x		x	x
B	x	x		x
C	x	x	x	
D		x	x	x

$k = 4, b = 5, t = 5, r = 4$

A	x	x	x	x	
B	x	x	x		x
C	x	x		x	x
D	x		x	x	x
E		x	x	x	x

$k = 4, b = 7, t = 7, r = 4$

A		x	x	x			x
B	x	x		x		x	
C	x		x			x	x
D		x	x		x	x	
E				x	x	x	x
F	x		x	x	x		
G	x	x			x		x

Fisher and Yates' Tables give a number of other interesting solutions. For example, 9 treatments can be compared in blocks of 3 with 4 replications, or 13 treatments in blocks of 4 with 4 replications, or 16 treatments in blocks of 4 with 5 replications, or 21 treatments in blocks of 5 with 5 replications.

(d) **Other Uses for Symmetrical Incomplete Blocks**

It might be pointed out that though as indicated these designs were introduced to evade the difficulty of restricted block size, they can be adapted for other purposes. For example, if we had a two factor experiment, each factor at 7 levels, complete execution would require $7^2 = 49$ units. We could, however, obtain satisfactory estimates of the two factors by use of the design discussed, which involves only 21 runs, and which gives the variance of the difference between two corrected means as $6\sigma_k^2/7$. The complete experiment would have given it as $2\sigma_k^2/7$, so our error in the incomplete case is larger, but may still be small enough for our purposes.

The alternative classical solution of this problem would be to carry out the treatments T_1 to T_7 with B constant at B_A and B_A to B_G with T constant at T_1 which would require 13 units or runs. In the absence of replication the experiment is most unsatisfactory, for there is no estimate of error and no means of testing for significance. If we replicate all treatments, making a total of 26 runs, we then get the comparison of our means with a variance σ_k^2. Comparing with the balanced incomplete block arrangement, we have done 24% more work and got an error variance 14% larger.

CHAPTER XIV

CONFOUNDING: THE PROBLEM OF RESTRICTED BLOCK SIZE IN FACTORIAL EXPERIMENTS[1]

(a) The Algebraic Expressions for Factors

In Chapter I we mentioned that for factorial experiments of the type 2^n (n factors all at 2 levels) the number of runs required, being 2^n, rapidly increased and for 4, 5 and 6 factors is 16, 32 and 64 respectively. These numbers may be too large to get into a single block, and the problem then arises of how to split the experiment up into smaller units.

Let us introduce an appropriate symbolism. Let the small letters p, q, r, etc., stand for the condition that the factor referred to is at its upper level. For example rs would mean that p and q are at their lower levels and r and s at their upper levels. Let the capital letter P denote the difference between the sum of all the upper levels of P and the sum of all the lower levels of P, and similarly for the other factors. Then for a three factor experiment,

$$P = pqr + pq + pr + p - qr - q - r - 1$$

where 1 implies all the factors at their lower levels. Algebraically, this is equivalent to

$$P = (p - 1)(q + 1)(r + 1)$$

and we can show that

$$Q = (p + 1)(q - 1)(r + 1),$$
$$R = (p + 1)(q + 1)(r - 1).$$

The first order interaction PQ is given by the difference between P at the lower level of Q, namely,

$$pr + p - r - 1$$

and P at the upper level of Q, namely,

$$pqr + pq - qr - q.$$

This gives

$$PQ = pqr + pq - qr - q - pr - p + r + 1$$

and algebraically this is equivalent to

$$PQ = (p - 1)(q - 1)(r + 1).$$

It will be noted that we get exactly the same result if we regard PQ as the difference between Q at the lower level of P, namely,

$$qr + q - r - 1$$

and Q at the upper level of P, namely,

$$pqr + pq - pr - p:$$

for this gives

$$\begin{aligned} PQ &= pqr + pq - qr - q - pr - p + r + 1 \\ &= (p - 1)(q - 1)(r + 1). \end{aligned}$$

Similarly

$$QR = (p + 1)(q - 1)(r - 1)$$
$$RP = (p - 1)(q + 1)(r - 1).$$

(1) For discussions of confounding see R. A. Fisher: "The Design of Experiments," Chapter VI (Oliver and Boyd), and F. Yates: "The Design and Analysis of Factorial Experiments" (Imperial Bureau of Soil Science).

The second order interaction PQR is rather more complicated : we can regard it as the difference between PQ at the lower level of R and PQ at the upper level of R.

The former is

$$(PQ)_{R_1} = pq - q - p + 1$$

and the latter is

$$(PQ)_{R_2} = pqr - qr - pr + r$$

so the difference is

$$PQR = pqr - qr - pr + r - pq + q + p - 1$$
$$= (p - 1)(q - 1)(r - 1).$$

As with a first order interaction, so with a second order interaction there are complementary ways of looking at it ; we might have regarded it as the difference between QR at P_1 and QR at P_2, or as the difference between RP at Q_1 and RP at Q_2.

(b) Confounding with Three Factors

Now consider that we have a three factor experiment, which will take $2^3 = 8$ runs, and we need to put this experiment not into one block of 8 runs but into 2 blocks of 4 runs, the block size admitting only up to 4 runs. If we consider that we are mainly interested in the main effects and the first order interactions, and are willing to sacrifice the second order interaction to achieve this end, we can allocate the treatments to the two blocks as in Table 14.1.

Table 14.1

Block 1	Block 2
pqr	1
r	qr
p	pr
q	pq

The second order interaction PQR is now lost as it is identical with the possible block differences, for the effect

$$pqr + r + p + q - 1 - qr - pr - pq$$

is both PQR and the difference between Block 1 and Block 2. This confusing of effects with block differences is known as "confounding."

We have now to assure ourselves that our estimates of the main effects and first order interactions are not affected by possible block differences. Suppose that Block 2 has a bias such that all the four results contained in it come out d higher than they would have done if they had been in Block 1.

We have

$$P = pqr + (pq + d) + (pr + d) + p - (qr + d) - q - r - (1 + d)$$
$$= pqr + pq + pr + p - qr - q - r - 1$$

as before, the biases d vanishing, and similarly for the two other main effects.

Also

$$PQ = pqr + (pq + d) - (qr + d) - q - (pr + d) - p + r + (1 + d)$$
$$= pqr + pq - qr - p - pr - p + r + 1$$

as before, the biases d again vanishing, and similarly for the other two first order interactions.

(c) Confounding with Four Factors

With four factors, the total number of runs required is $2^4 = 16$. The main effects are of the type

$$P = (p - 1)(q + 1)(r + 1)(s + 1),$$

the first order interactions of the type

$$PQ = (p - 1)(q - 1)(r + 1)(s + 1),$$

the second order interactions of the type

$$PQR = (p - 1)(q - 1)(r - 1)(s + 1),$$

and the third order interaction is

$$PQRS = (p - 1)(q - 1)(r - 1)(s - 1).$$

If we expand the latter it becomes

$$PQRS = pqrs - pqr - pqs + pq - prs + pr + ps - p - qrs + qr + qs - q + rs - r - s + 1.$$

If we wish to confound in 2 blocks of 8, and select PQRS as the term to be confounded, then we merely need to place all those terms with a + sign in one block and all those with a — sign in the other block, as in Table 14.2.

Table 14.2

Block 1	pqrs + pq + pr + ps + qr + qs + rs + 1
Block 2	pqr + pqs + prs + qrs + p + q + r + s

To confound in 4 blocks of 4, we need to select 3 terms to correspond to the 3 degrees of freedom that we confound with block differences. It is found that while we can select any two arbitrarily, the third is then uniquely determined. The third is determined by the rule that we multiply the first two together by the ordinary laws of algebra, but wherever a squared term appears we place it equal to unity. Thus if the two selected are PQ and RS, then the third is PQRS: if the two selected are PQR and QRS, then the third is PS.

A little experiment will show that with 4 factors to be confounded in 4 blocks of 4 it is impossible to avoid including one first order interaction amongst the three that are to be confounded.

One method of dividing the treatments into their appropriate blocks is to expand two of the selected interactions which are being confounded, as in Table 14.3.

Table 14.3

PQR	pqrs — pqs + pqr — pq — qrs + qs — qr + q
QRS	pqrs — pqs — pqr + pq + qrs — qs — qr + q
PQR cont	— prs + ps — pr + p + rs — s + r — 1
QRS cont	— prs + ps + pr — p — rs + s + r — 1

Where one treatment has the same plus sign in both expansions, we place it in one block. Similarly — —, + —, and — + form the other blocks, as in Table 14.4.

Table 14.4

Block 1 + +	Block 2 — —	Block 3 + —	Block 4 — +
pqrs	pqs	pqr	pq
q	qr	qs	qrs
ps	prs	p	pr
r	1	rs	s

There is an alternative method of writing down the treatment which in the more complicated cases is less troublesome. We consider the three interactions which we have selected for confounding, here

PQR, QRS, PS.

We place in the first block those treatments which have an even number of letters in common with the letters of these three terms. The treatment (1) is obviously satisfactory, for it has none in common (and zero is an even number). The treatment q r is also satisfactory, for it has 2 letters in common with both PQR and QRS and none in common with PS. The two others satisfying the condition are prs and pqs. This has given us one block, actually equivalent to Block 2 in Table 14.4. To get the next block, we select any treatment which has not yet occurred, say p, and multiply each of the terms in our first block by this, using the convention as before that e.g. $p^2 = 1$. Thus we get

$$\begin{aligned} pqs &\times p = p^2\,qs = qs \\ qr &\times p = qpr \\ prs &\times p = p^2\,rs = rs \\ 1 &\times p = p \end{aligned}$$

Accordingly, (p, rs, qpr and qs) form our second block, which actually is Block 3 of Table 14.4. The next block is formed by selecting a treatment which has not yet occurred, say q, and multiplying the term of the first block in turn. This will give us Block 1 of Table 14.4. Selecting any treatment not yet mentioned, say s, and carrying out the same operation given as Block 4.

(d) Confounding with Five Factors

With five factors we require a total of $2^5 = 32$ runs. Accordingly there are a number of possibilities according to the size of block we have available.

For splitting into 2 blocks of 16 we obviously choose to confound the highest order interaction, PQRST. To allocate the treatments into the two blocks, we can expand $(p - 1)(q - 1)(r - 1)(s - 1)(t - 1)$ and place all treatments with a + sign in one block and all those with a — sign in the other block. Alternatively, we get the same result by taking for one block all those treatments with an even number of letters in common with PQRST: these are (1) (no letter in common), the ten treatments of the type pq, qr, pr, ps, etc., and the five treatments of the type pqrs, qrst, etc.

For splitting into 4 blocks of 8, the best set of interactions to be selected for confounding is of the type

PQR, RST, PQST

which avoids losing any first order interaction. For allocation into the four blocks, we can expand any two, say PQR and RST, and distribute the treatments according to whether their signs in the two expansions are + +, + —, — +, or — —, as in the previous section. Alternatively, we can take as the first block those treatments with an even number of letters in common with the interactions selected for confounding. These are

(1), pq, st, pqst, qrs, qrt, prs, prt.

The subsequent blocks are obtained by multiplying each of these treatments by p for the second block, s for the third block, and r for the fourth block.

For splitting into 8 blocks of 4, the best we can do is to lose 2 first order nteractions. A typical set is

PQ, RS, PRT, QRT, PST, QST, PQRS

One method of building up the treatment combinations for the eight blocks is to expand any three (the third not being the product of the first two: e.g. if we select PQ and RS as the first two, then the third cannot be PQRS) and then the eight blocks are made up according to whether a treatment has the signs in the three expansion + + +, + + —, + — —, + — +, — + +, — + —, — — —, or — — +. The alternative method is, however, less arduous. Our first block would be

(1), pqt, rst, pqrs.

and the other seven are obtained by multiplying by treatments not hitherto mentioned. For example, to get our next block we can multiply by p, getting

p, qt, prst, qrs.

For the third block we can multiply by q, getting

q, pt, qrst, prs,

and so on, till all treatments have occurred.

(e) Confounding with Six Factors

With six factors we require $2^6 = 64$ runs. In confounding in 2 blocks of 32 we obviously choose the highest order interaction PQRSTU to be confounded. For four blocks of 16 the most satisfactory set for confounding is

PQRS, RSTU, PQTU,

and for 8 blocks of 8

PQR, RST, PSU, QTU, PQST, QRSU, PRTU.

In all these cases we avoid losing any first order interaction. To get the 64 runs into 16 blocks of 4, however, losing 3 first order interactions is unavoidable. A typical set of 15 interactions for confounding is

PQ, RS, PRT, QRT, PST, QST, PQRS, TU, PQTU, RSTU,
PRU, QRU, PSU, QSU, PQRSTU.

For allocating the treatments to their appropriate blocks the same method as hitherto can be applied. The first block is

(1) pqrs, rstu, pqtu

and the subsequent blocks can be obtained by mutliplication.

(f) Computation of the Results of a Confounded Experiment: An Example

In a confounded experiment the computation proceeds exactly as though the experiment had not been confounded, with the sole difference that we do not compute those interactions which we have confounded. Instead, we take the block totals, square them, divide by the number of treatments occurring in each block, and subtract the usual correcting factor (grand total squared over grand total number of observations). The degrees of freedom for this sum of squares is of course one less than the number of blocks. We would get an identical result if we calculated the sum of squares for the interactions being confounded, and then pooled them.

As an example, let us consider an experiment on a process employing a mixed catalyst made up of three components. We wish to vary catalyst component A at 4 levels and components C and D each at 2 levels, and we measure the yield as the dependent variable. A straightforward factorial experiment would require $4 \times 2 \times 2 = 16$ runs. However, it was necessary to confound the experiment in blocks of 4, 4 blocks thus being required.

The first problem is how to confound with a factor at 4 levels. Yates has given a method by which it can be regarded as two factors each at 2 levels. If we regard the two factors as A′ and A″, with suffices 1 and 2 to indicate their lower and upper levels, and if the four levels of the four level factor are a_1 to a_4, then Table 14.5 gives the appropriate allocation.

Table 14.5

	A'_1	A'_2
A''_1	a_2	a_3
A''_2	a_1	a_4

With this allocation

$$A' = a_4 + a_3 - a_2 - a_1$$
$$A'' = a_4 - a_3 - a_2 + a_1$$

and the interaction of A′ and A″, which we may call A‴, is

$$A''' = a_4 - a_3 + a_2 - a_1$$

Accordingly, the linear component is 2A′ + A‴, the quadratic component is A″, and the cubic component is 2A‴ — A′. For confounding we assume that the cubic component is negligible and confound A‴, this leaving us estimates of the linear and quadratic components.

Reference to Section (c) will show that with four factors (all at two levels) being confounded one first order interaction must be lost: we select A‴ as this (equivalent to A′A″). The other two most suitable interactions for confounding are clearly A′CD and A″CD.

The allocation of treatments to the four blocks proceeds in the usual manner, and is set out with the yields obtained in Table 14.6.

Table 14.6

Block 1		Block 2		Block 3		Block 4	
(1)	24	a′	25	a″	56	c	48
cd	31	a′cd	23	a″cd	41	d	29
a′a″d	6	a″d	24	a′d	27	a′a″cd	23
a′a″c	14	a″c	36	a′c	40	a′a″	25
	75		108		164		125

The symbolism for treatments is such that, for example, a′a″ implies both A′ and A″ at their upper levels; reference to Table 14.5 shows that $A'_2A''_2$ corresponds to a_4, i.e. the highest level of the four-level factor. Factors C and D are of course at their lower levels. The treatment a″cd has C and D at their upper levels: a″ implies $A'_1A''_2$ (i.e. A′ at its lower level and A″ at its upper level), and Table 14.5 gives this as a_1.

The last line in Table 14.6 gives the block totals, and the sum of squares for Blocks is of course

$$\frac{1}{4}(75^2 + 108^2 + 164^2 + 125^2) - \frac{(75 + 108 + 164 + 125)^2}{16} = 1028.500$$

and this sum of squares has 3 degrees of freedom.

The remainder of the analysis proceeds in the usual fashion. It is interesting to note that if we calculate the three interactions confounded, we get for their sums of squares—

A′A″	324.000
A′CD	2.250
A″CD	702.250

and this total agrees with that obtained above.

If we wish to obtain a check on the correctness of the computation, we can calculate the highest order interaction, A′A″C D, directly rather than the usual manner of obtaining it by difference. We expand (a′ — 1) (a″ — 1) (c — 1) (d — 1) as a′a″c d + a′c + a′d + a″c + a″d + a′a″ + cd + 1 — a′cd — a″cd — a′a″c — a′a″d — a′ — a″— c — d.

Going through the table of results (Table 14.6) we obtain as this total (—12). The sums of squares for A′A″CD is the square of this result divided by the number of observations concerned, or $(-12)^2/16 = 9.000$. This checks with the figure found by difference from the total sum of squares. In any factorial experiment with factors at 2 levels it is open to us, if we prefer, to calculate all the sums of squares in this manner.[2]

The table of analysis of variance is in Table 14.7.

Table 14.7

Source of Variance	Degree of Freedom	Sums of Squares
Blocks	3	1028.500
A { Linear Component A′	1	702.250
A { Quadratic Component A″	1	30.250
C	1	100.00
D	1	256.000
A′C	1	2.250
A′D	1	12.250
A″C	1	72.250
A″D	1	6.250
C D	1	36.000
A′A″C	1	36.000
A′A″D	1	25.000
Residual	1	9.000
Total	15	2316.000

The interpretation of this table is quite straightforward. The Residual, which of course is A′A″C D, can be pooled with the two second order interactions A′A″C and A′A″D to give a mean square of 23.333 with 3 degrees of freedom which we use for error. We then find all the first order interactions to be non-significant. Of the main effects, D is significant at the 1% level, C non-significant, the linear component of A is significant at the 0.1% level and the quadratic component of A, measuring the possible curvature, is non-significant. We can then proceed to calculate the relevant averages and attach the appropriate standard errors to them.

It is noteworthy in Table 14.7 that the Mean Square for Blocks, 1028.000/3 = 342.667, is highly significant (0.1%). With confounding the estimate of error obtained by pooling all the non-significant first order interactions is 18.178 (with 7 degrees of freedom). If confounding had not been used, but instead the 16 treatments allocated at random, then the sum of squares due to difference between blocks would have appeared in this pooled residual error, which would then have been 115.575 with 10 degrees of freedom. The gain in accuracy through the use of confounding, which reduced the error mean square to 18.178, is thus very great, and without it the experiment would have been almost valueless.

Finally, it is of interest to note how such an experiment as this could have been tackled traditionally. The best that could have been done would be to put the four level factor A into two blocks, C and D being constant. The third block could have contained C replicated twice (two observations at each of the two levels), A and D being constant, and the fourth block could have been used similarly

[2] A systematic method of making these calculations is given by F. Yates "Design and Analysis of Factorial Experiments" (Imperial Bureau of Soil Science), pages 15 and 28.

for D. Such an experiment would only give half the accuracy for estimating A and one quarter the accuracy for estimating C and D as the factorial confounded experiment. Further, it would have given no estimates at all of the possible existence of interactions. The gain through the use of the factorial confounded design is thus very considerable.

(g) Partial Confounding

It will be clear that if we cannot afford to lose any of the first order interactions, and the confounding that we are forced to adopt through the restricted block size is going to lose one or more of them, then it we replicate further we can choose to confound interactoins other than those which we lost in the first replication. This technique is known as "partial confounding." Details will be found in :—

Yates : "Design and Analysis of Factorial Experiments" (Imperial Bureau of Soil Science). Sections 4 and 5.

Goulden : "Methods of Statistical Analysis" (John Wiley). Page 162.

(h) Other Confounding Possibilities

Yates (c.f. reference in preceding section) has set out the possibilities of confounding when factors at more than two levels are concerned. Amongst the schemes he describes are the confounding of the $3 \times 3 \times 3$ and the $3 \times 3 \times 3 \times 3$ experiments in respectively 3 and 9 blocks of 9 runs. Mixed experiments of the type $3 \times 2 \times 2$, $3 \times 2 \times 2 \times 2$, $3 \times 3 \times 2$, and $3 \times 3 \times 3 \times 2$ all confounded in blocks of 6 runs are also described.

(i) Double Confounding[3]

Sometimes in a factorial experiment we have a double restriction imposed on the system. For example, in a 2^5 experiment (5 factors all at 2 levels, requiring a total of 32 runs) we may have 4 reactors which may be different. Accordingly we confound in 4 blocks of 8, there being 8 runs on each of the 4 reactors. However, our batches of raw material may not be large enough to carry out the whole experiment. We then need to confound the experiment in an additional way. The problem is soluble if we make it the inverse of the first type of confounding. Thus, if the first confounding is in 4 blocks of 8 then the second must be in 8 blocks of 4. There is the further restriction that no interaction confounded in the second set must occur in the first set, and vice versa.

For the confounding in 8 blocks of 4 let us select for confounding

PQ, RS, PRT, QST, QRT, PST, PQRS,

and for the confounding in 4 blocks of 8 we can choose

PQR, RST, PQST,

none of the second set occurring in the first.

To allocate the treatments, we can first set out them in the usual manner for confounding in 8 blocks of 4, as in Table 14.8.

Table 14.8

Batch 1	Batch 2	Batch 3	Batch 4	Batch 5	Batch 6	Batch 7	Batch 8
(1)	p	q	r	s	t	pr	qr
pqrs	qrs	prs	pqs	pqr	pqrst	qs	ps
rst	prst	qrst	st	rt	rs	pst	qst
pqt	qt	pt	pqrt	pqst	pq	rqt	prt

[3] c.f. R. A. Fisher, "The Design of Experiments," 3rd edition, p. 116.

We do likewise for the 4 blocks of 8, as in Table 14.9.

Table 14.9

Reactor 1	(1)	pq	st	prst	qrt	prt	prs	qrs
Reactor 2	p	q	pst	qst	pqrt	rt	rs	pqrs
Reactor 3	s	pqs	t	pqt	qrst	prst	pr	qr
Reactor 4	r	pqr	rst	pqrst	qt	pt	ps	qs

We now superimpose Tables 14.8 and 14.9 on top of each other. Treatment (1) belongs to Batch 1 and Reactor 1, and is entered in Table 14.10 accordingly. Treatment pqrs belongs to Batch 1 and Reactor 2, and is entered thus. Treatment rst belongs to Batch 1 and Reactor 4, and so on.

Table 14.10

	Batch 1	Batch 2	Batch 3	Batch 4	Batch 5	Batch 6	Batch 7	Batch 8
Reactor 1 ..	(1)	qrs	prs	st	pqst	pq	qrt	prt
Reactor 2 ..	pqrs	p	q	pqrt	rt	rs	pst	qst
Reactor 3 ..	pqt	prst	qrst	pqs	s	t	pr	qr
Reactor 4 ..	rst	qt	pt	r	pqr	pqrst	qs	ps

Table 14.10 will be found to satisfy the condition of both Tables 14.8 and 14.9, and accordingly is the correct allocation of treatments. The analysis of variance proceeds normally, all the interactions being confounded not being mentioned specifically in the table of analysis of variance but their Sums of Squares and Degrees of Freedom being lumped together under the description "Blocks."

It will be noted that, if we were confounding in 8 blocks of 4, the imposition of the second restriction leads to no increase in the number of first order interactions being lost.

Double confounding is not very practical in the 2^4 experiment, but works well in the 2^5 as described above, and also in the 2^6, where there are two possibilities, either confounding in 8 blocks of 8 and 8 blocks of 8 or in 16 blocks of 4 and 4 blocks of 16.

For the former case, one set of 8 interactions for confounding in

PQRS, RSTU, PQTU, PRT, QST, PSU and QRU

and another non-overlapping set is

PQRU, PRST, QSTU, PQS, RSU, RQT and PTU.

Thus the double restriction can be applied without losing any first order interactions.

For double confounding in 16 Blocks of 4 and in 4 blocks of 16, one set of interactions for confounding is

PQ, RU, PRT, QST, QRT, PST, PQRS, TU,
PQTU, RSTU, PRU, QSU, QRU, PSU, PQRSTU,

and the other set, non-overlapping, is

PQRU, PRST, QSTU.

Accordingly, if we are confounding in 16 Blocks of 4, we lose 3 first order interactions, and the introduction of the second restriction in no way increases the loss, so can always be carried out when convenient or necessary.

CHAPTER XV

GENERAL CONCLUSIONS

(a) Investigation of Multi-Variable Processes

The reader will have noticed that we have discussed two different techniques for the investigation of multi-variable systems, namely multiple correlation and the factorial experiment.

Multiple correlation is appropriate where we have a considerable mass of data on the system under investigation, the various independent variables being at random and at all levels. Such data arises from the normal running of a plant: in particular, on a modern plant with automatic recorders kept in proper working condition such data should be very easily collected.

The factorial experiment is appropriate where we can make a deliberate experiment upon a system, controlling the independent variables at the levels laid down by the factorial design. The execution of such an experiment generally calls for careful supervision and hence tends to be relatively costly.

The multiple correlation approach suffers from the disadvantage that initially one is restricted to the assumption that the dependent variable is a linear function of the independent variables which are also assumed to be acting independently.

It is, however, possible to evade some of these difficulties arising from non-linearity by use of the various forms of transformation mentioned in Chapter IX (b) and Chapter X (b). It will be noted that the satisfactory use of these devices is based on our initially selecting the appropriate transformation, either from physico-chemical knowledge of the system, or from an intelligent or lucky inspection of the data. If we have to try first one transformation, then another and so on till we get a good fit the amount of work is excessive.

The difficulty with regard to the independence of the independent variables can be partially circumvented by the addition of product terms as additional independent variables, e.g. if our dependent variable is y and we have independent variables x_1 and x_2 we can include the third variable $(x_1 x_2)$, i.e. we fit an equation of the form

$$y = b_1 x_1 + b_2 x_2 + b_{1\,2}(x_1 x_2)$$

However, if there are three independent variables and we wish to check on the possible interactions of all of them, the equation we fit is

$$y = b_1 x_1 + b_2 x_2 + b_3 x_3 + b_{1\,2}(x_1 x_2) + b_{2\,3}(x_2 x_3) + b_{3\,1}(x_3 x_1)$$

The labour of calculating all the relevant sums of squares and sums of products and then solving the six simultaneous equations would be very heavy and only in very important cases could it be justified.

With the factorial experiment, our initial assumptions are very general and we are quite prepared to see any of the first order interactions significant, and we have made no assumptions as to linearity. This generality means that a factorial experiment could only give confusing results if every factor was interacting strongly with all the others, a very rare occurrence, and even then one which could probably be made clearer by a logarithmic transformation. Further, if some of our factors are at more than two levels we can readily check on the possible non-linearity of the effects by the methods of Chapter XII (c). The total computation required is very much less than with multiple correlation.

The factorial experiment has the further advantage that it can generally be increased very appreciably in accuracy by the device of confounding.

Taking an overall view, there can be no doubt that the factorial experiment is to be greatly preferred to an examination of existing data by mutliple correlation. In addition to all the advantages set out above, the experiment has the further advantage that it is not liable to error through the presence of unsuspected correlated variables: this is the distinction between experiment and observation discussed in Chapter IX (k).

In the intermediate case, where some variables can be controlled at the levels laid down by a factorial design but where some of them are more difficult to control, the most appropriate technique would be covariance: there are no published references referring to industrial problems but the technique is described in the references below.[1]

(b) The Advantages of Planning Experiments

It will have been apparent that none of these statistical designs for experiments can be applied without the appropriate forethought and planning. They cannot be superimposed on a hotch-potch of random results.

The implication of this are rather far-reaching. For example, the traditional style of experimenting by trying first one thing, then if that does not work then something else, and so on, in fact the policy of proceeding by small steps, is quite unsuitable. On the contrary, we require to sit down and appraise all the points that appear to be of interest, or likely to be of interest in the future, and then experiment on them all simultaneously. We thus move in jumps rather than in steps. The great advantage of moving in jumps is that the information given by a jump adds up to very much more than that given by its component steps, though requiring no more effort.

To take an example of this, consider the case discussed in Chapter XIII (a) where we tested 7 treatments in blocks of 3. The variance of the comparison of any two corrected means was $(6/7)\ \sigma_k^2,\ = 0.857\sigma_k^2$, where σ_k^2 was the error variance of a single observation within blocks.

Now suppose that instead of starting off the experiment with the full number of treatments (7) we had begun with only 4 and had afterwards decided to test the remaining 3. Our first 4 could be tested with the design given in Table 13.3, when the variance of the comparison of any two of these means would be

$$2 \times \frac{k\,(t-1)}{N\,(k-1)}\ \sigma_k^2 = 2 \times \frac{3\,(4-1)}{3 \times 4\,(3-1)}\ \sigma_k^2 = 0.75\sigma_k^2$$

This compares favourably with the figures of $0.857\sigma k^2$ for the whole experiment. However, when we come to the 3 additional treatments, it is impossible to execute them in such a manner that when added to the existing data we get the same design as that used for testing 7 treatments. Accordingly the best we can do is to select one treatment as a "standard" (say treatment T_4) to occur in both experiments, and with this standard and the remaining 3 treatments we carry out a further balanced incomplete block of 4 treatments in blocks of 3, requiring 3 replications. The error variance of the comparison of any two of the four treatments T_4 to T_7 in $0.75\sigma_k^2$ as it was for any two of the four treatments T_1 to T_4. However, when we wish to compare any of the three treatments T_1 to T_3 with any of the three T_5 to T_7, this can only be done via T_4, and the error variance of these comparisons is $2 \times 0.75\sigma_k^2 = 1.5\sigma_k^2$, nearly double that of $0.857\sigma_k^2$ for the experiment in one stage. The overall average variance of a comparison in the two stage experiment is actually $1.071\sigma_k^2$.

When we consider that the experiment in two stages has taken 24 runs as compared with 21 for the experiment in one stage, it is evident that the latter has been much more satisfactory.

In parenthesis, a comparison might be made with the classical type of experiment using a single standard throughout. The nearest approach to a balanced design calls for 6 blocks, all containing the standard and two of the remaining 6 treatments. Each of the latter therefore occurs twice. The total number of runs

[1] For a description of the method of covariance see R. A. Fisher: "Statistical Methods for Research Workers," Section 49.1 (Oliver and Boyd). K. Mather: "Statistical Analysis in Biology," Section 34 (Methuen). G. W. Snedecor: "Statistical Methods," Chapter 12 (Iowa State College Press).

required is 6 × 3 = 18, which is slightly less than the 21 for the balanced incomplete blocks. The accuracy is very much less. There are three separate types of comparison in this classical design :—

(a) Between any treatment and the standard. These have variances $0.667\sigma_k^2$

(b) Between any two treatments which occur in the same block. These have variances $1.333\sigma_k^2$.

(c) Between any two treatments not in the same block. These have variances approximately $4.0\sigma_k^2$. The overall average is approximately $2.285\sigma_k^2$. The comparison of this classical design with a "standard" with the balanced incomplete block is thus seen to be very unfavourable to the former, when it is remembered that in the latter all comparisons have the variance $0.857\sigma_k^2$.

In the same manner, it can be shown that one large factorial experiment is much more satisfactory than two smaller ones. For example, with 6 factors all at 2 levels, it is much better to have then in one full experiment requiring $2^6 = 64$ runs[2] than to divide the experiment into two parts, each with 3 factors, requiring for the two parts a total of $2 \times 2^3 = 16$ runs. The former requires appreciably more work, but in return yields the following advantages :—

(a) The main effects are determined with 8 times the accuracy.

(b) All the 15 possible first order interactions are evaluated with considerable accuracy: the two stage experiment only estimates 6 of these 15, and then only with one-eighth the accuracy.

(c) All the 20 possible second order interactions are estimated : in the two stage experiment only 2 are estimated, and then these estimates have to be used as error so are of no value as regards estimating the interactions themselves.

(d) All the 15 possible third order interactions are estimated. There are still 7 degrees of freedom left for error : if we use these plus the greater part of the 15 third order interactions for error we will have the latter with about 20 degrees of freedom. This is much more satisfactory than in the two-stage experiment where we start off with a second order interaction with only 1 degree of freedom as error.

(c) Conclusions

These sections on the design of experiments have been written rather as though it were a fully-developed subject like Euclid's Geometry. This is not the case, however : these statistical designs have hitherto only been employed in the chemical industry to a very limited extent, their development taking place in the science of agriculture, where there is now a body of experience available stretching over twenty years. The methods are clearly capable of transplantation on the lines indicated. but we must guard against an undue literalism in their application. In the chemical industry certain aspects will need to be developed, and others perhaps to be modified as not suitable in the changed conditions. Thus, for example, it seems that for the presentation of final results on which action may be taken the 5% level of significance is inadequate, and we really require the 1% or better. In general, therefore, caution should be used in their interpretation till there is a greater foundation of experience, but to date no incident has come to the author's notice which suggests that there are any pitfalls.

[2] Methods have been developed recently for factorial experiments with large numbers of factors which allow us to obtain satisfactory estimates of the main effects and lower order (first and second) interactions with only a fraction of the full number of runs ; c.f. D. J. Finney, Annals of Eugenics, Volume 12, page 291, 1945.

APPENDIX

TABLE I

Table of t

Degrees of Freedom	t				
	0.10	0.05	0.02	0.01	0.001
1	6.31	12.71	31.82	63.66	636.62
2	2.92	4.30	6.97	9.93	31.60
3	2.35	3.18	4.54	5.84	12.94
4	2.13	2.78	3.75	4.60	8.61
5	2.02	2.57	3.37	4.03	6.86
6	1.94	2.45	3.14	3.71	5.96
7	1.90	2.37	3.00	3.50	5.41
8	1.86	2.31	2.90	3.36	5.04
9	1.83	2.26	2.82	3.25	4.78
10	1.81	2.23	2.76	3.17	4.59
11	1.80	2.20	2.72	3.11	4.44
12	1.78	2.18	2.68	3.06	4.32
13	1.77	2.16	2.65	3.01	4.22
14	1.76	2.15	2.62	2.98	4.14
15	1.75	2.13	2.60	2.95	4.07
16	1.75	2.12	2.58	2.92	4.02
17	1.74	2.11	2.57	2.90	3.97
18	1.73	2.10	2.55	2.88	3.92
19	1.73	2.09	2.54	2.86	3.88
20	1.73	2.09	2.53	2.85	3.85
21	1.72	2.08	2.52	2.83	3.82
22	1.72	2.07	2.51	2.82	3.79
23	1.71	2.07	2.50	2.81	3.77
24	1.71	2.06	2.49	2.80	3.75
25	1.71	2.06	2.48	2.79	3.73
26	1.71	2.06	2.48	2.78	3.71
27	1.70	2.05	2.47	2.77	3.69
28	1.70	2.05	2.47	2.76	3.67
29	1.70	2.04	2.46	2.76	3.66
30	1.70	2.04	2.46	2.75	3.65
40	1.68	2.02	2.42	2.70	3.55
60	1.67	2.00	2.39	2.66	3.46
120	1.66	1.98	2.36	2.62	3.37
∞	1.65	1.96	2.33	2.58	3.29

Abridged from Table III of "Statistical Tables for Biological, Agricultural and Medical Research." (R. A. Fisher and F. Yates : Oliver and Boyd).

TABLE II

Table of χ^2

Degrees of Freedom	0.99	0.98	0.95	0.90	0.50	0.10	0.05	0.02	0.01	0.001
1	0.000	0.001	0.004	0.015	0.455	2.71	3.84	5.41	6.64	10.83
2	0.020	0.040	0.103	0.211	1.386	4.61	5.99	7.82	9.21	13.82
3	0.115	0.185	0.352	0.584	2.366	6.25	7.82	9.84	11.34	16.27
4	0.297	0.429	0.711	1.064	3.357	7.78	9.49	11.67	13.28	18.47
5	0.554	0.752	1.145	1.610	4.351	9.24	11.07	13.39	15.09	20.52
6	0.872	1.134	1.635	2.204	5.35	10.65	12.59	15.03	16.81	22.46
7	1.239	1.564	2.167	2.833	6.35	12.02	14.07	16.62	18.48	24.32
8	1.646	2.032	2.733	3.490	7.34	13.36	15.51	18.17	20.09	26.13
9	2.088	2.532	3.325	4.168	8.34	14.68	16.92	19.68	21.67	27.88
10	2.558	3.059	3.940	4.865	9.34	15.99	18.31	21.16	23.21	29.59
11	3.05	3.61	4.57	5.58	10.34	17.28	19.68	22.62	24.73	31.26
12	3.57	4.18	5.23	6.30	11.34	18.55	21.03	24.05	26.22	32.91
13	4.11	4.76	5.89	7.04	12.34	19.81	22.36	25.47	27.69	34.53
14	4.66	5.37	6.57	7.79	13.34	21.06	23.69	26.87	29.14	36.12
15	5.23	5.99	7.26	8.55	14.34	22.31	25.00	28.26	30.58	37.70
16	5.81	6.61	7.96	9.31	15.34	23.54	26.30	39.63	32.00	39.25
17	6.41	7.26	8.67	10.09	16.34	24.77	27.59	31.00	33.41	40.79
18	7.02	7.91	9.39	10.87	17.34	25.99	28.87	32.35	34.81	42.31
19	7.63	8.57	10.12	11.65	18.34	27.20	30.14	33.69	36.19	43.82
20	8.26	9.24	10.85	12.44	19.34	28.41	31.41	35.02	37.57	45.32
21	8.90	9.91	11.59	13.34	20.34	29.61	32.67	36.34	38.93	46.80
22	9.54	10.60	12.34	14.04	21.34	30.81	33.92	37.66	40.29	48.27
23	10.20	11.29	13.09	14.85	22.34	32.01	35.17	38.97	41.64	49.73
24	10.86	11.99	13.85	15.66	23.34	33.20	36.42	40.27	42.98	51.18
25	11.52	12.70	14.61	16.47	24.34	34.38	37.65	41.57	44.31	52.62
26	12.20	13.41	15.38	17.29	25.34	35.56	38.89	42.86	45.64	54.05
27	12.88	14.12	16.15	18.11	26.34	36.74	40.11	44.14	46.96	55.48
28	13.56	14.85	16.93	18.94	27.34	37.92	41.34	45.42	48.28	56.89
29	14.26	15.57	17.71	19.77	28.34	39.09	42.56	46.69	49.59	58.30
30	14.95	16.31	18.49	20.60	29.34	40.26	43.77	47.96	50.89	59.70

Abridged from Table IV of "Statistical Tables for Biological, Agricultural and Medical Research." (R. A. Fisher and F. Yates : Oliver and Boyd).

TABLE III

Tables of Variance Ratio (i)

N_2 \ N_1	0.20 Significance Level								
	1	2	3	4	5	6	12	24	∞
1	9.5	12.0	13.1	13.7	14.0	14.3	14.9	15.2	15.6
2	3.6	4.0	4.2	4.2	4.3	4.3	4.4	4.4	4.5
3	2.7	2.9	2.9	3.0	3.0	3.0	3.0	3.0	3.0
4	2.4	2.5	2.5	2.5	2.5	2.5	2.5	2.4	2.4
5	2.2	2.3	2.3	2.2	2.2	2.2	2.2	2.2	2.1
6	2.1	2.1	2.1	2.1	2.1	2.1	2.0	2.0	2.0
7	2.0	2.0	2.0	2.0	2.0	2.0	1.9	1.9	1.8
8	2.0	2.0	2.0	1.9	1.9	1.9	1.8	1.8	1.7
9	1.9	1.9	1.9	1.9	1.9	1.8	1.8	1.7	1.7
10	1.9	1.9	1.9	1.8	1.8	1.8	1.7	1.7	1.6
11	1.9	1.9	1.8	1.8	1.8	1.8	1.7	1.6	1.6
12	1.8	1.8	1.8	1.8	1.7	1.7	1.7	1.6	1.5
13	1.8	1.8	1.8	1.8	1.7	1.7	1.6	1.6	1.5
14	1.8	1.8	1.8	1.7	1.7	1.7	1.6	1.6	1.5
15	1.8	1.8	1.8	1.7	1.7	1.7	1.6	1.5	1.5
16	1.8	1.8	1.7	1.7	1.7	1.6	1.6	1.5	1.4
17	1.8	1.8	1.7	1.7	1.7	1.6	1.6	1.5	1.4
18	1.8	1.8	1.7	1.7	1.6	1.6	1.5	1.5	1.4
19	1.8	1.8	1.7	1.7	1.6	1.6	1.5	1.5	1.4
20	1.8	1.8	1.7	1.7	1.6	1.6	1.5	1.5	1.4
22	1.8	1.7	1.7	1.6	1.6	1.6	1.5	1.4	1.4
24	1.7	1.7	1.7	1.6	1.6	1.6	1.5	1.4	1.3
26	1.7	1.7	1.7	1.6	1.6	1.6	1.5	1.4	1.3
28	1.7	1.7	1.7	1.6	1.6	1.6	1.5	1.4	1.3
30	1.7	1.7	1.6	1.6	1.6	1.5	1.5	1.4	1.3
40	1.7	1.7	1.6	1.6	1.5	1.5	1.4	1.4	1.2
60	1.7	1.7	1.6	1.6	1.5	1.5	1.4	1.3	1.2
120	1.7	1.6	1.6	1.5	1.5	1.5	1.4	1.3	1.1
∞	1.6	1.6	1.6	1.5	1.5	1.4	1.3	1.2	1.0

Abridged from Table V of "Statistical Tables for Biological, Agricultural and Medical Research." (R. A. Fisher and F. Yates: Oliver and Boyd).

Table of Variance Ratio (ii)

N_2 \ N_1	0.05 Significance Level								
	1	2	3	4	5	6	12	24	∞
1	164.4	199.5	215.7	224.6	230.2	234.0	234.9	249.0	254.3
2	18.5	19.2	19.2	19.3	19.3	19.3	19.4	19.5	19.5
3	10.1	9.6	9.3	9.1	9.0	8.9	8.7	8.6	8.5
4	7.7	6.9	6.6	6.4	6.3	6.2	5.9	5.8	5.6
5	6.6	5.8	5.4	5.2	5.1	5.0	4.7	4.5	4.4
6	6.0	5.1	4.8	4.5	4.4	4.3	4.0	3.8	3.7
7	5.6	4.7	4.4	4.1	4.0	3.9	3.6	3.4	3.2
8	5.3	4.5	4.1	3.8	3.7	3.6	3.3	3.1	2.9
9	5.1	4.3	3.9	3.6	3.5	3.4	3.1	2.9	2.7
10	5.0	4.1	3.7	3.5	3.3	3.2	2.9	2.7	2.5
11	4.8	4.0	3.6	3.4	3.2	3.1	2.8	2.6	2.4
12	4.8	3.9	3.5	3.3	3.1	3.0	2.7	2.5	2.3
13	4.7	3.8	3.4	3.2	3.0	2.9	2.6	2.4	2.2
14	4.6	3.7	3.3	3.1	3.0	2.9	2.5	2.3	2.1
15	4.5	3.7	3.3	3.1	2.9	2.8	2.5	2.3	2.1
16	4.5	3.6	3.2	3.0	2.9	2.7	2.4	2.2	2.0
17	4.5	3.6	3.2	3.0	2.8	2.7	2.4	2.2	2.0
18	4.4	3.6	3.2	2.9	2.8	2.7	2.3	2.1	1.9
19	4.4	3.5	3.1	2.9	2.7	2.6	2.3	2.1	1.9
20	4.4	3.5	3.1	2.9	2.7	2.6	2.3	2.1	1.8
22	4.3	3.4	3.1	2.8	2.7	2.6	2.2	2.0	1.8
24	4.3	3.4	3.0	2.8	2.6	2.5	2.2	2.0	1.7
26	4.2	3.4	3.0	2.7	2.6	2.5	2.2	2.0	1.7
28	4.2	3.3	3.0	2.7	2.6	2.4	2.1	1.9	1.7
30	4.2	3.3	2.9	2.7	2.5	2.4	2.1	1.9	1.6
40	4.1	3.2	2.9	2.6	2.5	2.3	2.0	1.8	1.5
60	4.0	3.2	2.8	2.5	2.4	2.3	1.9	1.7	1.4
120	3.9	3.1	2.7	2.5	2.3	2.2	1.8	1.6	1.3
∞	3.8	3.0	2.6	2.4	2.2	2.1	1.8	1.5	1.0

Abridged from Table V of "Statistical Tables for Biological, Agricultural, and Medical Research." (R. A. Fisher and F. Yates : Oliver and Boyd).

Tables of Variance Ratio (iii)

N_2 \ N_1	0.01 Significance Level									
	1	2	3	4	5	6	8	12	24	∞
1	4052	4999	5403	5625	5764	5859	5981	6106	6234	6366
2	98.5	99.0	99.2	99.3	99.3	99.4	99.3	99.4	99.5	99.5
3	34.1	30.8	29.5	28.7	28.2	27.9	27.5	27.1	26.6	26.1
4	21.2	18.0	16.7	16.0	15.5	15.2	14.8	14.4	13.9	13.5
5	16.3	13.3	12.1	11.4	11.0	10.7	10.3	9.9	9.5	9.0
6	13.7	10.9	9.8	9.2	8.8	8.5	8.1	7.7	7.3	6.9
7	12.3	9.6	8.5	7.9	7.5	7.2	6.8	6.5	6.1	5.7
8	11.3	8.7	7.6	7.0	6.6	6.4	6.0	5.7	5.3	4.9
9	10.6	8.0	7.0	6.4	6.1	5.8	5.5	5.1	4.7	4.3
10	10.0	7.6	6.6	6.0	5.6	5.4	5.1	4.7	4.3	3.9
11	9.7	7.2	6.2	5.7	5.3	5.1	4.7	4.4	4.0	3.6
12	9.3	6.9	6.0	5.4	5.1	4.8	4.5	4.2	3.8	3.4
13	9.1	6.7	5.7	5.2	4.9	4.6	4.3	4.0	3.6	3.2
14	8.9	6.5	5.6	5.0	4.7	4.5	4.1	3.8	3.4	3.0
15	8.7	6.4	5.4	4.9	4.6	4.3	4.0	3.7	3.3	2.9
16	8.5	6.2	5.3	4.8	4.4	4.2	3.9	3.6	3.2	2.8
17	8.4	6.1	5.2	4.7	4.3	4.1	3.8	3.5	3.1	2.7
18	8.3	6.0	5.1	4.6	4.3	4.0	3.7	3.4	3.0	2.6
19	8.2	5.9	5.0	4.5	4.2	3.9	3.6	3.3	2.9	2.5
20	8.1	5.9	4.9	4.4	4.1	3.9	3.6	3.2	2.9	2.4
22	7.9	5.7	4.8	4.3	4.0	3.8	3.5	3.1	2.8	2.3
24	7.8	5.6	4.7	4.2	3.9	3.7	3.3	3.0	2.7	2.2
26	7.7	5.5	4.6	4.1	3.8	3.6	3.3	3.0	2.6	2.1
28	7.6	5.5	4.6	4.1	3.8	3.5	3.2	2.9	2.5	2.1
30	7.6	5.4	4.5	4.0	3.7	3.5	3.2	2.8	2.5	2.0
40	7.3	5.2	4.3	3.8	3.5	3.3	3.0	2.7	2.3	1.8
60	7.1	5.0	4.1	3.7	3.3	3.1	2.8	2.5	2.1	1.6
120	6.9	4.8	4.0	3.5	3.2	3.0	2.7	2.3	2.0	1.4
∞	6.6	4.6	3.8	3.3	3.0	2.8	2.5	2.2	1.8	1.0

Abridged from Table V of "Statistical Tables for Biological, Agricultural and Medical Research." (R. A. Fisher and F. Yates : Oliver and Boyd).

Table of Variance Ratio (iv)

N_2 \ N_1	0.001 Significance Level									
	1	2	3	4	5	6	8	12	24	∞
1		varying from 400,000 to 600,000								
2	998	999	999	999	999	999	999	999	999	999
3	167	148	141	137	135	133	131	128	126	123
4	74.1	61.3	56.2	53.4	51.7	50.5	49.0	47.4	45.8	44.1
5	47.0	36.6	33.2	31.1	29.8	28.8	27.6	26.4	25.1	23.8
6	35.5	27.0	23.7	21.9	20.8	20.0	19.0	18.0	16.9	15.8
7	29.2	21.7	18.8	17.2	16.2	15.5	14.6	13.7	12.7	11.7
8	25.4	18.5	15.8	14.4	13.5	12.9	12.0	11.2	10.3	9.3
9	22.9	16.4	13.9	12.6	11.7	11.1	10.4	9.6	8.7	7.8
10	21.0	14.9	12.6	11.3	10.5	9.9	9.2	8.5	7.6	6.8
11	19.7	13.8	11.6	10.4	9.6	9.1	8.3	7.6	6.9	6.0
12	18.6	13.0	10.8	9.6	8.9	8.4	7.7	7.0	6.3	5.4
13	17.8	12.3	10.2	9.1	8.4	7.9	7.2	6.5	5.8	5.0
14	17.1	11.8	9.7	8.6	7.9	7.4	6.8	6.1	5.4	4.6
15	16.6	11.3	9.3	8.3	7.6	7.1	6.5	5.8	5.1	4.3
16	16.1	11.0	9.0	7.9	7.3	6.8	6.2	5.6	4.9	4.1
17	15.7	10.7	8.7	7.7	7.0	6.6	6.0	5.3	4.6	3.9
18	15.4	10.4	8.5	7.5	6.8	6.4	5.8	5.1	4.5	3.7
19	15.1	10.2	8.3	7.3	6.6	6.2	5.6	5.0	4.3	3.5
20	14.8	10.0	8.1	7.1	6.5	6.0	5.4	4.8	4.2	3.4
22	14.4	9.6	7.8	6.8	6.2	5.8	5.2	4.6	3.9	3.2
24	14.0	9.3	7.6	6.6	6.0	5.6	5.0	4.4	3.7	3.0
26	13.7	9.1	7.4	6.4	5.8	5.4	4.8	4.2	3.6	2.8
28	13.5	8.9	7.2	6.3	5.7	5.2	4.7	4.1	3.5	2.7
30	13.3	8.8	7.1	6.1	5.5	5.1	4.6	4.0	3.4	2.6
40	12.6	8.2	6.6	5.7	5.1	4.7	4.2	3.6	3.0	2.2
60	12.0	7.8	6.2	5.3	4.8	4.4	3.9	3.3	2.7	1.9
120	11.4	7.3	5.8	5.0	4.4	4.0	3.5	3.0	2.4	1.6
∞	10.8	6.9	5.4	5.6	4.1	3.7	3.3	2.7	2.1	1.0

Abridged from Table V of "Statistical Tables for Biological, Agricultural and Medical Research." (R. A. Fisher and F. Yates: Oliver and Boyd).

TABLE IV

Table of the Correlation Coefficient

Degrees of Freedom	r				
	0.10	0.05	0.02	0.01	0.001
1	.988	.997	.999	1.000	1.000
2	.900	.950	.980	.990	.999
3	.805	.878	.934	.959	.992
4	.729	.811	.882	.917	.974
5	.669	.754	.833	.874	.951
6	.621	.707	.789	.834	.925
7	.582	.666	.750	.798	.898
8	.549	.632	.716	.765	.872
9	.521	.602	.685	.735	.847
10	.497	.576	.658	.708	.823
11	.476	.553	.634	.684	.801
12	.457	.532	.612	.661	.780
13	.441	.514	.592	.641	.760
14	.426	.497	.574	.623	.742
15	.412	.482	.558	.606	.725
16	.400	.468	.543	.590	.708
17	.389	.456	.528	.575	.693
18	.378	.444	.516	.561	.679
19	.369	.433	.503	.549	.665
20	.360	.423	.492	.537	.652
25	.323	.381	.445	.487	.597
30	.296	.349	.409	.449	.554
35	.275	.325	.381	.418	.519
40	.257	.304	.358	.393	.490
45	.243	.287	.338	.372	.465
50	.231	.273	.322	.354	.443
60	.211	.250	.295	.325	.408
70	.195	.232	.274	.302	.380
80	.183	.217	.256	.283	.357
90	.173	.205	.242	.267	.337
100	.164	.195	.230	.254	.321

Abridged from Table VI of "Statistical Tables for Biological, Agricultural and Medical Research." (R. A. Fisher and F. Yates: Oliver and Boyd).

TABLE V

Factors for Control Charts

Number in Sample	$A'_{0.025}$	$A'_{0.001}$	$D'_{0.975}$	$D'_{0.999}$	d_n
2	1.229	1.937	2.81	4.12	1.13
3	0.668	1.054	2.17	2.98	1.69
4	0.476	0.750	1.93	2.57	2.06
5	0.377	0.594	1.81	2.34	2.33
6	0.316	0.498	1.72	2.21	2.53
7	0.274	0.432	1.66	2.11	2.70
8	0.244	0.384	1.62	2.04	2.85
9	0.220	0.347	1.58	1.99	2.97
10	0.202	0.317	1.56	1.93	3.08

Abridged from B. S. 600R "Quality Control Charts". (B. P. Dudding and W. J. Jennett. British Standards Institution.)

Printed in the U.S.A. by DORAY PRESS, NEW YORK, N. Y,

Printed in the United Kingdom by
Lightning Source UK Ltd., Milton Keynes
136670UK00001B/41/A